AUDIT SAMPLING

AN INTRODUCTION TO STATISTICAL SAMPLING IN AUDITING

ACCOUNTING TEXTBOOKS FROM JOHN WILEY & SONS

AUDIT SAMPLING

AN INTRODUCTION TO STATISTICAL SAMPLING IN AUDITING

SECOND EDITION

Dan M. Guy

D. R. Carmichael

JOHN WILEY & SONS
New York
Chichester
Brisbane
Toronto
Singapore

Library of Congress Cataloging in Publication Data:

Guy, Dan M.
Audit Sampling: An Introduction to Statistical Sampling in Auditing

   1. Auditing—Statistical methods. 2. Sampling
(Statistics) I. Carmichael, D. R. (Douglas R.),
1941–   . II. Title.

HF5667.G87 1986   657′.45′015195   85-26570
ISBN 0-471-81540-3

Printed in the United States of America

10 9 8 7 6 5 4 3 2

ABOUT THE AUTHORS

Dan M. Guy, is Vice President, auditing, at the American Institute of Certified Public Accountants. He received his A.B. and M.B.A. degrees from East Carolina University and his Ph.D. from the University of Alabama. He is a Texas CPA.

Prior to joining the AICPA, he was a member of the faculty at Texas Tech University for seven years. He was also on the faculty of the University of Texas at Austin for one year. During his academic career, he taught basic and advanced auditing courses. He is the author of numerous articles published in **The CPA Journal, The Journal of Accountancy, Management Accounting, The Practical Accountant, Financial Executive,** and other professional journals. He is also a coauthor of the **Guide to Compilation & Review Engagements** (Practitioners' Publishing Company).

D. R. Carmichael, Ph.D., CPA, is the Wollman distinguished professor of accountancy at the Baruch College of the City University of New York. Until December, 1982, he was Vice President, auditing, at the AICPA. For most of his thirteen years at the AICPA he headed the staff of the auditing standards division and was personally involved in the development of over 60 pronouncements on auditing standards and procedures. Mr. Carmichael is one of the country's most prolific writers on auditing, having written or cowritten eight books and over 70 articles on accounting or auditing subjects.

Both authors participated in the development of Statement on Auditing Standards No. 39, *Audit Sampling*.

PREFACE

The second edition of this book has been retitled Audit Sampling and the original title, *An Introduction to Statistical Sampling in Auditing,* has become the subtitle. This change was made to recognize the fundamental position of Statement on Auditing Standards No. 39, *Audit Sampling,* that the same underlying logic applies to both statistical and nonstatistical sampling.

SAS No. 39 equates statistical and nonstatistical sampling in a common approach and imposes the same essential requirements on all audit samples. The requirements and particularly the new terms introduced by SAS No. 39 have been integrated throughout the second edition.

The second edition, like the first, is written from the viewpoint of financial auditors. Although the focus is on use of sampling in the audit of financial statements by an independent auditor, much of the discussion is equally useful to internal auditors. The material presented can be easily understood by the entry-level auditing student, is useful as a supplement to a basic auditing text, and can be covered in 8 to 12 classroom hours. It may also be used in an advanced or graduate auditing course (i.e., a second auditing course). By no means, however, is the text intended to be a three-hour course in itself.

This book will be particularly beneficial in an advanced auditing course, where coverage is often given to topics such as SEC accounting, audit report writing, and legal liability. It will also be useful to practitioners who are considering the use of statistical sampling in their firms. Much of the material was originally developed and extensively tested for CPE training courses. The material is written from the viewpoint of people who have a basic knowledge of business statistics (i.e., one undergraduate course).

Educational material pertaining to statistical auditing generally is included in lengthy, technical books designed for reference, or is presented in one or sometimes two chapters of a basic auditing text. The latter treatment is designed to be a very brief introduction to the subject. This book occupies a middle ground between the highly technical presentation and an introduction. It is designed to reduce the gap between textbooks that give only introductory coverage to statistical sampling and the basic level of professional knowledge that is required to cope with statistical sampling applications in an audit.

The organization of the book is as follows. Chapter 1 explains the essential aspects of audit sampling and presents an overview of statistical sampling in auditing. Throughout the book, statistical sampling is planted firmly in an auditing context, not as an auxiliary subject. Chapter 2 discusses sample selection for both statistical and nonstatistical sampling. Chapter 3 is entitled "Attribute Sampling" and discusses fixed-sample-size, stop-or-go, and discovery sampling. The purpose of Chapter 4 is to review fundamental variable sampling concepts and to illustrate unstratified mean per unit, stratified mean per unit, and difference estimation. Ratio estimation is also discussed briefly. Chapter 5 deals with variable sampling in an audit decision framework and explains the audit risk model. Chapter 6 explains sampling probability proportionate to size (or dollar unit sampling). Finally, Chapter 7 concludes with a brief summary, a discussion of statistical auditing policies, and an explanation of a formal approach to nonstatistical sampling. All chapters are preceded by learning objectives and are followed by a glossary and review questions. Selected chapters have case studies to be solved. In addition, the appendices contain calculation worksheets, a list of equations, additional reading references, and statistical sampling on the CPA examination. Solutions to the review questions and case studies are found in the Instructor's Manual, which is available from the publisher.

In teaching this material in an advanced undergraduate auditing course meeting 1½ hours per class, we have found the following schedule desirable.

Class Meeting No.	Topic	Chapter Assignment
1	Review of Statistical Sampling	Chapters 1-2
2	Attribute Sampling Review	Chapter 3
3	Variable Sampling: Accounting Estimation	Chapter 4
4	Empress Cosmetique Case	—
5	Variable Sampling: Audit Hypothesis Testing	Chapter 5
6	Audit Hypothesis Problems and Cases	—
7	Probability Proportionate to Size Sampling	Chapter 6
8	Audit Sampling Policies	Chapter 7

The above schedule requires 12 classroom hours. A shorter version of the material may be presented by starting with Chapter 4, or reducing coverage of Chapters 4 and 5 to one period each.

Our appreciation and thanks are extended to the following individuals.

Doyle Z. Williams (University of Southern California) contributed the "Empress Cosmetique" case in Chapter 4. William C. Dent and Frederick A. Hancock (Alexander Grant & Co.) contributed extensively to the entire book. Much of the probability proportionate to size sampling material in Chapter 6 was originally compiled by Donna C. McNeil (Peat, Marwick, Mitchell Co.). Also, Scott B. Henry, David H. Souser, and Larry B. White (while students at Texas Tech University) made numerous suggestions concerning readability. We also benefited from the statistical sampling material and training course in audit sampling developed by Ernst & Whinney, and we thank them for their willingness to share their materials and to contribute to educational institutions. We are also grateful to the American Institute of Certified Public Accountants, for permission to use selected CPA Examination problems and to reproduce SAS No. 39. CPA Examination problems are identified as AICPA adapted.

We are also appreciative of reviewers: Wayne C. Alderman (Auburn University), Andrew H. Barnett (San Diego State University), R. K. Mautz (University of Michigan), Ceil Pillsbury (DePaul University), Larry Rittenberg (University of Wisconsin, Madison), Jack Robertson (University of Texas, Austin), Brad Schwieger (St. Cloud State University), and, especially, Bart H. Ward (University of Oklahoma). Many of their recommended changes were incorporated.

Notwithstanding the involvement and contributions of others, the responsibility for any deficiencies in this book remains solely our own.

Dan M. Guy
D. R. Carmichael

CONTENTS

OVERVIEW OF AUDIT SAMPLING

Learning Objectives

After a careful study and discussion of this chapter, you will be able to:

1. Define audit sampling and distinguish statistical and nonstatistical sampling.
2. List and define three types of attribute sampling models.
3. List and define three types of variable sampling models.
4. Cite the important AICPA developments in statistical sampling.
5. Discuss the advantages and disadvantages of statistical sampling relative to nonstatistical sampling.
6. Define nonsampling and sampling error.
7. Identify areas of professional judgment inherent in using statistical sampling.
8. List and describe characteristics of application areas where statistical sampling may be efficient and effective.
9. Relate statistical sampling to generally accepted auditing standards.

Audit sampling, according to SAS No. 39 (AU 350.01),[1] is defined as follows:

Audit sampling is the application of an audit procedure to less than 100 percent of the items within an account balance or class of transactions for the purpose of evaluating some characteristics of the balance or class.

Some auditing procedures are not susceptible to application by sampling. For example, inquiry, observation, analytical review procedures, and general procedures such as reading minutes and contracts do not involve sampling. Also, as is explained in more detail in Chapter 7, sampling is not involved when the auditor applies a procedure *only* to the significant items in an account balance.

NONSTATISTICAL AND STATISTICAL AUDIT SAMPLING

When an auditor uses audit sampling, the same basic requirements apply whether the approach to sampling is statistical or nonstatistical. SAS No. 39 (AU 350.03) states:

There are two general approaches to audit sampling: nonstatistical and statistical. Both approaches require that the auditor use professional judgment in planning, performing, and evaluating a sample. . . . The guidance in this section applies equally to nonstatistical and statistical sampling.

Until recently, nonstatistical sampling was called judgment sampling, but as the previously quoted passage states, both approaches require judgment.

Whenever an auditor uses audit sampling (statistical or nonstatistical), the following basic requirements apply:

- *Planning*   When planning an audit sample, the auditor should consider the relationship of the sample to the relevant specific audit or internal control objective and consider certain other factors that influence sample size.
- *Selection*   Sample items should be selected so that the sample can be expected to be *representative* of the population. All items in the population should have an opportunity to be selected. (The methods that meet this requirement for representative selection are explained in Chapter 2.)
- *Evaluation*   The auditor should *project* the error results of the sample to the items from which the sample was selected.

These basic requirements are necessarily an integral part of statistical sampling. Their application to nonstatistical sampling is relatively new in

---

[1] SAS No. 39, **Audit Sampling,** is reproduced in Appendix E.

auditing practice. The rationale of SAS No. 39 for imposing these basic requirements on all audit samples is that there is an underlying logic for sampling that holds true whether the sampling approach is statistical or nonstatistical.

The essential features of *statistical* sampling are:

- The sample items should have a known probability of selection, that is, random selection.
- The sample results should be evaluated mathematically, that is, in accordance with probability theory.

Just because one of these requirements is met does not mean that the application is statistical. For example, practitioners and others will sometimes state that they are using statistical sampling solely because a random number table is employed to select the sample. However, this is not statistical sampling; no attempt has been made mathematically to evaluate sample findings (requirement no. 2).

A block sample is a good illustration of a selection method that is unacceptable for audit sampling. A block sample includes all items in a selected time period. For example, if the auditor selects all checks issued for the months of March and June for verifying cash disbursements *for the year,* the sample is not statistical. That is, the sample results cannot be mathematically projected to the population of cash disbursements for the whole year because the sample selected cannot be expected to be representative. Checks from other months had no chance of being selected.

Figure 1.1 illustrates the two types of audit sampling: nonstatistical and statistical. It also shows that representative sampling, whereby the sample items are randomly or haphazardly[2] selected from the population, is not equivalent to statistical sampling because the sample is not mathematically evaluated. Sampling concepts such as representative sampling are sometimes confused with statistical sampling. Figure 1.1 clearly depicts that a statistical sample has to be *selected randomly* and *evaluated mathematically.*

TYPES OF STATISTICAL SAMPLING MODELS

There are two broad categories of statistical sampling: attribute or proportional sampling and variable or quantitative sampling. Attribute sampling is used primarily in tests of internal controls. In contrast, variable sampling is most frequently used to test the monetary value of account balances.

---

[2] Haphazard selection is explained in Chapter 2. Essentially, it means selecting items without conscious bias, but not using a formal random-based selection method.

FIGURE 1.1 DISTINCTION BETWEEN TYPES OF AUDIT SAMPLING

	Example Audit Application	Sample Selection	Sample Evaluations
Representative (nonstatistical) sample	Fifty sales invoices processed during year	Random or haphazard	Judgmental
Statistical sample	Sixty sales invoices processed during first 10 months of year.	Random	Mathematical

ATTRIBUTE SAMPLING MODELS

"Attribute sampling" is used in practice to refer to three different, but related types of proportional sampling.

1. *Attribute sampling* (or fixed sample-size attribute sampling) is a sampling model that is used to estimate the rate (%) of occurrence of a specific quality (attribute) in a population. It answers the question "how many." It is one of the most common statistical sampling models in auditing. An attribute sampling model might be used to estimate the number of invoices paid twice. Attribute sampling would help the auditor answer the question "how often." The auditor using attribute sampling might conclude: "I am 95 percent confident that the true error rate of double payment in the population falls between 2 and 6 percent."

2. *Stop-or-go sampling* is a sampling model that helps prevent over-sampling (for attributes) by permitting the auditor to halt an audit test at the earliest possible moment. Stop-or-go sampling is a widely used type of attribute sampling in some large CPA firms. It is used when the auditor believes that relatively few errors are expected to be found in the sampling population. In a stop-or-go sampling application, the auditor might conclude: "I am 95 percent confident that no greater than 5 percent of cash discounts are being lost."

3. *Discovery sampling* is a sampling model that is appropriate when the expected occurrence rate is extremely low (near zero). Discovery sampling is used when the auditor desires a specified chance of observing at least one example of an occurrence (e.g., payroll padding) if the true proportion of occurrences is greater than specified.

VARIABLE SAMPLING MODELS

In contrast to attribute sampling, variable or quantitative sampling is employed when the auditor wishes to estimate (or project) a quantity. For example, if students wanted to employ a sample to estimate the total dollar amount of money in their auditing class for a given day, a variable sampling model could be used. On the other hand, if students wished to estimate the percentage of people in their auditing class 6 feet tall or over, the appropriate approach would be an attribute sampling model.

Like the term "attribute sampling," "variable sampling" is used in practice to refer to a number of different types of quantitative sampling models. The primary models discussed in this book are described below.

1. *Unstratified mean per unit* is a statistical model whereby a sample mean is calculated and projected as an estimated total. For example, if students use unstratified mean per unit to estimate the dollar amount of money in their auditing class, the results might be: Ten students out of a class of 78 students are selected. They have a total of $150 that yields a mean of $15 per student. The mean of $15 times 78 produces an estimated total for the class of $1170.

2. *Stratified mean per unit* is a statistical model in which the population is divided into different groups (strata) and samples are drawn from the various groups. Stratified mean per unit sampling is used to produce a smaller (more efficient) overall sample size relative to unstratified mean per unit. In the auditing classroom illustration, to apply stratified mean per unit the auditing students might be divided into two groups—students that work part-time and students that are not presently employed.

3. *Difference estimation* is a statistical model used to estimate the total difference between audited values and book (unaudited) values based on differences obtained from sample observations. The estimated population difference (sample mean difference times population size) is added or subtracted from the total book value to produce an estimate of the true population total. Difference estimation cannot be applied to the auditing classroom illustration. To apply difference estimation, a book value and an audit value must exist for each student. This is discussed in detail in Chapter 4 and a similar estimation method—ratio estimation—is introduced and discussed briefly.

In addition to the three variable sampling models defined above, probability proportionate to size sampling is discussed in Chapter 6. It is a hybrid model combining characteristics of attribute and variable sampling. Unstratified mean per unit, stratified mean per unit, and difference estimation sampling are often distinguished from probability proportionate to size sampling by calling them "classical variable sampling models." They are called classical methods because they are based on normal distribution theory.

HISTORICAL DEVELOPMENTS OF STATISTICAL SAMPLING IN AUDITING

In 1962, the first official American Institute of Certified Public Accountants (AICPA) literature on statistical sampling was published (*Journal of Accountancy*, February 1962, pp. 60–62) by the Subcommittee on Statistical Sampling, a standing subcommittee of the Auditing Standards Board. (In 1985, the name of this subcommittee was changed to the Audit Testing Subcommittee.) The subcommittee concluded that statistical sampling is permitted under generally accepted auditing standards. Also, the report stressed that *statistical sampling* does not eliminate judgment. Some practitioners are wary about using statistical sampling in auditing because of an erroneous belief that its use encroaches on professional judgment. In this book we demonstrate that statistical sampling actually sharpens the professional judgment of auditors and enhances understanding of the audit process.

Statements on Auditing Procedure No. 33, published in 1963, indicated that a practitioner might consider using statistical sampling in certain circumstances.[3] However, the circumstances were not defined.

In determining the *extent* of a particular audit test and the method of selecting items to be examined, the auditor *might* consider using statistical sampling techniques which have been found to be advantageous in certain instances. The use of statistical sampling *does not reduce* the use of judgment by the auditor but provides certain statistical measurements as to the results of audit tests, which measurements may not otherwise be available (emphasis supplied).[4]

SAP No. 36, "Revision of Extensions of Auditing Procedures Relating to Inventories," published in 1966, indicates that clients are not required to take a 100 percent inventory if they use a valid and reliable statistical model.[5] The auditor, of course, has a responsibility to review the application to ascertain if it is, in act, valid and reliable. The ramifications of SAP No. 36 are discussed in Chapter 4 in connection with the Empress Cosmetique case.

In 1967, the AICPA started publishing the professional educational series entitled *An Auditor's Approach to Statistical Sampling*. To date, the following volumes have been published.[6]

---

[3] Statements on auditing procedure are now referred to as statements on auditing standards (SAS).

[4] **AICPA Professional Standards,** Volume 1 (Chicago: Commerce Clearing House, Inc., 1978), AU 330.14. (This section has been superseded, but is quoted because of its historical interest.)

[5] AU 331.11. SAP No. 36 also was codified in SAS No. 1.

[6] Volumes 2 and 4 in the series are combined in the updated revision of Volume 2.

Volume 1 *An Introduction to Statistical Concepts and Estimation of Dollar Values* (1967)

Volume 2 *Sampling for Attributes: Estimation and Discovery* (1974)

Volume 3 *Stratified Random Sampling* (1968)

Volume 5 *Ratio and Difference Estimation* (1972)

Volume 6 *Field Manual for Statistical Sampling* (1974)

In 1972, SAP No. 54, "The Auditor's Study and Evaluation of Accounting Control," was issued with an appendix on the use of statistical sampling in audit tests. The appendix explained the relationship of statistical terms to established auditing concepts such as materiality and risk, and provided guidance on the incorporation of statistical sampling in planning and applying audit procedures. Although use of statistical sampling was clearly permitted, it was not required.

In 1975, the AICPA published Auditing Research Monograph No. 2, *Behavior of Major Statistical Estimators in Sampling Accounting Populations*, by John Neter and James K. Loebbecke. Auditing Research Monograph No. 2 discusses variable sampling as applied to accounting populations. It contains several policy overtones that are important to students of auditing and practitioners. These policy recommendations are discussed in Chapter 7.

Statistical Auditing, an AICPA practitioner's handbook, was published in 1978. *Statistical Auditing* was designed to extend the series *An Auditor's Approach to Statistical Sampling* and as a comprehensive reference book for practitioners. The professional education series introduces basic statistical concepts, and *Statistical Auditing* helps practicing accountants and auditors implement statistical sampling in audit engagements.

In 1981, SAS No. 39 (AU 350), "Audit Sampling," moved statistical sampling from the subordinate status of an appendix to the body of the statement, and equated statistical and nonstatistical sampling in a common approach. Basically, the SAS says that there is an underlying rationale for sampling in auditing that is applicable whether the sampling is statistical or nonstatistical.[7]

WHAT ARE THE ADVANTAGES OF STATISTICAL SAMPLING?

Statistical sampling:

1. Allows auditors to calculate sample reliability and the risk of reliance on the sample. (Conceptually, this is the *sole* distinction between statistical sampling and nonstatistical sampling.)

---

[7] See Appendix E.

2. Requires auditors to plan their approach in a more orderly manner than when an informal nonstatistical sampling approach is used.

3. Permits auditors to optimize the sample size given the mathematically measured risk they are willing to accept. In this way both overauditing and underauditing can be avoided.

4. Enables auditors to make objective statements about the sampled population on the basis of the sample. In other words, the sample findings can be projected to the population and sampling risk can be explicitly considered by using accepted mathematical calculations.

Auditors who have used statistical sampling report the following benefits:[8]

- They tend to develop better working paper documentation.
- Their audit work is of higher quality than before the use of statistical sampling (i.e., more objective and defensible).
- They are more capable of rendering suggestions to clients.
- They have greater confidence about the audit opinion.
- They save time by eliminating transactions compliance tests that have no influence on substantive audit procedures.

Many audit tests do not involve sampling, such as footing of journals, reviewing records, searching for unusual relationships, and inquiring of client personnel. Also, in some instances, the cost of performing statistical sampling may exceed the benefits. An auditor should remember that statistical sampling is a tool that is useful in some, but not all situations. Whether statistical sampling should be used is a question that depends primarily on audit judgment and audit objectives, giving consideration to differential costs and cost trade-offs (i.e., opportunities for cost reduction in other aspects of the audit).

THE RISK OF SAMPLING

Traditionally, the basis for determining the extent of an audit examination has been the degree of reliability (assurance) that the auditor requires about the financial information recorded in the accounts. The auditor always has some idea, on a judgment basis, of what this degree of assurance is. In statistical sampling applications, the auditor must use judgment in selecting a desired level of reliability, but he or she should be able to mathematically determine the *extent of testing* that is necessary to achieve the desired

---

[8] James P. Bedingfield, "The Current State of Statistical Sampling and Auditing," **Journal of Accountancy** (December 1975), p. 53.

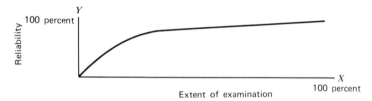

FIGURE 1.2 RELATIONSHIP BETWEEN EXTENT OF EXAMINATION AND RELIABILITY

reliability. Figure 1.2 indicates the degree of reliability that can normally be achieved in terms of the extent of examination. The Y axis (Figure 1.2) reflects the reliability achieved; the X axis reflects the extent of examination (sample size).

Complete confidence can only be approached with a complete examination, but the curve shows that a small test can achieve a relatively high degree of reliability and that, beyond a certain point, additional testing improves reliability by only a very small amount. This fact is the basic justification for test examinations. The risk of sampling is the complement of reliability, that is, one minus reliability is risk. The auditor, knowing that some risk is always involved when a test instead of a complete examination is made, has always consciously or unconsciously been aware of the characteristics of this curve. With the use of statistical sampling techniques the auditor can, in a given situation, mathematically determine the extent of testing necessary to provide a desired degree of reliability. Conversely, the auditor, by using statistical sampling, can determine the degree of risk associated with the extent of testing. The risk of sampling also is present for a nonstatistical sample and the auditor has to hold this risk to a relatively low level. However, a nonstatistical sample does not permit objective measurement of the risk of sampling.

WHAT IS NONSAMPLING ERROR?

Two concepts that are very important in any audit sampling application are nonsampling error and sampling error. The risk of sampling creates the possibility of sampling error. If all items rather than a sample were examined, there would be no sampling error. However, there is also a nonsampling risk that creates the possibility of nonsampling error. Examples of nonsampling error are as follows:

- Failure to define the population properly.
- Failure to define clearly the nature of an audit exception.
- Failure to recognize an error when one exists in the sample.

- Failure to obtain a random start.
- Failure to draw a random sample (or a sample that can be expected to be representative).
- Failure to evaluate findings properly.

In contrast, a sampling error occurs when a sample indicates characteristics that are not the actual (true) characteristics of the population. Conceptually, sampling error represents the difference between findings based on sample results versus findings based on examination of all the population items. Nonsampling errors are human errors and can be reduced, deleted, or prevented. Sampling errors are due entirely to chance. They are inherent in any sampling process, statistical or otherwise. Sampling error can be precisely measured and, hence, controlled when statistical sampling is used.

Nonsampling error can be reduced to a very low level by proper engagement planning, supervision, and review. Control of sampling error is discussed in detail later. The control of sampling error is accomplished in statistical applications through establishing appropriate relationships among sample size, characteristics of the population being sampled, and the degree of reliance being placed on nonsampling audit procedures.

In addition to the types of nonsampling errors that arise in using statistical sampling listed earlier, there are other nonsampling errors that are inherent in the auditing process. A selected audit procedure may not be effective in identifying an internal control deviation or a monetary misstatement. For example, an auditor may examine vouchers to determine if they were properly approved before cash was disbursed. If the only evidence of approval is the controller's signature on a voucher, there is a risk that the disbursement was not approved, even though the signature appears. Reliance on the controller's signature entails additional risk that cannot be statistically controlled. Consequently, audit risk can never be reduced below nonsampling risk, even if 100 percent of the items are audited.

In auditing, sampling risk and nonsampling risk have been defined in terms related to audit objectives and conclusions. According to SAS No. 39 (AU 350.10 and .11):

Sampling risk arises from the possibility that, when a compliance or a substantive test is restricted to a sample, the auditor's conclusions may be different from the conclusions he would reach if the test were applied in the same way to all items in the account balance or class of transactions. . . .

Nonsampling risk includes all aspects of audit risk that are not due to sampling. An auditor may apply a procedure to all transactions or balances and still fail to detect a material misstatement or a material internal accounting control weakness. Nonsampling risk includes the possibility of selecting audit procedures that are not appropriate to achieve the specific objective.

The specific types of sampling risk associated with compliance tests and substantive tests are explained in Chapters 3 and 4.

STATISTICAL SAMPLING AND PROFESSIONAL JUDGMENT

Statistical sampling does not eliminate professional judgment. For example, the auditor has to decide whether to use nonstatistical or statistical sampling (assuming, of course, that he or she elects to sample in the first place). There are also areas in a statistical sampling model where judgment must be exercised and quantified. Some of them are:

Population definition   The auditor must define the population in terms of its size, the characteristics of significance to the auditor, and what constitutes an error.

Sampling model   The auditor must determine the type of sampling model to be used (e.g., an attribute sampling model or a variable sampling model).

Selection technique   The auditor must decide which sampling selection process is to be used (e.g., computer generation, random number table selection, or systematic selection).

Error analysis   Statistical sampling findings must be evaluated both *quantitatively* and *qualitatively*. The primary input into the auditor's qualitative evaluation is his or her professional judgment and experience, not statistical sampling.

WHERE CAN YOU APPLY STATISTICAL SAMPLING?

According to a survey of CPAs in public accounting practice conducted in 1975, statistical sampling is used in the following areas:[9]

Compliance	Substantive
Cash disbursements	Accounts and notes receivable
Sales	Inventory
Payroll	Revenues and expenses
Cash receipts	Accounts and notes payable
Voucher system	Property, plant, and equipment
Purchasing	Cash

[9] James P. Bedingfield, "The Current State of Statistical Sampling and Auditing," Journal of Accountancy (December 1975), p. 51.

In a survey of internal auditors, Rittenberg and Schwieger found that statistical sampling is applied to areas such as:[10]

Confirmations (receivables, mortgages, notes, securities, etc.)

Inventories (test counts, observations, etc.)

Transactions testing (voucher testing, order processing, etc.)

Accounts payable and other disbursements work

Payroll tests

Insurance claims and processing procedures

Purchase order and procurement analysis

Tests of billing process and sales analysis

Adequacy of documentation (loans, securities, etc.)

Fixed asset work

These applications were used in financial auditing, operational auditing, EDP auditing, special investigations, and external auditor assistance.

Surveys identify characteristics that make certain compliance tests and substantive tests targets for potential statistical sampling applications. Populations characterized by large volume, homogeneous transactions, and material totals lend themselves to statistical sampling models.

The 1975 survey of CPAs identified "estimation sampling for attributes," "estimation sampling for variables," and "stratified sampling for variables" as the three most widely used statistical sampling models.

In an AICPA study conducted in 1978, Akresh reported:[11]

- Use of statistical sampling is increasing. Also, it was not typically used by CPA firms until the early 1970s.
- Most firms that use statistical sampling primarily use attribute sampling.
- Variable sampling is not used often, and most of the use is by the largest CPA firms.

The survey of internal auditors found that attribute sampling was the most frequently used statistical sampling model, followed by discovery, stop-or-go, and dollar unit sampling (referred to here as probability proportionate to size sampling).

Another interesting point also emerged from the 1975 survey: the primary drawback to the use of statistical sampling was "the lack of adequate training." A second prominent reason for not using statistical sampling was the belief held by some of the responding CPA practitioners that statistical

---

[10] Larry Rittenberg and Bradley J. Schwieger, "Use of Statistical Sampling Tools—Parts I and II," **The Internal Auditor** (August 1978), p. 31.

[11] Abraham D. Akresh, "The Use of Statistical Sampling in the Accounting Profession," unpublished manuscript.

sampling was not as relevant for firms servicing small clients. As Chapters 3 and 4 demonstrate, statistical sampling is useful for clients of all sizes. The most pervasive drawback to more extensive use of statistical sampling in auditing is that statistical sampling techniques are not as widely understood as they should be.

The authors' own experience indicates that since the issuance of SAS No. 39 the use of statistical sampling has increased and that the PPS method, explained in Chapter 6, is now more widely used than variable sampling.

RELATIONSHIP OF STATISTICAL SAMPLING TO AUDITING STANDARDS

The 10 generally accepted auditing standards are authoritative guides for measuring the quality of audit performance. The second sentence in the scope paragraph of the unqualified audit opinion indicates that the examination was performed in accordance with generally accepted auditing standards. In this section we view the 10 standards in a statistical sampling context.

GENERAL STANDARDS

1. The examination is to be performed by a person or persons having adequate technical training and proficiency as an auditor.
2. In all matters relating to the assignment, an independence in mental attitude is to be mantained by the auditor or auditors.
3. Due professional care is to be exercised in the performance of the examination and the preparation of the report.

STANDARDS OF FIELD WORK

1. The work is to be adequately planned and assistants, if any, are to be properly supervised.
2. There is to be a proper study and evaluation of the existing internal control as a basis for reliance thereon and for the determination of the resultant extent of the tests to which auditing procedures are to be restricted.
3. Sufficient competent evidential matter is to be obtained through inspection, observation, inquiries, and confirmations to afford a reasonable basis for an opinion regarding the financial statements under examination.

STANDARDS OF REPORTING

1. The report shall state whether the financial statements are presented in accordance with generally accepted accounting principles.
2. The report shall state whether such principles have been consistently observed in the current period in relation to the preceding period.
3. Informative disclosures in the financial statements are to be regarded as reasonably adequate unless otherwise stated in the report.
4. The report shall either contain an expression of opinion regarding the financial statements, taken as a whole, or an assertion to the effect that an opinion cannot be expressed. When an overall opinion cannot be expressed, the reasons therefor should be stated. In all cases where an auditor's name is associated with financial statements, the report should contain a clear-cut indication of the character of the auditor's examination, if any, and the degree of responsibility he is taking.

In viewing the 10 standards from a statistical sampling perspective, general standard no. 1 and all three field work standards take on special meaning. For instance, auditors, if they elect to use statistical sampling, should have adequate knowledge and training in the sampling model they use (e.g., attribute or variable). The practicing CPA also should be given on-the-job training in addition to formal training in the statistical sampling area. The CPA should continually read and study current sampling literature in order to understand the limitations and pitfalls of statistical sampling. It is also imperative that the partner reviewing a staff application of statistical sampling be knowledgeable and proficient in the area of attribute or variable sampling.

The field work auditing standards really have new meaning when they are considered in a statistical sampling context. Figure 1.3 depicts the special meaning the field work standards have when statistical sampling is applied to important areas in an audit engagement.

CHAPTER ORGANIZATION

The order of presentation of the topics discussed in the chapters that follow is:

FIGURE 1.3 RELATIONSHIP OF STATISTICAL SAMPLING TO FIELD WORK AUDITING STANDARDS

Standards of Field Work	Audit Tasks	Statistical Sampling Tasks
The work should be adequately planned and assistants, if any, should be properly supervised.	Plan work. Supervise assistants. Review work.	Define population and errors. Specify decision criteria in terms of risk and precision (tolerable rate or tolerable error) Evaluate results both quantitatively and qualitatively.
There should be a proper study and evaluation of internal control as a basis for reliance and for determination of the resultant extent of the tests to which auditing procedures should be restricted.	Perform preliminary evaluation of internal control if controls are to be relied on. Document system. Apply walk through. Perform detail compliance tests. Determine extent of substantive tests based on final evaluation of control.	Identify areas of reliance in terms of attributes to be tested. Select appropriate attribute sampling model. Vary substantive sample size inversely with reliance placed on internal control.
Sufficient competent evidential matter should be obtained through inspection, observation, inquiries, and confirmations to afford a reasonable basis for an opinion regarding the financial statements under examination.	Obtain evidential matter by substantive tests. Evidence should be: 1. Relevant. 2. Sufficient. 3. Competent. Evidence must establish a reasonable basis for opinion.	Sample for variables. Specify risk level and precision limits (tolerable error). Determine extent of audit tests. Evaluate sample results mathematically.

Each chapter is preceded by learning objectives to aid in identifying the important material in the chapter and facilitate studying for examinations. Each chapter is also followed by a glossary of new terms, review questions, and case problems (for selected chapters).

GLOSSARY

Attribute   A qualitative characteristic of an item that distinguishes the item from other items: for example, the absence of an approval signature required on a purchase order or a variance between a sales invoice and the amount recorded in a sales journal.

Attribute sampling   A statistical model used to statistically estimate the actual and the upper precision limit of the occurrence rate of the attribute.

Audit sampling   The application of an audit procedure to less than 100 percent of the items within an account balance or class of transactions for the purpose of evaluating some characteristic of the balance or class.

Block sample   A sample including all items in a selected time period, numerical sequence, or alphabetical sequence: for example, selecting 50 checks in sequence for testing or testing one entire week. (It is not acceptable to select a block sample and to project the results to the entire population.)

Compliance tests   Tests that are used to determine whether internal controls actually exist and are working effectively.

Difference estimation   A statistical model used to estimate the total difference between audited and book values based on differences obtained from sample observations. The estimated population difference $\hat{D}$ is added/subtracted to the footed book value to yield a point estimate of the population total.

Discovery sampling A special case of attribute sampling that is used to determine a specified probability of finding at least one example of an occurrence (attribute) in a population. Also referred to as *exploratory sampling*.

Nonsampling error An error that actually exists in a sample but is not identified as an error because of the auditor's failure to recognize the error. Naturally, the statistical results are incorrect if nonsampling errors occur.

Nonstatistical sample A representative audit sample that is evaluated judgmentally rather than mathematically.

Random sample A sample that can be evaluated statistically because each item in the population has a known probability of being selected.

Representative sample An audit sample that is selected either randomly or by the haphazard selection method (see Chapter 2).

Sampling error The chance that a representative sample will lead to the wrong conclusion or an inaccurate projection. Sampling error is inherent in any sampling process, nonstatistical or statistical, where less than 100 percent of the items are examined. Sampling error results when a nonrepresentative sample characteristic is extrapolated to a population.

Statistical sampling A sampling plan applied in such a manner that the laws of probability can be used to make statements about a population. Statistical sampling is the whole process by which the size of a sample is determined, items are selected and examined, and results are evaluated.

Stop-or-go sampling A type of attribute sampling that permits sampling to halt if a certain number (including zero) of occurrences are observed. The sampling units are examined in groups until the cumulative evidence is sufficient to achieve a defined precision and reliability. Also referred to as *sequential sampling*.

Stratified mean per unit A statistical model in which the population is divided into strata and samples are drawn from the various strata. Stratification, properly applied, reduces the sample size relative to unstratified mean per unit.

Substantive tests Tests of details of account balances and analytical tests (i.e., the review of significant ratios and trends and resulting investigation of unusual fluctuations and questionable items). Substantive tests are sometimes referred to as ''tests of bona fides'' and ''year-end tests.''

Unstratified mean per unit A statistical model whereby a sample mean is calculated and projected as an estimated total. Also referred to as *simple extension*. Unstratified simple extension tends to produce inefficient sample sizes relative to stratified simple extension.

Variable sampling A statistical model used to project a quantitative characteristic, such as a dollar amount. Variable sampling includes unstratified mean per unit, stratified mean per unit, and difference estimation.

REVIEW QUESTIONS

1-1. Indicate whether each of the following is true (T) or false (F).

    A. If an auditor selects a sample randomly, he or she is using statistical sampling.

    B. Two broad classes of statistical sampling models are attribute sampling and discovery sampling.

    C. The AICPA requires the use of statistical sampling in selected situations.

    D. Nonstatistical sampling permits objective determination of sample risk.

    E. The failure to define the nature of an audit error is an example of a sampling error.

    F. Statistical sampling requires that selected audit judgments be quantified but not eliminated.

    G. If an auditor examines 100 percent of the items in a population, uncertainty is not eliminated.

1-2. Two requirements must be met for a sampling application to qualify as a statistical sample. What are these two requirements?

1-3. List three types of attribute sampling models.

1-4. List three types of variable sampling models.

1-5. List four audit areas where attribute sampling might be used for compliance testing.

1-6. List four areas where variable sampling might be used for substantive testing.

1-7. How can nonsampling error be controlled?

1-8. Cite four advantages of statistical sampling relative to nonstatistical sampling.

1-9. Statistical sampling does not eliminate professional judgment. Identify four areas involving professional judgment that are inherent in a statistical sampling application.

1-10. "Audit risk" cannot be eliminated even if the total population is audited. Why?

1-11. Which of the 10 generally accepted auditing standards are primarily affected by the use of statistical sampling in an audit engagement?

CASE

CASE 1-1 Is Sampling Involved?
(estimated time to complete: 15 minutes)

The following list contains examples of tests an auditor might perform in an examination of financial statements. For each test listed, identify whether the procedure usually involves sampling, and if it does, state whether attribute or variable sampling would be typically used.

A. Tests of recording of shipments.
B. Comparison of financial information with budgeted information.
C. Tests of controls over payroll and related personnel policy systems.
D. Obtaining written representations from management.
E. Inspecting land and buildings.
F. Completing an internal accounting control questionnaire.
G. Tests of controls over inventory pricing.
H. Tests of recorded payroll expense.
I. Observing cash-handling procedures.
J. Tests of the amount of transactions that are not supported by proper approval.
K. Selecting one transaction to obtain an understanding of the entity's system of internal accounting control.

Organize your answer as follows:

Procedure	Involves Sampling? (Yes or No)	Attribute/ Variable/ Not Applicable

2
SELECTING A RANDOM SAMPLE

Learning Objectives

After a careful study and discussion of this chapter, you will be able to:

1. Define random sampling, sampling with replacement, and sampling without replacement.
2. Use a random-number table to select a random sample.
3. Discuss the use of the computer to generate random numbers.
4. Use systematic sampling or random systematic selection to generate sample elements.
5. Illustrate sampling probability proportionate to size as a sample selection technique.
6. Cite the advantages of stratified sample selection.
7. Describe the haphazard selection method that is permissible for a nonstatistical sample.

Chapter 1 delineates two requirements that must be met before a sampling model can be statistical. These requirements are: (1) the sample must be randomly selected, and (2) the sample results must be mathematically evaluated. This chapter explains and illustrates the first requirement.

Statistical sampling requires that a sample be selected in an unbiased way. That is, the sample must be random. Six techniques are available to aid the auditor in generating a random sample. They are: random number table selection, computer selection, systematic selection, random systematic selection, probability proportionate to size selection, and stratified selection. We discuss each of these selection techniques in this chapter. The selection techniques presented are used whenever it is desirable to produce a random sample, usually without regard to whether the sampling model is an attribute or a variable sampling application. In fact, the selection techniques can also be used for nonstatistical as well as statistical sampling.[1]

DEFINITION OF RANDOM SAMPLE, POPULATION, AND SAMPLING FRAME

If the auditor wishes to measure a sampling risk when less than 100 percent of a population is examined, a random (probability) sample must be used. Recall from Chapter 1, that nonstatistical samples are those where the inclusion or exclusion of individual sampling elements depends on professional judgment. Such judgment samples may indeed yield good estimates or correct decisions, but with this type of sampling technique, the accountant or auditor has no objective method for evaluating the adequacy of the sample.

Of course, because of sampling risk, an accountant or auditor may decide that a complete enumeration is desirable. Often the accountant will decide that at least part of the population should be examined 100 percent. Because of cost and time considerations, however, the decision to sample a portion of a population and to accept some sampling risk is usually made. In such situations, proper sample design is of utmost importance.

Auditors must exercise caution to avoid projecting sample results to a population if all population items did not have a chance of being included in the sample. In other words, it is improper to conclude that all vouchers for cash disbursements processed during the year are properly supported if the sample was selected only from vouchers processed in July. Likewise, it would be improper to conclude that all sales were properly recorded if the sample were selected only from charge sales and excluded cash sales.

---

[1] According to Rittenberg and Schwieger, many internal auditors use a statistical (random) selection process to reduce bias in their samples. However, they do not use statistical evaluation. See Larry E. Rittenberg and Bradley J. Schwieger, "Use of Statistical Sampling Tools—Parts I and II," **The Internal Auditor** (August 1978), p. 28.

A *simple **random sample*** may be defined as a sample that is selected in such a way that every element in the population has an equal chance of being selected. The *population* is the universe or field about which the auditor desires certain information. The population the auditor wishes to generalize about must be defined in advance. There are two stipulations the auditor should adhere to when defining a population:

- The population should be relevant to the audit objectives.
- The population definition should enable anyone to tell whether an item belongs or does not belong to the population.

The following examples illustrate population definition.

Population definition	Items included
All accounts receivable as of year end	Accounts with zero balances, positive balances, and negative balances
All accounts receivable appearing in the year-end trial balance	Accounts with positive or negative balances
All checks written for the year	All checks, including voided and unrecorded checks

In addition to very carefully defining the population, the auditor must define the sampling frame in advance. The sampling frame is a listing or other physical representation of the individual items in the population. For example, in testing physical inventory there are three possible sampling frames: (1) an inventory listing, (2) the perpetual inventory records, or (3) the physical item of inventory. The major requirement in selecting a sampling frame is to make certain that the frame is a complete representation of all of the items in the sampled population. However, frames may contain units that do not belong to the population. For example, a listing of accounts receivable may contain zero and credit balance accounts, even if the auditor is interested in only the positive balances. If a zero balance or credit balance account is selected, it is excluded from the sample and another item is drawn.

SAMPLING WITH OR WITHOUT REPLACEMENT

Sampling with replacement is a sample selection method that permits a selected sample item to be returned to the population and reselected. In other words, the same item may be included in the sample more than once.

Sampling without replacement is a technique where once an item is selected, it is removed from the population and cannot be selected again. The item can be included only once in a sample selection.

To illustrate sampling with or without replacement, let us assume that we have a goldfish bowl that contains 100 marbles numbered from 1 to 100. If sampling with replacement is employed in drawing a random sample of 20 marbles, marble 54 may be selected as the first sample item and, again, as say, the eighteenth sample item. If it is, marble 54 is included twice in the total sample of 20. On the other hand, if we are sampling without replacement, marble 54, once selected, is removed from the goldfish bowl and cannot be reselected.

Because of logic and sample efficiency (smaller sample size), sampling without replacement is more applicable to accounting and audit sampling problems. Consequently, throughout this book sampling without replacement is assumed unless otherwise stated.

RANDOM NUMBER TABLES

A random, as opposed to an arbitrary or judgmental, selection of the sample offers the best chance that the sample will be unbiased. A random number table is one device for helping to achieve randomness. Such a table is composed of randomly generated digits 0 through 9. Each digit should appear in the table approximately the same number of times, and the order in which they appear is random. Columns in the table are purely arbitrary and otherwise meaningless. Columns do, however, make random number tables easier to read.

In using a random number table to determine which population items will be included in a sample, once an item has been randomly selected to be part of the sample, it cannot be ignored or excluded for any reason. Selected random numbers should be documented in audit work papers by identifying each of the following:

1. *Correspondence*—defines the relationship between population sampled and random number table.

2. *Route*—specifies selection path. The auditor may go up or down the columns—left or right. Any route desired can be selected as long as it is consistently followed until all required numbers are drawn.

3. *Starting point*—identifies row, column, digit starting position, as well as source (book) and page number of selection route.

4. *Stopping point*—facilitates adding new sample items, if needed.

To establish correspondence, each population item must have a unique number in the random number table. It must be possible to read the random number table and arrive at the proper sample element. To illustrate, assume that an auditor is examining a population of sales invoices numbered from 1 to 750. To establish correspondence, it is necessary to use a three-digit number scheme in the random number table.

In selecting a route to identify sample elements, the only stipulation is to document the route definition in the audit work papers so that a reviewer could, if necessary, reproduce the exact sample selection. Another point to remember is that the route used should not be cumbersome or complex. A complex route definition increases the probability of human error (non-sampling error).

To determine a starting point, the random number table that consists of many pages may be opened at random and the random stab method used to define row, column, and digit starting position. In the unlikely event an entire random number table is exhausted in meeting the needs of a large sample, the table should not be used again. In that instance, a larger random number table should be used. Auditors are not likely to encounter this problem, however.

USING A RANDOM NUMBER TABLE

Figure 2.1 on page 25 is an illustrative page from a random number table. It is included to show the efficient use of a table of this kind. Figure 2.1 should not be used in actual practice, since it is only one page from a table that contains 3000 rows of random numbers. Note that Figure 2.1 contains 45 rows and 10 columns.

To demonstrate the use of the table in Figure 2.1, we present a series of four illustrations. Assume a route definition as follows: Read down the column to the bottom of the table. After reaching the bottom of the page, start with the next column by using the same digit starting position.

Illustration No. 1

Select a sample of four items from prenumbered canceled checks numbered from 1 to 500. Start at row 5, column 1, digit starting position 1. Select three-digit numbers. Items selected are:

      145 (sample item no. 1)

      516 (discard because check numbers do not go beyond 500)

      032 (sample item no. 2)

      246 (sample item no. 3)

      840 (discard)

      181 (sample item no. 4)

FIGURE 2.1 ILLUSTRATIVE PAGE FROM A RANDOM NUMBER TABLE

Table of Random Numbers

	(01)	(02)	(03)	(04)	(05)	(06)	(07)	(08)	(09)	(10)
(0001)	9492	4562	4180	5525	7255	1297	9296	1283	6011	0350
(0002)	1557	0392	8989	6898	1072	6013	0020	8582	5059	9324
(0003)	0714	5947	2420	6210	3824	2743	4217	3707	5894	0040
(0004)	0558	8266	4990	8954	7455	6309	9543	1148	0835	0808
(0005)	1458	8725	3750	3138	2499	6017	7744	0485	3010	9606
(0006)	5169	6981	4319	3369	9424	4117	7632	5457	0608	4741
(0007)	0328	5213	1017	5248	8622	6454	8120	4585	3295	0840
(0008)	2462	2055	9782	4213	3452	9940	8859	1000	6260	2851
(0009)	8408	8697	3982	8228	7668	8139	3736	4889	7283	7706
(0010)	1818	5041	9706	4646	3992	4110	4091	7619	1053	4020
(0011)	1771	8614	8593	0930	2095	5005	6387	4002	7498	0066
(0012)	7050	1437	6847	4679	9059	4139	6602	6817	9972	5360
(0013)	5875	2094	0495	3213	5694	5513	3547	9035	7588	5994
(0014)	2473	2087	4618	1507	4471	9542	7565	2371	3981	0812
(0015)	1976	1639	4956	9011	8221	4840	4513	5263	8837	5868
(0016)	4006	4029	7270	8027	7476	7690	6362	1251	9277	5833
(0017)	2149	8162	0667	0825	7353	4645	3273	1181	8526	1176
(0018)	1669	7011	6548	5851	8278	9006	8176	1268	7113	4548
(0019)	7436	5041	4087	1647	7205	3977	4257	9008	3067	7206
(0020)	2178	3632	5745	2228	1780	6043	9296	4469	8108	5005
(0021)	1964	3043	3134	8923	1019	8560	5871	7971	2233	7960
(0022)	5859	7120	9682	0173	2413	8490	6162	1220	3710	5270
(0023)	2352	1929	5985	3303	9590	6974	5811	4264	0248	4295
(0024)	9267	0156	9112	2783	2026	0493	9544	8065	4916	3835
(0025)	4787	0119	1261	5197	0156	2385	9957	0990	6681	2323
(0026)	5550	0699	8080	1152	6002	2532	3075	2777	8671	4068
(0027)	7281	9442	4941	1041	0569	4354	8000	3158	9142	5498
(0028)	1322	7212	3286	2886	9739	5012	0360	5800	9745	8640
(0029)	5176	2259	2774	3641	3553	2475	1974	4578	3388	6656
(0030)	2292	1664	1237	2518	0081	8788	8170	5519	0467	4646
(0031)	6935	8265	3393	4268	4429	1443	4670	4177	7872	9298
(0032)	8538	5393	8093	7835	0484	2550	0827	3112	1065	0246
(0033)	4351	0691	0592	2256	4881	4776	4992	2919	3046	3246
(0034)	6337	8219	9134	9611	8961	4277	6288	2818	1603	4084
(0035)	2257	1980	5269	9615	8628	4715	6366	1542	7267	8917

FIGURE 2.1 (Continued)

Table of Random Numbers

	(01)	(02)	(03)	(04)	(05)	(06)	(07)	(08)	(09)	(10)
(0036)	8319	9526	0819	0238	7504	1499	8507	9767	1345	7509
(0037)	1717	8853	2651	9327	7244	0428	6583	2862	1452	8061
(0038)	6519	9348	1026	4190	4210	6231	0732	7000	9553	6125
(0039)	1728	2608	6422	6711	1348	6163	4289	6621	0736	4771
(0040)	5788	5724	5388	5218	8929	3299	0945	6760	8258	5305
(0041)	7495	0547	0226	1188	1270	0689	5048	7689	9477	2210
(0042)	1519	1689	9573	7207	4188	1155	1366	1517	1943	2399
(0043)	0493	2858	2812	7122	4852	7317	6895	3666	5095	7681
(0044)	7235	8838	6680	7231	3713	9231	8510	6206	8596	3657
(0045)	2240	8303	9164	9119	3531	8567	9007	6877	5646	6305

TABLE SOURCE: From **Handbook of Sampling for Auditing and Accounting**, Second Edition by Herbert Arkin. Copyright © 1974 by McGraw-Hill Book Company, Inc. Used by permission of McGraw-Hill Book Company, Inc.

Caution

Do not use this illustration in an actual audit situation.

Illustration No. 2

To minimize discards in Illustration No. 1, table numbers greater than 500 can be reduced by 500 to produce a sample item within the population boundary of 1 to 500. The four sample items selected are:

145 (sample item no. 1)

016 (sample item no. 2 = 516 − 500)

032 (sample item no. 3)

246 (sample item no. 4)

340 (sample item no. 5 = 840 − 500)

Illustration No. 3

Select a sample of four items from a population of sales invoices numbered from 2586 to 8892. Start at row 12, column 8, digit starting position 4 (remember columns in the table are arbitrary and simply aid in table reading). Select four-digit numbers. Items selected are:

7997 (sample item no. 1)

5758 (sample item no. 2)

1398 (discard)

3883 (sample item no. 3)

1927 (discard)

1852 (discard)

8711 (sample item no. 4)

Illustration No. 4

Select four sales invoices numbered from 5000 to 12,000. Start at row 21, column 2, digit starting point 1. Rather than using a five-digit number, which produces a large number of discards, subtract a constant to get a population with four digits. If a constant of 3000 is used, the usable numbers selected from 2000 to 9000 are:

3043 (usable no. 1)

7120 (usable no. 2)

1929 (discard)

0156 (discard)

0119 (discard)

0699 (discard)

9442 (discard)

7212 (usable no. 3)

2259 (usable no. 4)

The above four usable sample items must be increased by 3000 to correspond with the selected population items. Thus, population items selected are:

6,043 (sample item no. 1 = 3,043 + 3,000)

10,120 (sample item no. 2 = 7,120 + 3,000)

10,212 (sample item no. 3 = 7,212 + 3,000)

5,259 (sample item no. 4 = 2,259 + 3,000)

Sometimes problems other than many discards arise from using a random number table. A population may have an alphabetical prefix instead of a consecutive numbering prefix. Inventory items, for example, are often not identified by a numerical numbering system. A possible solution to such a problem is to convert the alphabetical prefix to a numerical system by numbering the items consecutively.

Another problem sometimes develops when a population has overlapping sequences. For example, two checking accounts defined as one population may have number sequences from 500 to 800 and 300 to 500. A possible solution to this problem is to use proportional sampling. That is, since the first check number sequence contains 300 checks and the second check number sequence contains 200 checks, the total sample can be allocated 3/5 to the first batch of checks and 2/5 to the second batch of checks.

COMPUTER-GENERATED RANDOM NUMBERS

Computer generation of random numbers via time-sharing or generalized audit software is more efficient than using a random number table, because random number table selection produces more discards and human error. Thus, when available, computers should be used to generate random numbers.

Many accounting firms have random-number generation capabilities as part of their generalized audit software package. The audit software package is useful in accessing client files that are stored on data cards, magnetic tape, or disks. In addition to generalized audit software, many CPA firms have access to time-sharing programs. Time-sharing programs are very useful in producing random numbers for client applications when client files are not computerized.

To use a time-sharing terminal, the auditor:

- Sets the terminal's on/off switch to on.
- Dials the system's phone number.
- Waits for the printing of the sign-on message.
- Types an account number and any needed password.
- Waits for the printing of a confirming response.

After the confirming response indicating that the auditor is connected with the system, program execution is begun by keying a run command and the random number program name. An illustrative time-sharing application is shown in Figure 2.2 (italics indicate user inputs).

SYSTEMATIC SELECTION

In systematic selection, the auditor calculates a sampling interval and then selects the items for the sample based on the size of the interval. For example, if the population size N contains 1000 items and the sample size desired n is 100, the sampling interval is 10. A random start between 1 and 10 is selected as the first sample element. Afterward, every tenth item is selected.

FIGURE **2.2** ILLUSTRATIVE TIME-SHARING PROGRAM FOR RANDOM NUMBER GENERATION

This program generates your choice of:

1 ... Random days of the year
2 ... Random page and line numbers
3 ... Random document numbers from one population of broken sequences

Which do you want option 1, 2, or 3 to stop press escape key?   *2*
How many samples, pages, lines per page?   *20, 10, 50*
Thank you

Generation Order	Page and Line	
17	1	4
16	1	22
10	1	43
15	1	45
2	2	9
14	2	18
13	2	19
18	2	33
6	3	26
12	4	27
5	5	2
9	5	41
8	7	15
3	7	42
4	8	7
7	8	34
19	8	42
1	9	38
11	10	36

Random numbers printed 19*
Total population 500

 * The program rejects duplications, which results in sampling without replacement. Because of rejections, the number of samples printed may vary slightly from the number requested. The maximum number of random numbers obtainable by using this program is approximately 1200.

The primary advantage of systematic sampling is ease of use. However, a major problem is that it may produce a biased sample. To guard against a biased sample, the auditor should:

1. Be satisfied that the population is in random order.
2. Use more than one random start. (One large CPA firm uses five as a minimum number of starts. For illustrative purposes, we also use five.)
3. Continue sample selection until the population is exhausted.
4. Do not substitute one sample item for another (unselected) population item. (Population items that are not selected should not be substituted for sample items that are difficult to audit or locate.)
5. Use computer generation, if practical, instead of systematic sampling.

To illustrate point 2, using the sampling interval of 10 calculated above, the sampling interval is multiplied by the desired number of random starts to arrive at an adjusted sampling interval. Assuming five as the minimum number of random starts, the adjusted sampling interval is: 10 times 5 equals 50. Random numbers between 1 and 50 are selected to identify the first five sample elements. Afterward, every fiftieth item from each of the five starts is selected. To illustrate, assume that the following five random numbers between 1 and 50 were obtained from a random number table.

$$22 \quad 8 \quad 34 \quad 48 \quad 12$$

From lowest to highest these are arrayed as:

First five samples	8	12	22	34	48
Sampling interval	+50	+50	+50	+50	+50
6–10 samples	58	62	72	84	98
Sampling interval	+50	+50	+50	+50	+50
11–15 samples	108	112	122	134	148
	+50	+50	. . . .		+50
	n_{16}	n_{17}	. . . .		n_{100}

☐ = sample elements

Point 3 (continue sample selection until the population is exhausted) guards against a biased selection by requiring that sample selection continue until the last sample selected plus the sampling interval exceeds the last item in the population. If the auditor stops sampling when he or she reaches the desired sample size without sampling from the tail end of the population, the sample findings may not be representative.

According to point 4 (do not substitute one sample item for another), substitution is not permissible. If sample item 25 corresponds to an unusable item (say, a voided check), the auditor should not substitute item 24 or 26 or any other item. The sample size is simply reduced by one.

In this respect, the auditor should distinguish between legitimately voided or unused documents and missing supporting documentation. According to SAS No. 39 (AU 350.39):

Auditing procedures that are appropriate to achieve the objective of the compliance test should be applied to each sample item. If the auditor is not able to apply the planned audit procedures or appropriate alternative procedures to selected items, he should consider the reasons for this limitation and he should ordinarily consider those selected items to be deviations from the procedures for the purpose of evaluating the sample.

For substantive testing, SAS No. 39 (AU 350.25) states:

The auditor's treatment of unexamined items will depend on their effect on his evaluation of the sample. If the auditor's evaluation of the sample results would not be altered by considering those unexamined items to be in error, it is not necessary to examine the items. However, if considering those unexamined items to be misstated would lead to a conclusion that the balance or class is materially in error, the auditor should consider alternative procedures that would provide him with sufficient evidence to form a conclusion. The auditor should also consider whether the reasons for his inability to examine the items have implications in relation to his planned reliance on internal accounting control or his degree of reliance on management representations.

When applying systematic sampling, the sample will usually not be evenly divisible into the population as in the above examples. In these cases, the size of the skip interval should be rounded down to an integer. For example, if the population contains 10,069 items and the auditor wants to select 100 items with five multiple starts, the adjusted skip interval is 500 (10,069 ÷ 100 = 100 rounded × 5 = 500).

RANDOM SYSTEMATIC SELECTION

Samples may also be selected by the random systematic method. This method, as the name implies, is a combination of the random number and the systematic method. It is more random than the systematic method and sometimes involves less time than random number selection.

In systematic selection a fixed interval is used to choose items for the sample. In random systematic selection a variable interval is used. The variable intervals will have an average equal to the fixed interval (N/n = sample interval), as in the systematic method. To determine the variable intervals to be used, random numbers between one and two times the fixed (average) sampling interval are chosen. These random numbers (intervals) are then added together to determine the items to be selected.

If we return to the example used under systematic selection, the calculated sampling interval is 10 (1000/100 = 10). For random systematic selection, 100 random numbers between 01 and 20 (2 × 10) would be selected to represent the interval to be used. Assume the following random numbers from a random number table are selected as part of the 100: 8, 2, 14, 15, 3, and 8. The first sample item selected is 8, the second is 10 (8 + 2), the third is 24 (10 + 14), the fourth is 39 (24 + 15), the fifth is 42 (39 + 3), the sixth is 50 (42 + 8), and so forth. Of course, the auditor still needs 94 (100 − 6) more random numbers between 01 and 20 to complete the selection process.

SAMPLING PROBABILITY PROPORTIONATE TO SIZE

Sampling probability proportionate to size (also referred to as dollar unit sampling) gives units with larger recorded amounts proportionally more opportunity to be selected than units with smaller recorded amounts. A sales invoice with a $10,000 total would have a ten times greater chance of being selected than an invoice with $1000 total. Thus, sampling probability proportionate to size is a random process, because each recorded dollar in the population has an equal chance of selection. It is not, however, a random *unit* process because each sales invoice does not have an equal probability of selection. Before applying sampling probability proportionate to size, negative amounts should be removed from the population.

To apply sampling probability proportionate to size, the following sequence of steps must be followed.

1. Select random numbers according to desired sample size from a random number table. Each random number should contain as many digits as are contained in the total recorded amount (omit negative amounts).
2. Arrange the selected random numbers in ascending order.
3. Prepare a listing of the cumulative recorded amounts.
4. Find the location in the cumulative listing of the selected random numbers and include the corresponding sampling unit in the sample.

To illustrate, if the recorded amount of sales invoices is $5000 and a sample size of four is desired, the auditor selects four random numbers with four digits not greater than 5000 from a random number table. Assume that these numbers are 0350, 4741, 0040, and 0808. In ascending order, they are 40, 350, 808, and 4741. The sample selected should contain the 40th cumulative dollar, the 350th cumulative dollar, the 808th cumulative dollar, and the 4741st cumulative dollar. The dollar selected acts as a hook to drag in the sales invoice in which it is located. If the population of $5000 of sales invoices containing 12 invoices appears as follows, units 1, 1, 3, 12 will be selected as sample items.

Unit-number	Recorded amount	Cumulative amount
1	$500	$500
2	256	756
3	819	1575
4	125	1700
5	416	2116
6	215	2331
7	604	2935
8	245	3180
9	720	3900
10	404	4304
11	340	4644
12	356	5000

Note that sample item no. 1 is included twice because both the 40th cumulative dollar and the 350th cumulative dollar are contained within the same sampling unit. In using sampling probability proportionate to size, it is necessary to sample with replacement.

STRATIFIED SELECTION

Stratified selection is not itself a technique for drawing sample items. It is, however, a technique that is useful in improving the efficiency of sample design. By stratifying a population, the auditor can give greater representation to the larger recorded amounts. In fact, stratification allows the auditor to use a smaller sample size to achieve the planned level of sampling risk.

Stratified selection is used more often for variable sampling applications than for attribute applications. For example, in an audit of accounts receivable, the accountant may judgmentally decide to stratify the population and apply different sample selection techniques to the various strata. To confirm accounts receivable, he or she might stratify and test as follows:

Stratum	Size	Composition of stratum	Sample selection
1	22	All accounts over $5000	100% examination
2	586	All accounts between $1000 and $5000	Random number table
3	126	All accounts under $1000	Systematic selection
4	14	All accounts with credit balances	100% examination

Stratified selection has at least two major advantages from an audit perspective. It enables the auditor to relate sample selection to key and material items in the population and to use different audit techniques for each stratum. Stratification also improves the reliability of the sample and reduces the required sample size. If homogeneous items are grouped together, sample efficiency and effectiveness are increased.

Stratification is discussed and illustrated in Chapters 4 and 5. In addition, Chapter 6 considers "Sampling Probability Proportionate to Size," which is actually a type of stratified selection (units with larger recorded amounts are more likely to be selected). Because of the large sample sizes produced in variable sampling applications, *unrestricted random sampling* (when each unit has an equal chance of selection) is seldom used in audit situations.

REPRESENTATIVE SELECTION FOR NONSTATISTICAL SAMPLING

Naturally, any of the random-based selection methods also may be used for nonstatistical sampling. However, there is a method that produces a representative sample that is not one of the random-based methods. It is called haphazard selection and is described in the AICPA guide, *Audit Sampling*, as follows:

A *haphazard sample* consists of sampling units selected without any conscious bias, that is, without any special reason for including or omitting items from the sample. It does not consist of sampling units selected in a careless manner, and it is selected in a manner that can be expected to be representative of the population.[2]

---

[2] **Audit Sampling**, Audit and Accounting Guide, AICPA, New York, 1983, p. 29.

The key to haphazard selection is to avoid being biased by the nature, size, appearance, or location of items. For exmple, if the auditor selects invoices from a cabinet of drawers, the auditor should not select items only from the middle of the drawers because that would not give invoices in the first or last sections of the drawers a chance of selection.

Note that if the auditor only selects large or unusual items from the population or uses some other judgmental criterion for selection, the selection method has a conscious bias and cannot be considered a representative selection method.

The fact that judgmental selection is not acceptable for audit sampling does not mean that auditors should stop using judgment in selecting items. The point is only that the items selected using judgmental criteria are not necessarily representative of the population, and conclusions based on items selected judgmentally should not be extended to the population.

SAS No. 39 (AU 350.21) explains the matter as follows:

When planning a sample for a substantive test of details, the auditor uses his judgment to determine which items, if any, . . . should be individually examined and which items, if any, should be subject to sampling. The auditor should examine those items for which, in his judgment, acceptance of some sampling risk is not justified. . . . Any items that the auditor has decided to examine 100 percent are not part of the items subject to sampling.

SUMMARY

One of the most important ingredients of an effective statistical sampling application is a random sample. Without a random sample, sample results cannot be statistically evaluated.

Auditors use a variety of acceptable techniques to ensure that the sample selection process produces unbiased samples. Techniques introduced in this chapter include random number table selection, computer selection, systematic selection, random systematic selection, probability proportionate to size selection, and stratified selection. Generally, auditors use sampling without replacement. However, when proportionate to size selection is employed, sampling with replacement is appropriate. Sampling probability proportionate to size is discussed in detail in Chapter 6. For a nonstatistical sample, an auditor may use random or haphazard selection.

GLOSSARY

Biased sample A sample selected by a selection process that prevents each sample item from having an opportunity of being selected.

Correspondence   The defined relationship between the population sampled and a random number table.

Discards   Unusable numbers generated from a random number selection device (e.g., a random number table).

Haphazard Sample   A sample selected without any conscious bias that is expected to be representative of the population.

Population   All the items in the account or group being audited. Also referred to as *universe* and *field*.

Proportionate to size sampling   A sampling technique in which each population unit has a probability of being selected that is proportional to its recorded amount. Also frequently referred to as *dollar unit sampling*.

Random number table   A table composed of randomly generated digits 0 through 9 that can be used to generate random samples.

Random sample   A sample drawn from a population, each element of which has an equal probability of being selected; a valid statistical sample. Also commonly referred to as *probability sampling*.

Random-stab method   A technique whereby a random number table is opened randomly and a random stab is used to determine row, column and digit starting position.

Random systematic sampling   A systematic sample selection technique with a variable (random) rather than a fixed sampling interval.

Representative sample   A sample selected using haphazard selection or a random-based selection method.

Route   The predefined path to be followed through a random number table when selecting a sample.

Sampling frame   A listing or physical representation of a sampling unit. For example, for a test of cash disbursements, the individual check number could be a sampling frame.

Stratified selection   A sampling technique applied by grouping sampling units with similar characteristics into separate strata to reduce the variability among sampling units.

Systematic sampling   A method of selecting a sample n from a population N by first selecting a random number between 1 and N/n and then selecting every N/nth item.

With replacement   A sampling technique where any given item in the population may be included in the sample more than once.

Without replacement   A sampling technique where an item, once included in the sample, cannot be selected again. Sampling without replacement is ordinarily used in auditing.

REVIEW QUESTIONS

2-1. Indicate whether each of the following is true (T) or false (F).

   A. Statistical sampling requires that a sample be random.

   B. Valid sampling frames may contain units that do not belong to the population as defined.

   C. Sampling with replacement is more widely used by auditors than sampling without replacement.

   D. If a population is numbered from 6000 to 12,000, a five-digit number should be used to generate a sample from a random number table.

   E. Negative amounts should be eliminated from a population total before sampling proportionate to size is applied.

   F. A biased sample cannot be evaluated statistically.

   G. More than one random start should be used if systematic sample selection is employed.

   H. Random systematic selection is preferred relative to systematic selection with one random start.

   I. Computer time-sharing is generally a less efficient method used to generate random numbers relative to a random number table.

   J. Random sampling techniques can be used for judgmental samples.

   K. Haphazard selection cannot be used in statistical sampling.

2-2. Identify six sampling techniques that are useful in generating a random sample.

2-3. What other term(s) may be used for "random sample"? For "population"?

2-4. What two rules should be followed when a population is being defined?

2-5. To ascertain whether all shipments have been billed, what sampling frame should be used?

2-6. Identify the four items that should be documented in audit work papers if a random number table is used to generate a random sample.

2-7.   What rule should an auditor adhere to in specifying a route to follow in a random number table?

2-8.   How does the auditor determine the starting point in a random number table?

2-9.   For each of the following situations identify an effective method to select a random sample by using a random number table. Also, identify the discard range for each situation.

    A. Prenumbered disbursement vouchers numbered from 100 to 4892.

    B. Sales invoices numbered from 4562 to 13,482.

    C. Inventory listed on 52 pages, each with a maximum of 48 lines per page.

2-10. Identify the first 10 random numbers for a population numbered 201 to 942. Use the illustrative page from a random number table on page 24. The starting point is row 14, column 4, digit starting position 3. The route is down the table reading from left to right.

2-11. Why is computer generation generally more efficient than using a random number table?

2-12. What is the major distinction between systematic selection and random systematic selection?

2-13. A number of precautions must be taken when using systematic sampling to produce a random sample. What are they?

2-14. For a population numbered from 1 to 500 and a sample size of 50, what is the sampling interval for only one start? For two multiple starts? For six multiple starts?

2-15. If $N = 2000$, $n = 50$, and the sampling interval with one start $= 40$, what are the first four sample items using a random number start from 1 to 40 of 22?

2-16. Sales invoices of Muleshoe, Inc., are numbered from 1 to 15,000. The auditor has determined that 100 sample items are needed and that systematic sampling with five multiple starts will be used.

    A. What is the sampling interval for only one random start?

    B. What is the adjusted sampling interval (for five multiple starts)?

    C. How many items would be selected from a random number table? What is the selection range?

    D. Assuming that five items selected from a random number table are 700, 444, 15, 323, and 120, identify the first 15 sample items to be selected.

2-17. If a population N contains 100 checks and a sample n of 10 is desired, how many random numbers will be needed from a random number table for a random systematic sampling application? What is the range within which random numbers will be selected?

2-18. Systematic sampling is always applied in a sampling without replacement mode. Do you agree?

2-19. Describe the approach an auditor should follow if sampling proportionate to size is used.

2-20. If sampling proportionate to size is applied to a population of sales invoices totaling $148,562 and the reports are numbered from 1 to 5000, how many digits are needed to correspond the receiving report population to a random number table?

2-21. Contrast "unrestricted random sampling" with "stratified selection."

2-22. Use the computer facilities available at your university or a time-sharing terminal in a nearby CPA firm to produce random numbers for the following situations.

    A. Generate 10 random numbers for a population numbered 0260 to 8740. Your output report should list the random numbers in generation order and sequence, if those options are available to you.

    B. Generate 20 random numbers for an inventory stored in four separate warehouses. Each inventory listing for each warehouse contains a different number of pages. Each page, however, contains approximately 20 product lines.

Warehouse number	Number of pages—Inventory listing
1	280
2	82
3	240
4	124

3 ATTRIBUTE SAMPLING

Learning Objectives

After a careful study and discussion of this chapter, you will be able to:

1. Relate attribute sampling models to audit objectives.
2. Describe the relationship of attribute sampling to the auditor's study and evaluation of internal control.
3. Define and select appropriate attributes for compliance or special-purpose testing.
4. Identify areas of professional judgment inherent in an attribute sampling application.
5. Define and apply the concepts of risk of overreliance, tolerable rate, and expected rate.
6. Use fixed sample-size attribute sampling, stop-or-go sampling, and discovery sampling models to test accounting control procedures.
7. Perform error analysis and discuss its importance.
8. Provide suitable documentation in audit work papers of attribute sampling applications.
9. Describe how fixed sample-size attribute sampling and stop-or-go sampling results are evaluated and correlated with substantive tests.
10. Recognize the limitations of attribute sampling models.

This chapter defines, explains, and illustrates the three statistical sampling models categorized as "attribute sampling models." Also, a review of the audit process with particular emphasis on attribute sampling and internal control analysis is presented. The judgmental aspects of an attribute sampling application (e.g., setting tolerable rates) are discussed at appropriate points throughout the chapter.

ATTRIBUTE SAMPLING MODELS

As we discussed in Chapter 1, the term *attribute sampling* refers to one of three related sampling models.

1. *Fixed sample-size attribute sampling* also is called attribute estimation and is used primarily when the auditor wishes to test compliance with internal control [given that some errors (compliance deviations) are expected].
2. *Stop-or-go sampling* is sometimes defined as decision attribute sampling and is also sometimes called sequential sampling. It is appropriate when the auditor is concerned with whether or not the projected population error (deviation) rate exceeds a predefined error rate. It typically is used when the auditor expects a very low rate of errors.
3. *Discovery sampling* is used when the audit objective is to observe at least one deviation whenever the true deviation rate equals or exceeds some stated rate.

All three attribute sampling plans deal with *quality* characteristics. Attribute sampling relates to the question of "how many?", but variable sampling relates to the question "how much?". Fixed sample-size attribute sampling and stop-or-go models are used primarily by internal and independent auditors in *compliance testing* where the auditor desires to estimate the extent to which prescribed internal accounting control procedures are being followed.

Fixed sample-size attribute sampling and stop-or-go sampling might be used in the following areas:

- *Cash disbursements tests*—discounts not taken, invoices not properly approved, invoices not checked for numerical accuracy, or account distribution errors (both as to classification and posting).
- *Payroll tests*—errors in hours, rates, extensions, deductions, lack of appropriate approvals, or excessive vacation time.
- *Cash receipts tests*—erroneous discounts allowed, or entries posted to incorrect accounts or not recorded on a timely basis.

In executing a compliance test, the auditor is generally concerned with the frequency of deviations from prescribed control procedures (e.g., errors). In attribute sampling, items being tested or evaluated must be either in error (deviation) or not in error (compliance). There are no degrees of error. It is a yes or no situation. The objective of attribute sampling (attribute, stop-or-go, discovery) as it is used for compliance or special-purpose studies is to obtain a reasonable level of confidence that the population error rate is not beyond a certain level.

ATTRIBUTE SAMPLING AND THE STUDY AND EVALUATION OF ACCOUNTING CONTROL

The conceptually logical approach to the study and evaluation of accounting control is presented in the authoritative literature as SAS No. 1, Section 320, *The Auditor's Study and Evaluation of Internal Control.* Figure 3.1 is designed to illustrate the conceptually logical approach to internal control evaluation, especially as it relates to attribute sampling. The auditor makes an initial evaluation to decide if the system appears to permit any reliance. If the auditor decides that reliance might be efficient and effective, the auditor completes the review by transaction cycle. For each significant transaction cycle (e.g., payroll, acquisition and payment, sales and receivables), the auditor must understand the accounting system to determine what controls exist. After the control points are understood and documented, the auditor makes a preliminary evaluation of the strengths and weaknesses of the particular cycle (see Decision No. 2 in Figure 3.1).

An auditor's knowledge of the procedures prescribed by the client ordinarily is obtained by inquiry or reference to written instructions, and an understanding of their function and limitations is based on the auditor's training, experience, and judgment. On this basis, the auditor makes a preliminary evaluation of the effectiveness of the prescribed procedures, assuming that compliance with them is satisfactory. *Statistical sampling (i.e., attribute sampling) is not applicable to this phase of the evaluation.*

After the preliminary evaluation, the auditor must reach a decision as to which strengths (controls) he or she intends to rely on to *reduce* substantive tests. If a control does not leave an audit trail, attribute sampling cannot be used to test compliance. Pertinent strengths that leave an audit trail are tested, if the cost of testing does not exceed the benefit obtained from reduced substantive tests (see Decision No. 4 in Figure 3.1). According to SAS No. 39 (AU 350.32):

Sampling generally is not applicable to tests of compliance with internal accounting control procedures that depend primarily on appropriate segregation of duties or that otherwise provide no documentary evidence of performance. . . . When designing samples for the purpose of testing compliance with internal accounting control proce-

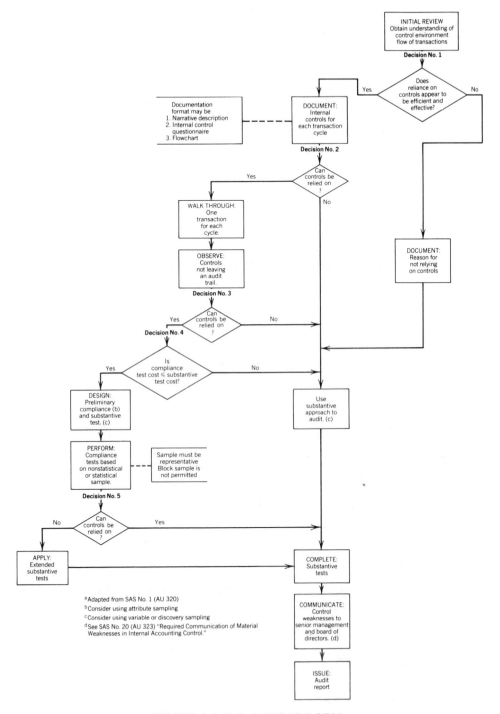

FIGURE 3.1 THE AUDIT PROCESS

dures that leave an audit trail of documentary evidence, the auditor ordinarily should plan to evaluate compliance in terms of deviations from . . . pertinent control procedures. . . .

As Figure 3.1 depicts, if Decision No. 4 is answered "yes," the auditor designs detailed compliance tests and substantive tests. The latter assume reliance on internal control and are, therefore, often referred to as *limited* substantive tests. After the detailed compliance tests are completed (perhaps based on fixed sample-size attribute or stop-or-go attribute sampling), the auditor again considers whether controls can be relied on (Decision No. 5 in Figure 3.1). If the compliance test results disclose that the deviation rate is not acceptable the control procedure tested cannot be relied on and the nature, extent, or timing of the related substantive tests should be modified to reflect the new information (*extended* substantive tests).

COMPLIANCE TEST PLANNING CONSIDERATIONS

Several matters need to be considered when a compliance test using audit sampling is planned. SAS No. 39 (AU 350.31) describes these matters:

- The relationship of the sample to the objective of the compliance test.
- The maximum rate of deviations from prescribed control procedures that would support the auditor's planned reliance.
- The auditor's allowable risk of overreliance.
- Characteristics of the population, that is, the items comprising the account balance or class of transactions of interest.

These considerations are identified by the following short-hand terms commonly used in SAS No. 39 (AU 350) and practice.

- Sample–objective relationship.
- Tolerable rate.
- Risk of overreliance.
- Expected rate.

The relationship between these terms and common statistical terms is explained in Figure 3.2.

ATTRIBUTE DEFINITION

An attribute must be carefully defined before an auditor begins to execute attribute sampling. Defining an attribute can be difficult and is a matter of

FIGURE 3.2 THE RELATION OF PROFESSIONAL AND STATISTICAL TERMS FOR ATTRIBUTE SAMPLING

Professional Terms [SAS No. 39 (AU 350)]	**Statistical Terms**
Sample–Objective Relationship	Attribute Definition and Population Definition
Tolerable Rate	Upper Precision Limit (UPL)
Risk of Overreliance	One minus Reliability
Expected Rate	Expected Rate of Occurrence

professional judgment. Considerable care must be exercised. For example, if the sampling unit is a check and the audit test is concerned with whether the check is properly supported, one of the attributes reviewed for proper support may be a receiving report. An error (deviation) may be defined as a check unsupported by a properly signed receiving report. Disbursements for services received (such as rent payments) are not typically supported by receiving reports. There are two ways that the auditor may handle this problem. First, the attribute definition may be structured so that checks selected relating to service acquisitions are excluded from the population. A second way to address this problem is to define the attribute broadly as a properly supported check with identification of what constitutes proper support. Thus, a check not requiring a receiving report but properly supported by a lease agreement would not be a control deviation. Of course, when performing audit tests, it is necessary for the auditor to be alert to the possibility of undefined errors. Audit awareness is essential in all sampling applications—statistical or nonstatistical.

POPULATION DEFINITION

In an attribute sampling application, the auditor should make certain that the population being sampled is homogeneous. Homogeneity means that all the items in the population should have similar characteristics. If, for example, export and domestic sales transactions for a given company are processed in a different manner, the auditor is faced with the evaluation of two different control systems and therefore two separate populations. Although the branch operations of a company may all be of a similar nature, the branches are run by different people. If the auditor is interested in the efficiency of the systems and staff of individual branches, he or she will be dealing with separate populations for each branch. On the other hand, if the auditor is not concerned about the individual branches but with the operations of the company as a whole, the company may be viewed as a single population.

JUDGMENT IN A STATISTICAL COMPLIANCE TEST

The importance of judgment in statistical sampling was considered in Chapter 1. As previously stated, statistical sampling does not eliminate professional judgment. However, it does require quantification of some of the auditor's judgmental decisions.

Figure 3.3 delineates the steps in a nonstatistical compliance test compared with those in a statistical compliance test. Note that quantification of judgment occurs at step 3 (setting risk of overreliance and tolerable rate), step 4 (determining sample size), and step 7 (evaluating sample findings quantitatively). Step 5 (pertaining to sample selection) also might be different in a statistical compliance test. As discussed in Chapter 2, before a sample can be evaluated statistically it should be selected randomly.

Step 5 in Figure 3.3 indicates that the compliance sample should be selected randomly from at least the first nine months of the fiscal year. The nine months criterion is a guide used by some practitioners. The rationale for its use is that year-end substantive tests include many transactions generated during the later months of the year and, therefore, will generate both substantive and compliance information (dual-purpose tests). Although AU 320.70 states that *ideally* compliance tests should encompass the entire period under examination, a shorter period, say, nine months, can be used as long as the auditor can justify and document his/her approach. Interim compliance tests are discussed in more detail in Chapter 7.

Step 3 of Figure 3.3 requires that for statistical compliance testing a risk of overreliance (reliability level) and a tolerable rate must be predefined. The risk of overreliance is determined in accordance with the maximum sampling risk that is acceptable. The tolerable rate is based on guidelines adopted from practice. Both risk of overreliance and tolerable rate (acceptable upper precision limit) are discussed and defined later in this chapter.

Step 7 of Figure 3.3 states that the sample findings must be evaluated quantitatively (statistically) and qualitatively. In fact, performing judgmental error analysis on each observed compliance deviation may be more strategically important to the auditor than a statistical projection based on the selected sample. For example, an auditor in a statistical compliance test may define an error as a sales invoice that is footed (totaled) incorrectly. Consequently, if in a sample of 100 sales invoices, two footing errors are observed—one for $10 and one for $5988—statistically, both errors are treated equally. However, audit judgment may indicate that even with a 2 percent deviation rate, an accounting system that permits a large error to go undetected cannot be trusted.

FIGURE 3.3 COMPARISON OF NONSTATISTICAL AND STATISTICAL COMPLIANCE TESTING

Steps in a Nonstatistical Compliance Test	Steps in a Statistical Compliance Test	Illustrative Statistical Compliance Test
1. Define the objective(s) of the audit test.	Same.	Ascertain if invalid (fictitious) employees are recorded in payroll journal.
2. Define the relevant population(s) from which to sample and the attributes to be tested.	Same.	All transactions recorded in the payroll journal from 1/1/8X through interim test date. Testable attributes are employee name and pay rate.
3. Determine the direction of the audit test—vouching or retracing data processing.	Determine the direction of the audit test—vouching or retracing data processing *and* set risk of overreliance and tolerable rate (acceptable upper precision limit), and expected deviation rate.	Vouch selected payroll transactions from payroll journal to personnel department records. Set reliability at 95% (5% risk of overreliance) and tolerable rate at 2%. Expected zero deviations.
4. Determine the sample size judgmentally or by reference to standard operating procedures of the CPA firm.	Determine the sample size using a mathematically derived sampling table.	Minimum sample size, if zero occurrences are observed, is 150 payroll transactions.
5. Select a representative sample using a random-based method or haphazard selection.	Select the sample at random from at least the first nine months of the fiscal year.	If test is at interim date, select sample from 1/1/8X through interim date. Use random number table for selection.

FIGURE 3.3 (Continued)

Steps in a Nonstatistical Compliance Test	Steps in a Statistical Compliance Test	Illustrative Statistical Compliance Test
6. Apply audit procedures to selected items—be alert for deviations not defined as testable attributes.	Same.	For each sample item, trace the employee name and pay rate to length of service records in personnel department.
7. Evaluate evidence from sample and ascertain impact on nature, timing, and extent of substantive auditing procedures.	Evaluate sample evidence quantitatively and qualitatively. Ascertain impact on nature, timing and extent of substantive auditing procedures.	Zero deviations noted; therefore, surprise payroll observation will not be performed.
8. Make final conclusion on reliance on control procedures tested.	Same.	Conclude that you are 95% certain that fictitious employees on the payroll for the period 1/1/8X through interim date do not exceed 2% of total payroll transactions.

SETTING RISK OF OVERRELIANCE (RELIABILITY LEVEL)

Generally, risk is the complement of reliability. In other words, one minus reliability is risk. The authoritative auditing literature [SAS No. 39 (AU 350)] is usually phrased in terms of risk, but in statistics the term *reliability* is more commonly used. Also, in statistics, the terms *reliability level* and *confidence level* are used interchangeably. Reliability refers to the probability of being right in placing reliance on an effective control procedure. For example, if an auditor selects a 95 percent reliability level, he or she has a 5 percent chance (risk) of accepting reliance on internal control when the control procedure is ineffective, given a certain tolerable rate (upper precision limit).[1] If the au-

---

[1] This assumes that the statistical evaluation and qualitative (judgmental) evaluation are the same.

FIGURE 3.4 RISKS OF OVERRELIANCE AND UNDERRELIANCE

Sample Results Indicate:	Control Procedure Tested Is:	
	Reliable	Unreliable
Accept	Correct Decision	Risk of Overreliance
Reject	Risk of Underreliance	Correct Decision

ditor decides that a 90 percent reliability level is acceptable, he or she has a 10 percent statistical chance of accepting reliance given a certain tolerable rate (upper precision limit) when he or she should not. In brief, the reliability level is the probability that the auditor's statistical conclusion will be correct. As Figure 3.4 depicts, the complement of reliability (1.0 − reliability) is the risk that the auditor will accept internal control reliance when, in fact, compliance deviations are excessive. This risk is referred to as the *risk of overreliance*.

Figure 3.4 shows another risk—the risk of underreliance. When an auditor encounters the risk of underreliance, the consequence is that substantive tests are unnecessarily large because reliance on internal control is rejected. The more serious error is relying on accounting control when the reliance is not justified—the risk of overreliance. In this book, attention is focused on controlling the risk of overreliance.[2]

According to policy guidelines in some major CPA firms, the minimum reliability level for compliance testing should be 90 percent. However, 95 percent reliability might be used if an attribute is critical to the scope of the remainder of the audit. When the auditor evaluates internal control attributes to determine the extent to which audit tests can be limited, a high reliability level (90 to 95 percent) generally should be used. The logic behind a high reliability level is that tests of compliance of internal control cannot be restricted, based on the assessment of internal control effectiveness. Also, compliance tests *per se* provide weaker evidence relative to substantive tests concerning the ultimate audit objective of determining if there is a material misstatement in financial statements.

A preliminary evaluation showing internal control to be weak would result in a decision not to perform detailed compliance tests. In other words, primary reliance will be placed on substantive tests.

---

[2] For a discussion of how to control the risk of underreliance, see Donald M. Roberts, **Statistical Auditing** (New York: AICPA, 1978), pp. 55–57.

TOLERABLE RATE (UPPER PRECISION LIMIT)

The tolerable rate [upper precision limit (UPL)] on compliance deviations represents a maximum error rate established so that the possibility of deviations in excess of that rate would cause the auditor to place less than the planned level of reliance on the internal control procedure being evaluated. For example, the following tolerable rates might be used:[3]

Reliance on internal control	Illustrative tolerable rates (acceptable UPL)
Little reliance based on the auditor's conclusions that substantive work will not be substantially or moderately reduced in reliance on internal control.	20% (or less) (consider omitting test)
Moderate reliance, based on the auditor's conclusion that substantive work will be reduced in reliance on internal control.	10% (or less)
Substantial reliance on internal control, based on the auditor's conclusion that substantive work may be reduced by one-half to two-thirds.	5% (or less)

Actually, in a fixed sample-size or stop-or-go attribute application two upper precision limits are generated. The one described thus far is *acceptable (or desired) UPL*. Acceptable UPL is predefined and is referred to as the tolerable rate in SAS No. 39 (AU 350). The second UPL, referred to herein as *achieved (or calculated) UPL*, is calculated after the selected sample has been audited by using an appropriate mathematical calculation or attribute sampling evaluation table. Generally, if reliance is to be placed on internal control, the tolerable rate (acceptable UPL) must be greater than or equal to the achieved UPL. However, the auditor's qualitative evaluation based on the statistical evaluation and error analysis may result in reliance on internal control, even though the specified tolerable rate (acceptable UPL) is less than achieved UPL or vice versa. The auditor's conclusion,

---

[3] For other suggestions on establishing tolerable rates, see Robert K. Elliott, "Basic Concepts of Statistics and Hypotheses Testing for Auditing," Chapter 9 of **Handbook of Modern Accounting,** edited by Sidney Davidson and Roman L. Weil, Second edition (New York: McGraw-Hill Book Company, © 1977).

especially when he or she accepts reliance on internal control when the quantitative (statistical) evaluation indicates a rejection decision, should be adequately documented in the audit work papers.

Other actions that can be considered when the tolerable rate (acceptable UPL) is less than the achieved UPL are:

1. Review the definition of a deviation (error) to make sure it is consistent with the original purpose of the audit test.
2. Review each sampling unit considered to be in error to be certain it is in error as defined. (This action reduces nonsampling errors as discussed in Chapter 1.)
3. Perform expanded substantive tests. (Do not rely on internal control to limit substantive tests.)
4. Increase the sample size until achieved UPL is less than or equal to the tolerable rate (normally, this will not be successful and is not cost effective except when the initial sample is small).

FIXED SAMPLE-SIZE ATTRIBUTE SAMPLING

As we previously discussed for internal control procedures that leave an audit trail, the extent of testing might be objectively determined by using fixed sample-size attribute sampling. Recall from Figure 3.3 that before the extent of testing decision is reached, the auditor must have already defined the objective(s) of the audit test, defined the population and testable attributes, and determined the direction of the audit test. To facilitate determination of the sample size for fixed sample-size attribute sampling, tables will be used. In addition, tables also will be used to evaluate sample findings.

Tables 1 to 6 are based on the binomial distribution. The tables are exact only when sampling is *with* replacement. When sampling *without* replacement is used, the hypergeometric distribution is appropriate. Tables are not, however, easily constructed for the latter. Although auditors usually sample without replacement, Tables 1 to 6 still may be used. When sampling without replacement, the binomial tables produce valid, but conservative results.

Fixed sample-size attribute sampling is employed when the auditor desires to estimate the population deviation rate (sample deviations divided by the sample size) and the achieved upper precision limit. In practice, the approach typically is used when the auditor expects some deviations in the population.

The first three tables (Tables 1 to 3) are used to determine sample size; Tables 4 to 6 are used to evaluate sample findings. *To determine sample size*

TABLE 1 Determination of Sample Size: Reliability, 90% (Risk of Overreliance 10%)

Expected Percent Rate of Deviation	Tolerable Rate: Percent Rate of Deviation									
	1	2	3	4	5	6	7	8	9	10
0.25	400	200	140	100	80	70	60	50	50	40
0.50	800	200	140	100	80	70	60	50	50	40
1.0		400	180	100	80	70	60	50	50	40
1.5			320	180	120	90	60	50	50	40
2.0		*	600	200	140	90	80	50	50	40
2.5			*	360	160	120	80	70	60	40
3.0				800	260	160	100	90	60	60
3.5				*	400	200	140	100	80	70
4.0					900	300	200	100	90	70
4.5					*	550	220	160	120	80
5.0						*	320	160	120	80
5.5						*	600	280	160	120
6.0							*	380	200	160
6.5							*	600	260	180
7.0								*	400	200
7.5								*	800	280
8.0									*	460
8.5									*	800
9.0										*
9.5										*

* Sample size more than 1000.

(Tables 1 to 3), three requirements must be estimated or known. The auditor must:

1. Establish the reliability level. This decision is based on the risk of overreliance that the auditor is willing to accept.
2. Estimate the population deviation rate in percent. To establish this the auditor may use prior knowledge or experience.
3. Define the tolerable rate (acceptable upper precision limit). This is a percent (rate) that is equated to the maximum permissible deviation rate. It is not one minus reliability.

   To illustrate fixed sample-size attribute sampling, assume that an auditor desires to test credit approvals on 20,000 sales invoices processed during the year. He/she desires a statistical sample that will give 95 percent

TABLE 2 Determination of Sample Size: Reliability, 95%
(Risk of Overreliance 5%)

Expected Percent Rate of Deviation	Tolerable Rate: Percent Rate of Deviation									
	1	2	3	4	5	6	7	8	9	10
0.25	650	240	160	120	100	80	70	60	60	50
0.50	*	320	160	120	100	80	70	60	60	50
1.0		600	260	160	100	80	70	60	60	50
1.5		*	400	200	160	120	90	60	60	50
2.0			900	300	200	140	90	80	70	50
2.5			*	550	240	160	120	80	70	70
3.0				*	400	200	160	100	90	80
3.5				*	650	280	200	140	100	80
4.0					*	500	240	180	100	90
4.5					*	800	360	200	160	120
5.0						*	500	240	160	120
5.5						*	900	360	200	160
6.0							*	550	280	180
6.5							*	1000	400	240
7.0								*	600	300
7.5								*	*	460
8.0									*	650
8.5									*	*
9.0										*
9.5										*

* Sample size more than 1000.

confidence that not more than 5 percent of the sales invoices were not approved. The auditor estimates from previous experience that about 1 percent of the sales invoices are in error (not approved).

Expected deviation = 1%

Tolerable rate = 5%

Reliability level (one minus risk of overreliance) = 95%

The appropriate table to use (Tables 1 to 3) is determined by the predefined reliability (one minus risk of overreliance). Table 2 corresponds with 95 percent reliability. According to Table 2, the required sample size (*n*) is 100. As shown at the top of page 54, this is determined by the intersection of 1 percent "expected percent rate of deviation" row with the 5 percent "tolerable rate" column.

To Determine Sample Size for 95% Reliability (5% Risk of Overreliance)

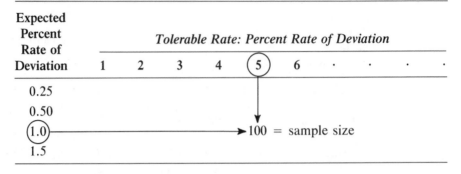

Expected Percent Rate of Deviation	Tolerable Rate: Percent Rate of Deviation									
	1	2	3	4	5	6	·	·	·	·
0.25										
0.50										
1.0					➤100 = sample size					
1.5										

TABLE 3 Determination of Sample Size: Reliability, 99% (Risk of Overreliance 1%)

Expected Percent Rate of Deviation	Tolerable Rate: Percent Rate of Deviation									
	1	2	3	4	5	6	7	8	9	10
0.25	*	340	240	180	140	120	100	90	80	70
0.50	*	500	280	180	140	120	100	90	80	70
1.0		*	400	260	180	140	100	90	80	70
1.5		*	800	360	200	180	120	120	100	90
2.0			*	500	300	200	140	140	100	90
2.5			*	1000	400	240	200	160	120	100
3.0				*	700	360	260	160	160	100
3.5				*	*	550	340	200	160	140
4.0					*	800	400	280	200	160
4.5					*	*	600	380	220	200
5.0						*	900	460	280	200
5.5						*	*	650	380	280
6.0							*	1000	500	300
6.5							*	*	800	400
7.0								*	*	600
7.5									*	800
8.0									*	*
8.5									*	*
9.0										*
9.5										*

* Sample size more than 1000.

TABLE 4 Evaluation of Results: Reliability, 90% (Risk of Overreliance 10%)

Number of Observed Deviations

Achieved Upper Precision Limit: Percent Rate of Deviation

Sample Size	1	2	3	4	5	6	7	8	9	10	12	14	16	18	20	25	30	35	40	45	50
10																0		1		2	
20											0				1	2		3	4	5	6
30								0				1		2		4	5	6	8	9	10
40						0			1		2	3			4	6	7	9	11	13	15
50					0			1			2	3	4	5		8	10	12	15	17	19
60				0		1		2			3	4	5	6	7	10	13	15	18	21	24
70				0		1		2		3	4	5	6	8	9	12	15	18	22	25	29
80			0			1		2	3	4	5	6	8	9	10	14	18	22	25	29	33
90			0		1		2	3	4		6	7	9	11	12	16	20	25	29	33	38
100			0		1	2	3	4	5		7	9	10	12	14	19	23	28	33	38	43
120		0		1	2	3	4	5	6	7	9	11	13	15	17	23	29	34	40	46	52
140		0	1	2	3	4	5	6	7	9	11	13	16	18	21	27	34	41	48	54	61
160		0	1	2	4	5	6	8	9	10	13	16	19	22	25	32	40	47	55	63	71
180		0	2	3	4	6	7	9	10	12	15	18	22	25	28	37	45	54	63	71	80
200	0	1	2	4	5	7	8	10	12	14	17	21	24	28	32	41	51	60	70	80	90
220		1	2	4	6	8	10	12	13	15	19	23	27	31	35	46	56	67	78	89	99
240	0	1	3	5	7	9	11	13	15	17	21	26	30	35	39	50	62	74	85	97	109
260	0	1	3	5	8	10	12	14	17	19	24	28	33	38	43	55	68	80	93	106	119
280	0	2	4	6	8	11	13	16	18	21	26	31	36	41	46	60	73	87	101	114	128
300	0	2	4	7	9	12	14	17	20	22	28	33	39	45	50	64	79	93	108	123	138
320	0	2	5	7	10	13	16	18	21	24	30	36	42	48	54	69	85	100	116	132	148
340	0	3	5	8	11	14	17	20	23	26	32	38	45	51	58	74	90	107	123	140	157
360	0	3	6	9	12	15	18	21	25	28	34	41	48	55	61	79	96	113	131	149	167
380	0	3	6	9	13	16	19	23	26	30	37	44	51	58	65	83	102	120	139	158	177
400	1	4	7	10	14	17	21	24	28	31	39	46	54	61	69	88	107	127	146	166	186
420	1	4	7	11	14	18	22	26	29	33	41	49	57	65	73	93	113	134	154	175	196
460	1	4	8	12	16	20	24	28	33	37	45	54	63	71	80	102	124	147	170	192	215
500	1	5	9	13	18	22	27	31	36	40	50	59	69	78	88	112	136	160	185	210	235
550	2	6	10	15	20	25	30	35	40	45	55	66	76	87	97	124	150	177	204	232	259
600	2	7	12	17	22	28	33	39	44	50	61	72	84	95	107	135	165	194	224	253	283
650	2	8	13	19	24	30	36	42	48	54	66	79	91	104	116	147	179	211	243	275	308
700	3	8	14	20	27	33	39	46	52	59	72	85	99	112	126	159	194	228	262	297	332
800	4	10	17	24	31	38	46	53	61	68	83	99	114	129	145	183	222	262	301	341	381
900	4	12	20	28	36	44	52	61	69	78	95	112	129	146	164	207	251	296	340	385	430
1000	5	13	22	31	40	49	59	68	77	87	106	125	144	164	183	232	280	330	379	429	479

In situations where the auditor does not know what the "expected deviation rate" is (1 percent above), a pilot sample of 50 may be selected to estimate the population deviation rate. To illustrate, if a sample of 50 is selected and one error is discovered for a given attribute, the estimated population deviation rate is 2 percent (1 ÷ 50). Assuming the reliability level desired is 90 percent (10 percent risk of overreliance) and the tolerable rate is 5 percent, the sample size from Table 1 is equal to 140.

To evaluate sample findings, Tables 4 to 6 are used. To illustrate, con-

TABLE 5   Evaluation of Results: Reliability, 95% (Risk of Overreliance 5%)

	Number of Observed Deviations																				
	Achieved Upper Precision Limit: Percent Rate of Deviation																				
Sample Size	1	2	3	4	5	6	7	8	9	10	12	14	16	18	20	25	30	35	40	45	50
10																	0		1		
20												0				1	2	3		4	5
30										0			1		2	3	4	5	7	8	10
40								0			1		2		3	5	6	8	10	12	14
50					0					1		2	3	4	5	7	9	11	13	16	18
60				0				1			2	3	4	5	6	9	11	14	17	20	23
70				0			1			2	3	4	5	7	8	11	14	17	20	24	27
80			0		1			2		3	4	5	7	8	9	13	16	20	24	28	32
90			0		1		2		3	4	5	6	8	9	11	15	19	23	27	32	36
100			0		1		2	3	4		6	8	9	11	13	17	22	26	31	36	41
120			0	1	2	3	4	5	6		8	10	12	14	16	21	27	33	38	44	50
140			0	1	2	3	4	5	6	7	10	12	14	17	19	26	32	39	46	52	59
160		0	1	2	3	4	5	6	8	9	12	14	17	20	23	30	38	45	53	61	69
180		0	1	2	3	5	6	8	9	11	14	17	20	23	26	35	43	52	60	69	78
200		0	1	3	4	6	7	9	11	12	16	19	23	26	30	39	48	58	68	77	87
220		0	2	3	5	7	8	10	12	14	18	22	25	29	33	44	54	64	75	86	97
240		1	2	4	6	8	10	12	14	16	20	24	28	33	37	48	59	71	83	94	106
260		1	3	4	7	9	11	13	15	17	22	26	31	36	41	53	65	77	90	103	116
280		1	3	5	7	10	12	14	17	19	24	29	34	39	44	57	71	84	98	111	125
300	0	1	3	6	8	11	13	16	18	21	26	31	37	42	48	62	76	91	105	120	135
320	0	2	4	6	9	11	14	17	20	22	28	34	40	45	51	66	82	97	113	128	144
340	0	2	4	7	10	12	15	18	21	24	30	36	42	49	55	71	87	104	120	137	154
360	0	2	5	8	10	13	17	20	23	26	32	39	45	52	59	76	93	110	128	146	163
380	0	2	5	8	11	14	18	21	24	28	34	41	48	55	62	80	98	117	135	154	173
400	0	3	6	9	12	15	19	22	26	29	37	44	51	59	66	85	104	123	143	163	183
420	0	3	6	9	13	16	20	24	27	31	39	46	54	62	70	90	110	130	151	171	192
460	0	4	7	11	15	18	22	26	31	35	43	51	60	68	77	99	121	143	166	188	211
500	1	4	8	12	16	21	25	29	34	38	47	56	66	75	84	108	132	157	181	197	221
550	1	5	9	14	18	23	28	33	38	43	53	63	73	83	94	120	146	173	200	227	255
600	1	6	10	15	20	26	31	36	42	47	58	69	80	92	103	132	161	190	219	249	279
650	2	6	12	17	23	28	34	40	46	52	64	76	88	100	112	143	175	207	239	271	303
700	2	7	13	19	25	31	37	43	50	56	69	82	95	108	122	155	189	223	258	292	327
800	3	9	15	22	29	36	43	51	58	65	80	95	110	125	141	179	218	257	296	336	376
900	4	10	18	26	34	42	50	58	66	74	91	108	125	142	159	203	247	291	335	379	424
1000	4	12	20	29	38	47	56	65	74	84	102	121	140	159	178	227	275	324	374	423	473

TABLE 6   Evaluation of Results: Reliability, 99% (Risk of Overreliance 1%)

Number of Observed Deviations

Achieved Upper Precision Limit: Percent Rate of Deviation

Sample Size	1	2	3	4	5	6	7	8	9	10	12	14	16	18	20	25	30	35	40	45	50
10																			0		
20																0	1		2	3	4
30													0			1	3	4	5	6	8
40											0		1		2	3	5	7	8	10	12
50									0		1		2		3	5	7	9	11	13	16
60							0				1	2	3		4	7	9	12	14	17	20
70						0				1	2	3	4	5	6	9	11	14	18	21	24
80					0				1		2	4	5	6	7	10	14	17	21	25	29
90					0				1	2	3	5	6	7	9	12	16	20	24	29	33
100				0			1		2	3	4	6	7	9	10	14	19	23	28	33	37
120				0	1	2		3		4	6	8	9	11	13	18	24	29	35	40	46
140			0	1	2	3		4		5	7	10	12	14	16	22	29	35	42	48	55
160			0	1	2	3		5	6	7	9	12	14	17	20	27	34	41	49	56	64
180			0	1	2	3	4	6	7	8	11	14	17	20	23	31	39	47	56	65	73
200			0	1	3	4	5	7	8	10	13	16	19	23	26	35	44	54	63	73	83
220			0	2	3	5	6	8	10	11	15	18	22	26	30	39	50	60	70	81	92
240		0	1	2	4	6	7	9	11	13	17	21	25	29	33	44	55	66	78	89	101
260		0	1	3	5	6	8	10	12	14	19	23	27	32	36	48	60	72	85	97	110
280		0	2	3	4	7	9	12	14	16	21	25	30	35	40	53	65	79	92	106	120
300		0	2	4	6	8	10	13	15	18	23	28	33	38	43	57	71	85	99	114	129
320		0	2	4	7	9	11	14	17	19	24	30	35	41	47	61	76	91	107	122	138
340		1	3	5	7	10	13	15	18	21	26	32	38	44	50	66	82	98	114	131	148
360		1	3	6	8	11	14	16	19	22	28	35	41	47	54	70	87	104	122	139	157
380		1	3	6	9	12	15	18	21	24	30	37	44	50	57	75	93	111	129	148	166
400		1	4	7	10	13	16	19	22	26	32	39	46	54	61	79	98	117	136	156	176
420		2	4	7	10	14	17	20	24	27	35	42	49	57	64	84	103	124	144	164	185
460	0	2	5	8	12	15	19	23	27	31	39	47	55	63	72	93	114	136	159	181	204
500	0	3	6	10	13	17	21	26	30	34	43	52	60	70	79	102	125	149	174	198	223
550	0	3	7	11	15	20	24	29	34	38	48	58	68	78	88	113	139	166	192	219	247
600	0	4	8	13	17	22	27	32	37	43	53	64	78	86	97	125	153	182	211	241	271
650	0	4	9	14	19	25	30	36	41	47	58	70	82	94	106	136	167	198	230	262	294
700	1	5	10	16	21	27	33	39	45	51	64	76	89	102	115	148	181	215	249	283	318
800	1	7	13	19	25	32	39	46	53	60	74	89	103	118	133	171	209	248	287	326	366
900	2	8	15	22	29	37	45	53	61	69	85	101	118	135	152	194	237	281	325	369	414
1000	2	9	17	25	34	42	51	60	69	78	96	114	133	151	170	218	266	314	363	412	462

sider the first example above where the sample size is calculated to be 100. Table 5 for 95 percent reliability (5 percent risk of overreliance) is the correct table to employ in evaluating the sample findings. If three deviations are found in the sample of 100, the achieved upper precision limit is 8 percent. This is determined by the intersection of the 100 sample size row with "3" deviations.

Sample Evaluation Table for 95 Percent Reliability (5% Risk of Overreliance)

Sample Size	Achieved Upper Precision Limit: Percent Rate of Deviation									
	1	2	3	4	5	6	7	8	·	·
10										
20										
·										
·										
·										
(100)								3 = observed number of deviations		

Other error findings from Table 5 for the sample size of 100 are evaluated as follows:

Deviations discovered	Achieved UPL on Deviation Rate
0	3%
1	5%
2	7%
6	12%

Of course, since the tolerable rate (acceptable UPL) was 5 percent, two or more deviations usually would cause the auditor to conclude that this aspect of internal control should not be relied on to limit substantive tests.

Notice that the achieved UPL incorporates an allowance for sampling risk. One deviation in a sample of 100 is a rate of 1 percent, but the upper limit on the deviation rate at a 5 percent risk of overreliance is 5 percent. The difference between the achieved UPL of 5 percent and the actual sample deviation rate of 1 percent (at a sample size of 100) is 4 percent. This is the allowance for sampling risk.

STOP-OR-GO ATTRIBUTE SAMPLING

Under fixed sample-size attribute sampling, the auditor examines a single sample of a specified size; under stop-or-go attribute sampling, the sample is selected in several steps; each step relies on the results of the previous step. The auditor may gain efficiency by applying stop-or-go sampling. Stop-or-go sampling is used when the auditor expects a zero or very low rate of compliance deviations. By selecting stop-or-go sampling, the auditor may halt sampling if zero or a defined number of occurrences are observed. The sample items are examined in groups until the cumulative evidence is sufficient to achieve a predefined reliability and an acceptable upper precision limit. In contrast, a fixed sample-size attribute application produces larger sample sizes, especially if the expected error rate is overstated. In a stop-or-go application, the auditor must specify:

1. Risk of overreliance (desired reliability) and
2. Tolerable rate (acceptable upper precision limit)

Tables 7 and 8 are presented to illustrate stop-or-go sampling. Again, sampling without replacement is assumed. That is, an item once selected is not replaced in the population for possible reselection.

Table 7 presents the minimum sample sizes that should be used for risks of overreliance of 10, 5, and 2.5 percent and the tolerable rates of 10 percent through 1 percent. The final sample may be larger than the initial sample specified in Table 7—if the auditor expects or finds deviations.

TABLE 7 Minimum Sample Size Table for Compliance Testing (Zero Expected Deviations)

	Sample Size Based on Risk of Overreliance		
Tolerable Rate	10%	5%	2.5%
10%	24	30	37
9	27	34	42
8	30	38	47
7	35	43	53
6	40	50	62
5	48	60	74
4	60	75	93
3	80	100	124
2	120	150	185
1	240	300	370

TABLE 8   Attribute Sampling Table for Determining
Stop-or-Go Sample Sizes and Upper Precision Limit of
Population Deviation Rate Based on Sample Results

Number of Deviations	Risk Factors for Risk of Overreliance of		
	10%	5%	2.5%
0	2.4	3.0	3.7
1	3.9	4.8	5.6
2	5.4	6.3	7.3
3	6.7	7.8	8.8
4	8.0	9.2	10.3
5	9.3	10.6	11.7
6	10.6	11.9	13.1
7	11.8	13.2	14.5
8	13.0	14.5	15.8
9	14.3	16.0	17.1
10	15.5	17.0	18.4
11	16.7	18.3	19.7
12	18.0	19.5	21.0
13	19.0	21.0	22.3
14	20.2	22.0	23.5
15	21.4	23.4	24.7
16	22.6	24.3	26.0
17	23.8	26.0	27.3
18	25.0	27.0	28.5
19	26.0	28.0	29.6
20	27.1	29.0	31.0
21	28.3	30.3	32.0
22	29.3	31.5	33.3
23	30.5	32.6	34.6
24	31.4	33.8	35.7
25	32.7	35.0	37.0
26	34.0	36.1	38.1
27	35.0	37.3	39.4
28	36.1	38.5	40.5
29	37.2	39.6	41.7
30	38.4	40.7	42.9
31	39.1	42.0	44.0
32	40.3	43.0	45.1
33	41.5	44.2	46.3
34	42.7	45.3	47.5
35	43.8	46.4	48.8

TABLE 8   (Continued)

Number of Deviations	Risk Factors for Risk of Overreliance of		
	10%	5%	2.5%
36	45.0	47.6	49.9
37	46.1	48.7	51.0
38	47.2	49.8	52.1
39	48.3	51.0	53.4
40	49.4	52.0	54.5
41	50.5	53.2	55.6
42	51.6	54.5	56.8
43	52.6	55.5	58.0
44	54.0	56.6	59.0
45	55.0	57.7	60.3
46	56.0	59.0	61.4
47	57.0	60.0	62.6
48	58.0	61.1	63.7
49	59.7	62.2	64.8
50	60.4	63.3	65.0
51	61.5	64.5	67.0

TABLE SOURCE   Adapted from a table developed by Marvin Tummins and Robert H. Strawser, "A Confidence Limits Table for Attribute Sampling," **Accounting Review** (October 1976), pp. 907–912.

Table 8 permits estimation of the population achieved UPL. An estimate of the achieved UPL is derived by dividing the proper *risk factor* taken from Table 8 by the sample size used to evaluate the population. The risk factor is determined by the intersection of the "risk" column with the "number of deviations" row. For example, using 5 percent risk of overreliance and a sample size of 200 with 14 deviations yields 22.0. This represents an achieved upper precision limit of 11 percent ($22.0 \div 200$).

Table 8 is particularly applicable when:

$$N > 1000$$
$$n > 20$$
$$n/N < 10\%, \text{ and}$$

Estimated population deviation rate < 20 percent, where:

$$N = \text{population size}$$
$$n = \text{sample size}$$

However, if Table 8 is used in other sampling situations, the only error made is a conservative estimate of the achieved UPL and an overestimate of the risk of overreliance. This, of course, means that the auditor may reject reliance on internal control precedures and apply unnecessary substantive procedures. In this situation, audit cost may increase but audit risk does not. As previously discussed, this concept is referred to as the risk of underreliance.

To apply stop-or-go sampling, the auditor typically initiates the application via a three-step process.

Step 1 Specify the tolerable rate (acceptable upper precision limit) and the risk of overreliance (reliability level) desired.
*For example, a 5 percent tolerable rate and a
5 percent risk of overreliance.*

Step 2 Use Table 7 to determine your initial sample.
Minimum sample from Table 7 = 60

Step 3 Construct a stop-or-go decision table as explained below.

If the auditor finds one deviation in a sample of 60, the achieved upper precision limit at a 5 percent risk of overreliance is 8 percent ($4.8 \div 60$). This is greater than the 5 percent tolerable rate specified in Step 1. Therefore, the auditor may decide to extend the sample by an additional 36 items to a total sample of 96 ($4.8 \div .05$ tolerable rate). If zero occurrences are observed in the 36 additional sample items, the auditor can conclude that he or she is 95 percent confident that the population deviation rate is not greater than 5 percent ($4.8 \div 96$). There is a 5 percent risk that the population deviation rate exceeds 5 percent.

If, on the other hand, the auditor finds two errors in the initial sample of 60, the achieved upper precision limit is 10.5 percent ($6.3 \div 60$). This is again greater than the 5 percent tolerable rate specified in Step 1. Therefore, the auditor may decide to extend the sample by an additional 66 ($6.3 \div .05$ tolerable rate minus 60). If zero deviations are observed in the 66 additional sample items, the auditor can conclude that he or she is 95 percent confident that the population deviation rate does not exceed 5 percent. If, instead, the auditor observed one more deviation (total deviations now equal three), the achieved upper precision limit is 6.2 percent ($7.8 \div 126$). He/she must then decide whether to extend the sample by an additional 30 items ($7.8 \div .05 = 156$ total sample). Another possibility the auditor has is to use the approximate sample deviation rate of 3 percent ($3 \div 126$) as an estimate of the expected deviation rate in order to use fixed sample-size attribute sampling. The sample size using Table 2 is 400.

In designing a stop-or-go application, the auditor will not typically extend the sample to more than three times the initial sample size. On reaching that point, the auditor might consider not relying on the tested attribute or shifting to fixed sample-size attribute sampling. Also, after each iteration the auditor should perform a *qualitative* error analysis. That is, does the nature and cause of deviations lead to the conclusion that a material error could exist in the financial statements and not be detected by the system? Qualitative analysis may indicate that the particular attribute cannot be relied on to limit substantive testing. In no circumstance should stop-or-go sampling be mechanically applied.

To apply stop-or-go sampling, the auditor may construct a decision table like the following:

Step	Cumulative Sample Size to Use:	Stop if Cumulative Deviations Are Equal to:	Sample More if Deviations Are:	Go to Step 5 if Deviations Are at Least:
1	60	0	1–4	4
2	96	1	2–4	4
3	126	2	3–4	4
4	156	3	4	4
5	Consider not relying on this aspect of internal control or use fixed sample-size attribute sampling.			

From the above discussion and illustrations, note that there are two ways that Table 8 may be used. First, in evaluation, to determine achieved UPL, the appropriate risk factor from the table is divided by the sample size.

$$\text{Achieved UPL} = \frac{\text{risk factor at desired risk of overreliance for deviations observed}}{\text{sample size}}$$

Second, in planning, to determine total sample size, the appropriate risk factor is divided by the tolerable rate (acceptable UPL).

$$\text{Sample size} = \frac{\text{risk factor at desired risk of overreliance for number of deviations expected}}{\text{tolerable rate}}$$

Table 8 is especially useful in practice, because any sample size (e.g., 53, 49, 86) can be evaluated. The practicing auditor's planned sample size is sometimes reduced because of discards or voids.

QUALITATIVE ANALYSIS IN ATTRIBUTE SAMPLING APPLICATIONS[4]

All errors detected while doing compliance testing, whether compliance deviations or monetary errors, should be analyzed regardless of *their statistical impact.* To determine what impact an error might have on audit scope, if any, is a very difficult problem. Given a certain type of error, the auditor has to determine the potential financial statement impact, the range and related probabilities of misstatement, and the type(s) of substantive test(s) that could be used to determine if the financial statements are misstated.

The basic decision model employed by auditors to analyze errors is presented in Figure 3.5. To distinguish a critical error from a noncritical error, the auditor should clearly understand the distinction between a compliance deviation and a monetary deviation. Compliance deviations do not necessarily produce monetary misstatements in the financial statements. For example, an unapproved disbursement voucher may nevertheless be a valid transaction that was properly paid and recorded. Compliance deviations increase the risk of monetary misstatements, but certainly not in a one-to-one ratio.

Some attributes are critical to audit scope, but others are not. For example, the failure of a client to take cash discounts may be evaluated in a disbursements test. Whether or not the client takes cash discounts has virtually no impact on audit scope. Of course, the failure to take cash discounts may be an item that should be included in a letter to management.

Some attributes are more critical than others. Generally, the more likely a compliance deviation is to produce a monetary deviation, the more critical it is. For example, the auditor may be more tolerant of a high error rate in credit limit reviews than for footings and extensions on sales invoices.

Statistical tests of compliance can be a primary source of reliance on internal controls. However, it is not true that sample results that indicate that the overall error rate in an accounting universe is no greater than 5 to 10 percent are invariably sufficient to justify substantial reliance on internal controls.

A random sample test, statistical or otherwise, cannot, in and of itself, be the sole source of the auditor's reliance on internal controls. If it were, he or she would need uneconomically large samples to support the conclusions. The primary source of reliance is, in fact, the auditor's entire study and evaluation of internal controls, and the results of the statistical test are simply one piece of corroborating evidence that, together with information

---

[4] Much of the material from this section is adapted from John C. Broderick, "Statistical Sampling", **Modern Auditing: The Arthur Young Approach,** a special edition of **The Arthur Young Journal** (Autumn/Winter 1972–1973), pp. 40–41, and Robert G. Taylor, "Error Analysis in Audit Tests," **Journal of Accountancy** (May 1974), pp. 78–82.

FIGURE 3.5 QUALITATIVE ANALYSIS MODEL

1. Define error as critical or noncritical to audit scope.
2. Determine the nature and cause of each critical error.
   a. Intentional or unintentional
   b. Carelessness or misunderstood instructions
   c. Frequent or infrequent
   d. Systematic or random
   e. Likely or actual dollar effect, if any
3. Evaluate the worst possible effect of each critical error.
4. Decide whether the critical errors were consistent or inconsistent with the preliminary evaluation of internal control and modify audit reliance accordingly.
5. Determine the effect of the deviations on other compliance and substantive tests. (Keep in mind that auditors are concerned with the population errors, not the sample errors.)
6. Suggest improved procedures to the client, preferably in writing.
7. **Remember:** Even when the statistical evaluation conclusions are within acceptable limits, error analysis should be performed in order to adhere to the due professional care standard. Moreover, nonfollow-up increases legal exposure.

from other procedures such as consideration of the competence of personnel and the results of observations and inquiries, supports the evaluation.

ILLUSTRATIVE ATTRIBUTE SAMPLING APPLICATION

To demonstrate work paper documentation and the relationship of compliance testing to substantive testing, a hypothetical detail sales test is illustrated. *The audit objective is to determine if internal controls are operating effectively and they are adequate to provide proper accounting control over shipments and billings to customers and the distribution thereof in the accounts. The population consists of sales invoices for the period 1/1/8X to 10/12/8X. The sampling frame is the sales invoice number recorded in the sales journal. Stop-or-go sampling will be used with 95 percent reliability or 5 percent risk of overreliance and 5 percent tolerable rate.* The following attributes were predefined.

1. Were supporting documents (customer purchase order, shipping document, billing document, and freight bill) agreed to sales invoice details?

2. Were prices in agreement with approved current price list in effect at date of sale or other price authorization, for example, sales contract, bid proposal, and the like?

3. Were the charges valued properly in the accounts receivable subsidiary ledger?

4. Were all documents tested for clerical accuracy?

5. Was credit memo for returns or allowances (if any) properly approved?

6. Was credit approved by the credit manager?

Actual test results were as follows:

Attribute Number	Actual Sample Size	Number of Deviations	Achieved UPL (in percent)
1	60	0	5
2	126	2	5
3	100	3	7.8
4	184	4	5
5	60	0	5
6	96	1	5

Before a reliance or nonreliance decision can be made concerning any of the six attributes tested, qualitative error analysis must be performed on *all* errors noted. Qualitative analysis data can be analyzed and documented as follows:

Attribute Number	Number of Deviations	Nature of Deviations	Effect on Audit Scope
1	—	—	—
2	2	In both instances the incorrect price was used. The priced items were understated by $15 per unit. The total underbilling was $1500.	Because of the potential significance of this deviation, the 50 largest sales transactions for the year should be reviewed for proper prices. Also, all sales invoices made to DZW, Inc., should be reviewed for correct price.

Attribute Number	Number of Deviations	Nature of Deviations	Effect on Audit Scope
3	3	In each instance, the amount was added to the receivable details of another company at the same address.	Sales made to Mason, Inc., are sometimes charged to Warner & Company, a parent holding company. No expansion of compliance or substantive tests is needed.
4	4	All four of the errors noted were extension errors apparently due to haste and multiplication mistakes. The extension errors were less than $100 each, except one which resulted in overbilling of $325.	Extension errors appear to be excessive, even though the achieved UPL is 5%. In extending audit scope in connection with attribute 2, also review the 50 largest sales transactions for computation errors.
5	0	—	—
6	1	Credit was not approved for a new customer.	Credit manager indicated that this rarely happens. Review five new customer invoices to test representation.

Based on quantitative evaluation and qualitative evaluation, attributes 1, 3, and 5 can be relied on to limit substantive tests (i.e., positive receivable confirmations). Attributes 2 and 4 cannot be relied on and, accordingly, audit scope should be modified as indicated. Attribute 6 must be tested further (as indicated) to determine if reliance can be placed on it. Also, as required by authoritative auditing literature, the auditor should consider whether material internal accounting control weaknesses exist related to attributes 2 and 4. These should be communicated to senior management and the board of directors.

DISCOVERY SAMPLING

Just as stop-or-go sampling is a special kind of attribute sampling, so is discovery sampling. In *selected* situations, the auditor may apply a discovery sampling technique. Discovery sampling is used when the auditor believes that the population error occurrence rate is near zero.[5] But in case the occurrence rate is not zero, discovery sampling applications are designed to yield a large enough sample size so at least one occurrence will be produced. Actually, two conditions should generally exist before discovery sampling is used. They are:

- When the auditor's best judgment of the population error occurrence rate is zero or near zero percent.
- When the auditor is looking for a *very* critical characteristic (e.g., payroll padding), that, if discovered, might be indicative of more widespread irregularities or serious errors in the financial statements.

Discovery sampling also is useful in substantive testing. If the auditor's objective is to discover at least one example of a type of error having a potentially material effect on an account balance, then discovery sampling should be considered. In this instance, discovery sampling may be more effective than trying to design a variable sampling application concerned with both error identification and estimation. In practice, discovery sampling often is used in confirming account balances in large banks and savings and loan institutions that have strong systems of internal control (i.e., few errors are expected).

In a discovery sampling application, the following prerequisites must be defined:

1. Characteristic to be evaluated.
2. Reliability desired.
3. Maximum acceptable occurrence rate (upper precision limit).
4. Definition and size of population.

Tables 9 to 11 (see pages 69–71) are discovery sampling tables.[6] To determine which of the three tables to use in a discovery sampling application, first define the population to be sampled and its size. Assume that for a given application, the auditor has a population size N equal to 6500 payroll checks; therefore, Table 10 is the correct table to use *to determine sample size*.

Next, the auditor defines reliability and maximum acceptable occurrence rate. Assume that reliability is set at 95 percent and maximum acceptable occurrence rate is set at 1 percent. To determine sample size, the auditor goes down the 1 percent column until the desired reliability factor is

---

[5] Typically, in discovery sampling applications, an error occurrence is defined as a monetary error or a compliance deviation.

[6] Tables 9 to 11 are taken from "Sampling for Attributes: Estimation and Discovery," Supplementary Section, **An Auditor's Approach to Statistical Sampling,** Volume 2 (New York: AICPA, 1974).

TABLE 9 Discovery Sampling Tables: Probability in Percent of Including at Least One Occurrence in a Sample (for Populations Between 2000 and 5000)

Sample Size	Upper Precision Limit: Critical Rate of Occurrence							
	0.3%	0.4%	0.5%	0.6%	0.8%	1%	1.5%	2%
50	14%	18%	22%	26%	33%	40%	53%	64%
60	17	21	26	30	38	45	60	70
70	19	25	30	35	43	51	66	76
80	22	28	33	38	48	56	70	80
90	24	31	37	42	52	60	75	84
100	26	33	40	46	56	64	78	87
120	31	39	46	52	62	70	84	91
140	35	43	51	57	68	76	88	94
160	39	48	56	62	73	80	91	96
200	46	56	64	71	81	87	95	98
240	52	63	71	77	86	92	98	99
300	61	71	79	84	92	96	99	99+
340	65	76	83	88	94	97	99+	99+
400	71	81	88	92	96	98	99+	99+
460	77	86	91	95	98	99	99+	99+
500	79	88	93	96	99	99	99+	99+
600	85	92	96	98	99	99+	99+	99+
700	90	95	98	99	99+	99+	99+	99+
800	93	97	99	99	99+	99+	99+	99+
900	95	98	99	99+	99+	99+	99+	99+
1000	97	99	99+	99+	99+	99+	99+	99+

Used with permission of the AICPA.

located (or the next highest reliability level if the one he or she is searching for is not in the table). The sample size *n* is 300.

The third step is to select 300 payroll checks at random from the population of 6500 payroll checks and to audit each sample item. Finally, the evaluation stage is reached. If no errors are discovered in the sample examined, the auditor can immediately state that the sampling plan criterion has been achieved. That is, the auditor can state that he or she is 95 percent certain that the worst likely error rate in the population does not exceed 1 percent.

On the other hand, if one or more errors are located, the auditor cannot make the above statistical statement. Perhaps no statistical conclusion will be expressed. Expanded audit procedures may be applied. Client employees under audit supervision might examine every one of the remaining population items. If the sole objective is discovery, the auditor may stop auditing

TABLE 10 Discovery Sampling Tables: Probability in Percent of Including at Least One Occurrence in a Sample (for Populations Between 5000 and 10,000)

Sample Size	*Upper Precision Limit: Critical Rate of Occurrence*							
	0.1%	0.2%	0.3%	0.4%	0.5%	0.75%	1%	2%
50	5%	10%	14%	18%	22%	31%	40%	64%
60	6	11	17	21	26	36	45	70
70	7	13	19	25	30	41	51	76
80	8	15	21	28	33	45	55	80
90	9	17	24	30	36	49	60	84
100	10	18	26	33	40	53	64	87
120	11	21	30	38	45	60	70	91
140	13	25	35	43	51	65	76	94
160	15	28	38	48	55	70	80	96
200	18	33	45	56	64	78	87	98
240	22	39	52	62	70	84	91	99
300	26	46	60	70	78	90	95	99+
340	29	50	65	75	82	93	97	99+
400	34	56	71	81	87	95	98	99+
460	38	61	76	85	91	97	99	99+
500	40	64	79	87	92	98	99	99+
600	46	71	84	92	96	99	99+	99+
700	52	77	89	95	97	99+	99+	99+
800	57	81	92	96	98	99+	99+	99+
900	61	85	94	98	99	99+	99+	99+
1000	65	88	96	99	99	99+	99+	99+
1500	80	96	99	99+	99+	99+	99+	99+
2000	89	99	99+	99+	99+	99+	99+	99+

Used with permission of the AICPA.

the sample items as soon as he or she finds an occurrence. For example, if the auditor merely wishes to find one error and to review the nature of the discrepancy, the sampling process might stop if the auditor observed an error in the tenth sample item, even though a sample size of 300 was indicated. Conversely, an error might not be discovered until the 299th item is randomly selected. The point is, if the auditor simply wants to find one error and evaluate it, the sampling process might stop and, as a result, the audit tests may be substantially modified.

In other discovery sampling situations, the auditor may continue with the sample selection, even though an error or deviation was found. The auditor then could use attribute tables (Tables 4 to 6 or Table 8) to project an error rate in the population.

TABLE 11 Discovery Sampling Tables: Probability in Percent of Including at Least One Occurrence in a Sample (for Populations over 10,000)

Sample Size	Upper Precision Limit: Critical Rate of Occurrence							
	0.01%	0.05%	0.1%	0.2%	0.3%	0.5%	1%	2%
50		2%	5%	9%	14%	22%	39%	64%
60	1%	3	6	11	16	26	45	70
70	1	3	7	13	19	30	51	76
80	1	4	8	15	21	33	55	80
90	1	4	9	16	24	36	60	84
100	1	5	10	18	26	39	63	87
120	1	6	11	21	30	45	70	91
140	1	7	13	24	34	50	76	94
160	2	8	15	27	38	55	80	96
200	2	10	18	33	45	63	87	98
240	2	11	21	38	51	70	91	99
300	3	14	26	45	59	78	95	99 +
340	3	16	29	49	64	82	97	99 +
400	4	18	33	55	70	87	98	99 +
460	5	21	37	60	75	90	99	99 +
500	5	22	39	63	78	92	99	99 +
600	6	26	45	70	84	95	99 +	99 +
700	7	30	50	75	88	97	99 +	99 +
800	8	33	55	80	91	98	99 +	99 +
900	9	36	59	83	93	99	99 +	99 +
1000	10	39	63	86	95	99	99 +	99 +
1500	14	53	78	95	99	99 +	99 +	99 +
2000	18	63	86	98	99 +	99 +	99 +	99 +
2500	22	71	92	99	99 +	99 +	99 +	99 +
3000	26	78	95	99 +	99 +	99 +	99 +	99 +

Used with permission of the AICPA.

RELATING ATTRIBUTE SAMPLING RESULTS TO MONETARY ERROR

It is difficult to make dollar conclusions (as opposed to proportion or percent conclusions) when any of the attribute sampling models (fixed sample-size, stop-or-go, or discovery) are used. Three techniques of *limited accuracy* to translate attribute information into dollar estimates are discussed below. Before studying these techniques, remember that the primary objective of attribute sampling is *not* dollar estimation.

1. If the sample deviation rate is 2 percent in a fixed sample-size application, and the achieved upper precision limit is 5 percent at 95 percent reliability, the auditor can be 95 percent sure that the maximum exposure of book value would be the total dollar amount of the largest 5 percent of the population items. To the extent that any of the largest 5 percent of the population items were found acceptable in the sample, the next items below that point would be included. A listing of population items in descending amount is needed to apply this estimate.

2. Another rough estimate of the probable dollar exposure might be computed by multiplying the sample mean ($\bar{x}$) in dollars by the sample deviation rate (deviations $\div$ n) by the number of items in the population. That is, $\bar{x}$ times (deviations $\div$ n) times N equals probable dollar exposure.

3. Conservative dollar conclusions also can be produced from a discovery sampling application *if no occurrences are found in the sample*. For example, if 300 payroll checks from a population of 6500 exhibited no calculation errors, at 95 percent reliability the auditor can conclude that no more than 1 percent of the checks are in error (65 checks). If the largest check is $1065, then payroll dollars exposed to errors probably do not exceed $69,225 (65 × $1065), with a risk of being incorrect of 5 percent.

Another major limitation of attribute sampling is that the achieved upper precision limit is not internal control risk. In a variable sampling application, one of the predefined items introduced into the sampling model will be a risk percentage for internal control. This risk percentage is based in part on the statistical evaluation of a compliance test, *and* input from judgment and other auditing procedures. This concept is discussed and explained in Chapter 5.

SUMMARY

Three kinds of attribute sampling models were introduced in this chapter. These models are useful in performing compliance testing or performing special studies.

Stop-or-go sampling will perhaps eventually become the most widely used attribute sampling model for audit compliance testing. Attribute sampling with a fixed sample size is used if the auditor wishes to project the sample occurrence rate as the population occurrence rate. Discovery sampling, on the other hand, is a special type of attribute sampling that is used when the occurrence is extremely critical to audit scope.

The key role played by audit judgment in an attribute sampling application is emphasized throughout this chapter. We also stress methods that the auditor can use to reduce judgmental failures that could weaken the effectiveness of attribute sampling. In fact, qualitative analysis is presented as being more important than its underlying statistical evaluation.

Fixed sample-size, stop-or-go, and discovery sampling may be summarized by typical application characteristics as follows:

Application Characteristic	Attribute Model		
	Fixed Sample Size	Stop-or-Go	Discovery
1. Typical sample size	Medium	Low	High
2. Types of testing	Compliance	Compliance	Special studies and substantive tests
3. Expected compliance deviations	Low	Zero or very low	Zero or near zero

The primary factors that influence compliance test sample size are:

Factor	Conditions Leading to		Relationship to Sample Size
	Smaller Sample Size	Larger Sample Size	
1. Planned reliance on internal control[1]	Lower reliance on internal control	Higher reliance on internal control	Direct
2. Allowable rate of deviation (tolerable rate)	Higher acceptable rate of deviation for planned reliance on internal control	Lower acceptable rate of deviation for planned reliance on internal control	Inverse
3. Allowable risk of overreliance	Higher risk of overreliance on internal control	Lower risk of overreliance on internal control	Inverse
4. Expected rate of population deviation.[2]	Lower expected rate of deviation in population	Higher expected rate of deviation in population	Direct
5. Number of items in population	Virtually no effect on sample size unless population is small		

[1] Compliance tests are not performed when no reliance on internal controls is planned.

[2] Larger samples are necessary when deviations occur. However, high deviation rates normally warrant little, if any, reliance on internal controls and, therefore, compliance testing might be omitted.

GLOSSARY

Acceptable upper precision limit   The statistical term for the predefined critical rate established so that the possibility of deviations in excess of that rate would cause the auditor to place less than full reliance on the control being evaluated. Also referred to as *ex ante* or *desired UPL*. In audit sampling, generally, the equivalent term is tolerable rate.

Achieved upper precision limit   A calculated upper precision limit determined from an audited sample. Also referred to as *ex post* or *computed UPL*.

Attribute sampling   See Chapter 1 glossary.

Compliance deviation   A failure to comply with or follow an internal control procedure. Also referred to as *procedural deviation* or simply *deviation*.

Confidence level   As used in attribute sampling, the probability of being correct in placing reliance on an effective internal control system. The term is used interchangeably with "reliability."

Critical error.   A compliance deviation that could cause material misstatements to occur in the financial statements.

Discovery sampling   See Chapter 1 glossary.

Error analysis   A judgmental study or determination of the cause (nature) of observed compliance deviations. Also referred to as qualitative analysis.

Expected rate   An estimate of a population compliance deviation rate based on prior knowledge or a pilot sample. The expected deviation rate is used to determine sample size in a fixed sample-size attribute application.

Initial sample size   The start or minimum sample size used in a stop-or-go sampling application. For 5 percent risk of overreliance (95 percent reliability) and 5 percent tolerable rate (upper precision limit), the minimum sample size is 60.

Occurrence   A compliance deviation. Also sometimes referred to as an *error*.

Precision   The range within which the sample result is expected to be accurate. For example, in a fixed sample-size attribute sampling model, precision is the difference between the sample error rate and the achieved upper precision limit.

Qualitative analysis   See error analysis.

Reliability level   See confidence level.

Risk of overreliance   The probability of deciding to rely on an aspect of internal control based on a compliance test when, in fact, compliance deviations exceed the tolerable rate. The complement of reliability is the risk of overreliance.

Risk of underreliance   As used in attribute sampling, the risk that the statistical test indicates unsatisfactory compliance when, in fact, compliance is satisfactory.

Stop-or-go sampling   See Chapter 1 glossary.

Tolerable rate   The maximum rate of deviations from a prescribed control procedure that the auditor would be willing to accept without altering his or her planned reliance on the control procedure. See also acceptable upper precision limit.

REVIEW QUESTIONS

3-1.   Indicate whether each one of the following statements is true (T) or false (F).

A. If the auditor expects zero or near zero errors in a sample, stop-or-go sampling should be used.

B. Performing a thorough qualitative analysis on each observed compliance deviation may be more informative than a quantitative projection of a sample.

C. It is not necessary to perform qualitative analysis if the achieved UPL is less than or equal to the tolerable rate (acceptable UPL).

D. If substantial reliance is to be placed on internal control, achieved UPL generally should not exceed 5 percent.

E. The risk of placing reliance on internal control when compliance deviations are excessive is referred to as the risk of underreliance.

F. If the tolerable rate (acceptable UPL) is less than the achieved UPL in a stop-or-go application, it is generally not in accordance with due professional care to increase the tolerable rate.

G. The minimum sample size for 95 percent reliability and 5 percent tolerable rate is 60.

H. Reliance may sometimes be placed on internal control, even though achieved UPL exceeds the tolerable rate.

I. To determine sample size for a discovery sampling application, the approximate population size must be known.

J. The decision to rely or not to rely on an internal accounting control procedure is based on the statistical tests.

K. The decision to use a fixed or a stop-or-go sampling application depends on which plan the auditor believes will be most efficient in the circumstances.

3-2. If the auditor's objective is to observe at least one occurrence if the true occurrence rate exceeds a defined level, _____ sampling should be used.

3-3. If the auditor is concerned with whether the population occurrence rate exceeds a predefined tolerable rate _____ sampling should be used.

3-4. If the auditor expects a 2 percent deviation rate, _____ sampling should be used.

3-5. In an attribute sampling application using check numbers as the sampling unit, what should the auditor do when "voided" checks are encountered?

3-6. Attribute sampling does not eliminate professional judgment. Identify the primary areas involving audit judgment in a typical attribute sampling application.

3-7. What is "risk of overreliance," and how is it controlled and calculated?

3-8. When the tolerable rate (acceptable UPL) is less than achieved UPL, a number of alternate actions are available to the auditor. Identify what actions could be considered acceptable by the auditor when acceptable UPL < achieved UPL.

3-9. For 90 percent reliability and acceptable UPL of 5 percent, what is the minimum sample size?

3-10. Construct a stop-or-go decision table for 5 percent risk of overreliance and 10 percent tolerable rate. Use the following format:

Step	Cumulative sample size to use	Stop if cumulative deviations are equal to	Sample more if deviations are	Go to step ___ if deviations are at least

3-11. Construct a stop-or-go decision table for 2.5 percent risk of overreliance and 5 percent tolerable rate. Use the format defined in question 3-10.

3-12. If a sample of 128 produced five deviations, what is the achieved UPL at 90 percent, 95 percent, and 97.5 percent reliability? Why is Table 8 easier to use for this evaluation?

3-13. If a sample of 15 produced 0 deviations, what is the achieved UPL at 10 percent, 5 percent, and 2.5 percent risk of overreliance? Why is a sample size of 15 insufficient?

3-14. A sample of 160 produces two deviations; what is the estimated population deviation rate?

3-15. What pilot size sample should be used to obtain an estimated occurrence rate if the auditor is attempting to project a sample occurrence rate to a population of vouchers and the expected occurrence rate is not known?

3-16. What is the fixed sample size for each of the following?

	Risk of overreliance	Tolerable rate	Expected deviation rate
A.	10%	7%	3.0%
B.	5%	5%	1.8%
C.	10%	4%	2.0%
D.	1%	6%	1.5%

3-17. Assume that the following control deviations were identified from the sample sizes determined in question 3-16. What is the achieved UPL for each situation?

	Deviations noted
A.	5
B.	2
C.	0
D.	4

3-18. What conditions should exist before discovery sampling is used?

3-19. Determine discovery sample sizes for each of the following situations.

	Population size	UPL	Reliability
A.	6,200	1%	90%
B.	5,000	0.5%	95%
C.	3,200	2%	98%
D.	10,649	0.3%	85%

3-20. If occurrences are observed in a discovery sampling application, what course of action should the auditor pursue?

3-21. Is it possible to convert an attribute sampling conclusion into a dollar or quantity estimate?

ATTRIBUTE SAMPLING CASES

CASE 3-1 MILLAR COMPANY, INC.
(estimated time to complete: 15 minutes)

Assume that you are working on the audit of Millar Company, Inc., and are examining checks for the presence of an approved supporting voucher. An unsupported check is thus a "deviation." The population is composed of the approximately 4000 checks that were processed by the client during the current year.

You decide that a deviation rate in the population as high as 5 percent would not require any extended audit procedures. However, if the population deviation rate is greater than 5 percent at 5 percent risk of overreliance you would want to extend the audit scope.

In each case situation below, identify the letter of the sample (i.e., A or B) which, in your judgment, provides better evidence that the deviation rate in the population is 5 percent or less. (Assume that each sample observation is selected randomly.)

Situation	Sample	Number of Invoices Examined	Number of Deviations Found in Sample	Percent of Sample Invoices in Error
1	A	75	1	1.3
	B	200	4	2.0
2	A	100	1	1.0
	B	125	3	2.4
3	A	150	2	1.3
	B	25	0	0.0
4	A	225	7	3.1
	B	200	4	2.0
5	A	250	6	2.4
	B	100	2	2.0

TABLE SOURCE Adapted from William R. Kinney, "Judgment Error in Evaluation Sample Results," **The CPA Journal** (March 1977), pp. 61–62.

CASE 3-2 EFT, INC.
(estimated time to complete: 20 minutes)

Calculate the achieved upper precision limits for the five situations presented in Case 3.1, using the appropriate attribute sampling table.

Record your solution and identify the letter of the sample that provides better evidence that the deviation rate in the population is 5 percent or less. Use 5 percent risk of overreliance.

Situation	Sample
1	A
	B
2	A
	B
3	A
	B
4	A
	B
5	A
	B

CASE 3-3 TECH PRODUCERS, INC.
(estimated time to complete: 20 minutes)

Tech Producers, a fast-growing electronics manufacturer, has approximately 2000 hourly employees who are paid weekly by check from a payroll imprest fund. In addition to the testing of payroll transactions throughout the year, the auditor, Terri Sinclair, has decided to test the current payroll period. Because of the many additions to the work force since last year, she is concerned with the possibility of payroll padding as well as less critical errors, such as minor mistakes in overtime computations, incorrect payroll deductions, and the like. Names will be drawn from the payroll journal at random.

In this particular engagement, the auditor believes that she should be reasonably satisfied that payroll padding to the extent of 10 or more fictitious or unauthorized employees at any one time would be detected by the system itself or by her examination.

Taking into consideration her other payroll testing procedures and her review of internal control procedures related to the payroll function, the auditor has decided to seek 90 percent assurance that the actual occurrence rate in the current payroll does not exceed 0.5 percent (10 ÷ 2000).

A. N = _____

Reliability = _____

UPL = _____

n = _____

B. Assuming that you find 0 occurrences in your sample, what probabilistic statement can you make?

C. Assuming that you find 1 occurrence, what action(s) should be taken?

D. Could you use an attribute table to evaluate discovery sampling findings?

CASE 3-4 CLIENT, INC.
(estimated time to complete: 10 minutes)

Client, Inc., operates out of four branches located in Denver, Dallas, New York, and Midland. You are designing a stop-or-go sampling plan to ascertain the effectiveness of internal control over credit sales. One of the problems that you are having is trying to determine how to allocate your total sample to the different branches. All branches have similar accounting systems, but process varying numbers of credit sales invoices during the year.

Branch	Number of sales invoices processed
Denver	16,000
Dallas	8,000
New York	14,000
Midland	2,000
	40,000

Assuming your sample size n is 100:

A. How would you allocate the sample to the four branches?

B. If it is necessary to determine the effectiveness of the system at each branch, how would you allocate the sample?

C. How would your answer change if it is known that the control systems in Denver and Dallas are especially reliable and the control system in New York and Midland are somewhat less reliable?

CASE 3-5 LEWIS & FOOT, CPAs
(estimated time to complete: 30 minutes)

Fred Hancock, a senior accountant with Lewis & Foot, CPAs, has just completed a professional development program in statistical sampling. He decided to use statistics in an audit engagement to which he is currently assigned.

He believed it would be appropriate to apply statistical sampling in a purchase transaction test. He decided that an 8 percent tolerable rate at a 5 percent risk of overreliance would be appropriate. The expected deviation rate was 4 percent, so he took a sample of 100.

Since Fred felt that the larger items deserved more attention than the smaller ones, he decided to include 60 items in the sample with a value of $5000 or more each; the remainder of the 100 items were valued at less than $5000 each. He was very careful to take a random sample of his test month for each of these two types of items.

When testing the sample he found only five errors. One error was a missing vendor's invoice, so he sent a confirmation to the vendor to make certain that it was a valid invoice. The confirmation indicated no errors. Two errors were simply missing approvals by the authorized official. Fred went to the official who agreed he had failed to sign the invoice because he had been on vacation in May. He reviewed the invoices and stated they were both valid and correct. The other two errors both involved dollar errors. One was an error in the extension of the invoice in the amount of $50 and the other a misclassification error of $850. Fred was not particularly concerned about the $50 error because it was not material, but the $850 was fairly large. Fortunately, it was a misclassification between expenses and did not affect net income. He decided to call the last two actual errors, and concluded that the achieved UPL was 6.3 percent at a 5 percent risk of overreliance.

Fred concluded that purchases for the year were almost certain to contain fewer errors than the allowable amount. As a result, he accepted the population and decided to reduce the tests in year-end accounts payable.

Fred was pleased with the use of statistical sampling because he had objective results. The reviewing partner, who could not attend the course because he was talking to a prospective client that day, also liked it because it reduced his exposure to legal liability and greatly reduced the time budget to complete the job.

Identify each weakness in this attribute sampling application and state why it is a weakness.

CASE 3-6 CPE ASSOCIATES
(estimated time to complete: 20 minutes)

CPE Associates is a partnership that provides discussion leaders and technical course materials on accounting, auditing, and taxation. The primary market served by CPE Associates is CPA firms that have requirements for professional personnel to obtain at least 40 hours of continuing professional education a year. CPE Associates has five partners and a staff of 10 people. The partnership uses prenumbered checks for all disbursements except for petty cash disbursements. For this year's annual audit you wish to use statistical sampling to ascertain if the cash disbursement system is functioning properly. Stop-or-go sampling with 5 percent risk of overreliance and 5 percent tolerable rate will be used. Identify the attributes that you will test in evaluating the effectiveness of the cash disbursement system. Your attribute definitions should be comprehensive. Assume that the sampling frame will be canceled checks.

CASE 3-7 TAYLOR & SONS, INC.

(estimated time to complete: 20 minutes)

You are getting ready to begin the audit of Taylor & Sons, Inc., for the year ended December 31, 19X1. You will function as senior on the engagement. In prior years, nonstatistical sampling was employed for all compliance testing on the Taylor engagement. In June of this year, however, your firm adopted a policy that all sample sizes for tests of compliance should be determined statistically, using a 5 percent risk of overreliance. The policy statement also stipulated that tolerable rate should be preset from 10 to 1 percent depending on the criticalness of the attribute being tested and the reliance being placed on internal control. Your audit program includes compliance tests for payroll and cash disbursements as presented below. Classify each test as "very critical," "moderately critical," or "least critical."

Selected payroll compliance tests	Selected cash disbursement compliance tests
1. Examine the time card for the approval of a foreman.	1. Examine voucher for supporting invoices, receiving reports, etc.
2. Account for a sequence of payroll checks in the payroll journal.	2. Examine supporting documents for evidence of cancellation (marked "paid").
3. Recompute hours on the time card.	3. Ascertain whether cash discounts were taken.
4. Compare the employee name in the payroll journal to personnel department records.	4. Review voucher for clerical accuracy.
5. Review overtime charges for approval of a foreman.	5. Agree purchase order price to invoice.

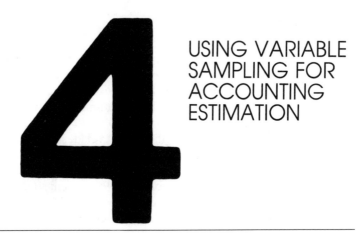

USING VARIABLE SAMPLING FOR ACCOUNTING ESTIMATION

Learning Objectives

After a careful study and discussion of this chapter, you will be able to:

1. Define variable sampling.
2. Define and apply selected statistical concepts such as standard deviation, the central limit theorem, and the distribution of sample means to accounting problems.
3. Distinguish the accounting estimation approach from the audit hypothesis approach.
4. Use variable sampling to project a book value (e.g., inventory balance).
5. Select the most efficient variable sampling model from among unstratified mean per unit, stratified mean per unit, difference estimation, and ratio estimation.

Variable sampling or quantitative estimation is a statistical technique used to estimate the dollar amount of an account balance or some other quantity. When it is used to estimate account balances, the computed result is stated in terms of the dollar amount of the point estimate (the sample mean times the population size) plus and minus the dollar amount of the precision interval at the confidence level desired. As an example, assume that an inventory balance is projected (based on a sample). If the point estimate is projected at $1,200,000 with a $150,000 computed precision interval at a confidence (or reliability) of 95 percent, this means the estimated true value of the inventory balance is between $1,050,000 and $1,350,000 at 95 percent reliability. Later in this chapter we learn how precision limits are calculated. Unlike attribute sampling, where the concern is primarily with the upper precision limit, variable estimation employs both an upper and lower precision limit—an account balance can be understated or overstated.

The primary purpose of this chapter is to review statistical concepts. Estimation sampling, as explained in this chapter, is primarily useful for accounting rather than auditing applications.

PRECISION AND RELIABILITY

Before we proceed, let us review the concepts of precision and reliability. *Precision,* expressed either as a dollar amount or a percentage, defines the maximum degree of error in either direction that will be acceptable. In statistical terms, the precision of an estimate describes the range of values, less and more than the point estimate, within which the true value is expected to fall. The lower and upper bounds of this range are referred to as *precision limits. Reliability,* on the other hand, expresses the probability that the precision interval contains the true value. Statistically, the reliability figure expresses the proportion of cases in which precision intervals would contain the true value if the same estimating procedures were employed a large number of times. Consequently, precision and reliability have no meaning for decision-makers unless paired with each other.

A REVIEW OF SELECTED STATISTICAL CONCEPTS

Sampling for variables is a more sophisticated statistical process than attribute, stop-or-go, or discovery sampling. To apply variable sampling properly, the accountant needs some familiarity with statistical theory and terminology. Of particular importance are the following concepts:

1. Mean.
2. Median.

3. Mode.
4. Standard deviation.
5. Skewness.
6. Normal distribution.
7. Distribution of sample means.
8. Central limit theorem.

MEAN

The mean is a measure of central tendency that is obtained by totaling all the values and dividing by the number of items. The mean of a *population* is expressed symbolically as $\bar{X}$. The mean of a *sample* is expressed symbolically as $\bar{x}$. To illustrate a sample mean calculation, assume that a sample of 10 items is selected. The numeric values are as follows:

$$\frac{x}{}$$

$10
18
15 Formula:
20
24 $\qquad \bar{x} = \dfrac{\Sigma_{x_j}}{n} = \dfrac{200}{10} = 20$
26
26
17
25
19

$\Sigma_{x_j} = \overline{\underline{\$200}}$

To calculate $\bar{X}$, you have to know the total dollars for every item in the population and the population size. The symbol x refers to an individual observation or sample item; n refers to sample size, and Σ is the summation sign.

MEDIAN

The median is that value for which half the values are above and half are below. In effect, the median divides the population into two equal sizes. Strictly speaking, a population (or sample) has a middle item only when it has an odd number of items. For an even number of items, the median can be defined as the average of the two middle numbers. The median for the 10 sample items is 19.5.

MODE

The value that occurs most frequently in a distribution is referred to as the mode. In the illustration of the mean, the mode is 26. The modal value(s) corresponds to the highest point(s) on a frequency distribution.

STANDARD DEVIATION

The standard deviation is a widely used statistic that is employed to measure the extent to which the values of the items are spread about the mean. To illustrate the calculation of the standard deviation, the sample items selected to illustrate a sample mean calculation are used.

x	$\bar{x}$	$x - \bar{x}$	$(x - \bar{x})^2$
10	20	-10	100
18	20	-2	4
15	20	-5	25
20	20	0	0
24	20	4	16
26	20	6	36
26	20	6	36
17	20	-3	9
25	20	5	25
19	20	-1	1

$$\Sigma(x - \bar{x})^2 = \underline{\underline{252}}$$

Equation:

$$SD = \sqrt{\frac{\Sigma(x - \bar{x})^2}{n - 1}}$$

$$SD = \sqrt{\frac{252}{9}} = 5.29$$

where:

SD = standard deviation

Notice that the equation for the standard deviation of a sample includes the term $n - 1$. Because the sample standard deviation is used as an estimate of the population standard deviation, the use of $n - 1$ in the denominator is imperative as an adjustment for bias.

The equation for the estimated population standard deviation presented in WORKSHEET 1 (Appendix A) is referred to as the shortcut computational equation. The result is the same as the previous equation. The shortcut computational equation is illustrated below:

x	x^2
10	100
18	324
15	225
20	400
24	576
26	676
26	676
17	289
25	625
19	361
200	4252

Computational equation:

$$\bar{x} = \frac{200}{10} = 20$$

$$SD = \sqrt{\frac{\sum_{j=1}^{n} x_j^2 - n\bar{x}^2}{n-1}}$$

$$SD = \sqrt{\frac{4252 - 10(20)^2}{10-1}}$$

$$SD = \sqrt{\frac{252}{9}} = 5.29$$

SKEWNESS

Skewness refers to the degree of asymmetry or lopsidedness of a distribution. Most accounting populations exhibit some degree of skewness. Skewness in accounting populations usually means the population contains a few very large items and many small items. Some skewness exists if there are extreme values at one end of a distribution with no counterbalancing values at the other end.

NORMAL DISTRIBUTION

The distribution following is, because of certain inherent characteristics described, a normal distribution. An important feature of this distribution is

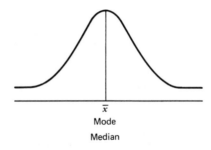

$\bar{x}$
Mode
Median

that the relative frequency of any interval can be determined by knowing only the sample mean $\bar{x}$ and the standard deviation SD. The interval from $\bar{x}$ ± 1 SD contains 68 percent of the items, $\bar{x}$ ± 1.96 SD contains 95 percent of the items, and ± 2.58 99 percent of the items.

DISTRIBUTION OF SAMPLE MEANS[1]

To illustrate the distribution of sample means, assume that we have a population N of nine different merchandise items. The population distribution is

$$\begin{array}{ccccc} & & \$20 & & \\ & \$16 & \$20 & \$24 & \\ \$12 & \$16 & \$20 & \$24 & \$28 \end{array}$$

The standard deviation of this distribution is $4.62.

If a sample size of 2 is selected from this population, there are 36 sample means based on all possible combinations of items, assuming sampling without replacement. These combinations appear as follows:

1. 12 and 16	10. 16 and 20	19. 16 and 24	28. 20 and 24
2. 12 and 16	11. 16 and 20	20. 16 and 24	29. 20 and 24
3. 12 and 20	12. 16 and 20	21. 16 and 28	30. 20 and 28
4. 12 and 20	13. 16 and 24	22. 20 and 20	31. 20 and 24
5. 12 and 20	14. 16 and 24	23. 20 and 20	32. 20 and 24
6. 12 and 24	15. 16 and 28	24. 20 and 24	33. 20 and 28
7. 12 and 24	16. 16 and 20	25. 20 and 24	34. 24 and 24
8. 12 and 28	17. 16 and 20	26. 20 and 28	35. 24 and 28
9. 16 and 16	18. 16 and 20	27. 20 and 20	36. 24 and 28

Given the 36 possible combinations of sample size 2, a mean for each combination may be calculated. The distribution of sample means that results is

$$\begin{array}{ccccccc} & & & 18 & 20 & 22 & & \\ & & & 18 & 20 & 22 & & \\ & & & 18 & 20 & 22 & & \\ & & & 18 & 20 & 22 & & \\ & & 16 & 18 & 20 & 22 & 24 & \\ & & 16 & 18 & 20 & 22 & 24 & \\ & 14 & 16 & 18 & 20 & 22 & 24 & 26 \\ & 14 & 16 & 18 & 20 & 22 & 24 & 26 \end{array}$$

[1]The illustrated distributions in this section are from Donald H. Taylor and G. William Glezen, **Auditing: Integrated Concepts and Procedures** (2nd ed.) [New York: John Wiley and Sons, Inc. © 1982], pp. 700–702.

The standard deviation of this distribution, which is called the *standard error of the mean*, is 3.06.

As shown above, the distribution of sample means will be normally distributed (bell-shaped distribution) if the sample is taken from a normally distributed population. However, as already stated, accounting populations usually are not normally distributed. For example, the population of nine items may be skewed to the right (large dollar items):

$$
\begin{array}{ccccccc}
 & & 20 & & & & \\
 & 14 & 20 & & & & \\
10 & 14 & 20 & 26 & 32 & 42 &
\end{array}
$$

However, even if the population distribution is skewed, the distribution of sample means will approach normality as the sample size increases. For example, a plotted distribution of sample means for all combinations of sample size 3 will be less skewed than one for a sample size of 2, and so on.

In variable sampling applications, the minimum sample size recommended is 30. Statisticians tell us that a sample of at least size 30 will produce a close approximation to normality, even if the population is skewed.

Accountants, of course, do not generate a distribution of sample means. They select one sample and project the same results to the sampled population. Likewise, accountants do not calculate the standard error of the mean based on all possible combinations of samples. An approximation of the standard error of the mean is the estimated population standard deviation (based on a sample) divided by the square root of the sample size. It is calculated by the following equation:

$$
\text{Standard error of the mean (estimated)} = \frac{SD}{\sqrt{n}}
$$

In summary, a distribution of sample means (mean calculated from many samples of the same size) has three properties:

1. The shape of the distribution is approximately normal if the sample is large enough.
2. The distribution is centered at the population mean $\overline{X}$.
3. The estimated standard error of the mean equals the estimated population standard deviation SD, divided by the square root of the sample size.

CENTRAL LIMIT THEOREM

For large sample sizes (typically, 30 is a reasonable minimum size), the distribution of sample means tends to be normally distributed, almost independently of the shape of the original population. The fact that sample means from a lopsided accounting population converge to a normal distribution is the reason why normal theory is useful in selected accounting or auditing applications. This chapter explains accounting applications and Chapter 5 explains auditing applications.

An accounting population may be skewed as follows:

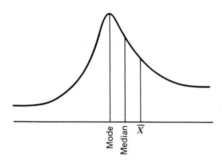

But *if the sample size* is large enough, the distribution of sample means from the skewed accounting population will be normal.

WHAT IS ACCOUNTING ESTIMATION?

In designing a variable sampling application, the accountant or auditor must consider whether the objective is: (1) to make an independent estimate of some amount (e.g., Lifo inventory), or (2) to test the reasonableness of a financial statement representation (e.g., the balance in accounts receivable). When an account balance is to be determined by statistical sampling, the accountant should use an *accounting estimation* approach. In these instances, the accountant generally intends to propose an adjustment to bring the account balance into agreement with the statistical estimate (point estimate). If an account balance does not exist, the point estimate is simply booked.

When an auditor desires to accept a client's representation without adjustment if it is reasonably correct, or to propose an adjustment only if it is probable that there might be a material error in the amount as stated by the client, an *audit hypothesis* approach should be used. The audit hypothesis approach statistically discriminates between the hypothesis that the amount as represented is correctly stated and the alternative hypothesis that the amount is materially misstated. Chapter 5 explains the audit hypothesis approach.

Remember that the purpose of the accounting estimation is to estimate some amount of interest to the accountant, such as the total cost of inventory on hand. This method is generally used when the resulting estimate is to be entered into the books and records as a substitute for a complete enumeration of the components of an account. Accounting estimation should *not* be used if the client has a book value that an auditor is trying to decide whether to accept or reject. If this type of decision is to be made, the audit hypothesis approach should be used.

The following statistical accounting estimation models are discussed in this chapter.

Unstratified mean per unit (unstratified MPU).

Stratified mean per unit (stratified MPU).

Difference estimation.

Ratio estimation.

Unstratified MPU generally is not efficient because the sample sizes generated are relatively large. It is presented in this chapter for illustrative purposes. The other models are easier to understand and apply when one has studied unstratified mean per unit. Ratio estimation is very similar to difference estimation; consequently, it is presented in a summary fashion without the operational aids (e.g., calculation worksheets) included for difference estimation.

UNSTRATIFIED MEAN PER UNIT

The unstratified MPU model is used to project an estimated value from a sample. This method also is called simple extension. After a sample is selected and a value determined for each sample item, the sample mean $\bar{x}$ of sample values is multiplied by the number of items in the population N to produce an estimate of the total dollar value of the sampled population.

Because mean per unit without stratification produces very large sample sizes relative to other sampling methods, as previously stated, its use in accounting or auditing is limited. The technique is appropriate when a book value for each population item is not available or when the footed total of the book value is not accurate. Mean per unit is seldom used without stratification, and generally important or material values (e.g., large dollar account balances) are treated separately. That is, large dollar balances or other key items (unusual, obsolete, etc.) are not included within the sampling frame.

In an unstratified MPU application the objective is to calculate a sample mean to project as the population total. Of course, the $\bar{x} \cdot N$ projection will not correspond exactly to the true (but unknown) population total. But the projection plus and minus a precision limit should contain the true population total with a defined reliability. Consequently, the projected or estimated population total, which is called the *estimated value*, must be paired with a reliability percentage and a precision limit.

Before he or she obtains an estimated value, the accountant has to determine the extent of testing. The sample size equation is derived from the mathematical definition of precision. Mathematically, precision is

$$A = U_R \cdot SE \cdot N$$

where

$$
\begin{aligned}
A &= \text{precision} \\
U_R &= \text{confidence level coefficient} \\
SE &= \text{estimated standard error of the mean, and} \\
N &= \text{population size}
\end{aligned}
$$

Given the mathematical definition of precision, the sample size equation can be derived as follows:

$$A = U_R \cdot SE \cdot N$$

$$A = U_R \cdot \frac{SD}{\sqrt{n}} \cdot N$$

$$\sqrt{n} \cdot A = U_R \cdot SD \cdot N$$

$$\sqrt{n} = \frac{U_R \cdot SD \cdot N}{A}$$

$$n' = \left(\frac{U_R \cdot SD \cdot N}{A} \right)^2$$

This is the equation for sample size assuming replacement, with n' denoting the sample size. The n' sample size is larger to compensate for the possibility of including the same sample item in the selection process more than once. If sampling is done without replacement, the sample size can be smaller. A finite population correction factor is applied to n' to yield n, which is sample size without replacement. This adjustment appears as follows:

$$n = \frac{n'}{1 + (n'/N)}$$

To determine the extent of testing (sample size) for an unstratified MPU application, the accountant must predefine U_R, SD, N, and A in the sample size equation. U_R is based on the amount of sampling risk the accountant is willing to accept. For example, if 95 percent reliability is selected ($U_R = 1.96$), there is a 5 percent chance that an estimated value $\pm$ precision will not contain the true population total. In an accounting estimation application a high reliability is usually selected. Otherwise, there will be a higher probability that the recorded point estimate (estimated value) will be materially misstated.

The standard deviation is determined by a pilot sample or the accountant's prior knowledge. Statisticians say that a sample of 30 is sufficient in most circumstances to estimate the standard deviation of a population.

N is determined by the sampling objective and is dependent on the part of the population that will be sampled. The total population may be divided into a sampled group and a 100 percent (nonsampled) group. In an accounting application, A (precision) is determined to be the amount material to the account balance in light of the amount that is material to the financial statements taken as a whole.

At this point the following variables have been predefined: U_R, SD, N, and A. By studying the equation for acceptable precision, you can see that we implicitly set an upper limit on SE.

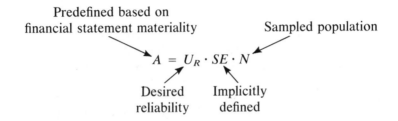

After the sample size is selected, acceptable precision A is compared with achieved precision A'. A is calculated based on the planned U_R, predefined N, and calculated SE (based on the final sample $SD \div \sqrt{n}$). If A' is greater than A, the sample size is insufficient because the precision limit is too wide. In this situation, the sample size would have to be increased to produce an A' equal to or below A. When the sample is deemed sufficient, the mean of the final sample is calculated to determine estimated value.

STEPS IN APPLYING UNSTRATIFIED MEAN PER UNIT

A 16-step approach to applying unstratified MPU is presented in this section. Afterward, we discuss stratified MPU, difference estimation, and ratio estimation.

Unstratified Mean per Unit

1. Define reliability level. Generally, a high reliability level should be used (99–90%).

2. Based on the following table, convert step $\boxed{1}$ into a U_R coefficient (reliability factor).

Reliability	U_R coefficient
.99	2.58
.95	1.96
.90	1.65

3. Set acceptable precision equal to the amount of material for the application.

$$\text{Acceptable precision} = A$$

Note: This is the *desired* precision and not a calculated amount.

4. Calculate required sample size *with replacement*.

$$n' = \left(\frac{U_R \cdot SD \cdot N}{A} \right)^2$$

where

$$
\begin{aligned}
n' &= \text{sample size with replacement} \\
SD &= \text{standard deviation}
\end{aligned}
$$

If the standard deviation SD is known from prior sampling work, use that as an estimate. If SD is unknown, an estimate must be made. To estimate SD:

A. Select a pilot random sample of 30 items from the population on a "without replacement" basis.

B. Use WORKSHEET 1 in Appendix A or the following equation to calculate SD:

$$SD = \sqrt{\frac{\sum_{j=1}^{n} x_j^2 - n\bar{x}^2}{n - 1}}$$

C. Substitute B into the n' equation.

5. Adjust step $\boxed{4}$ to sample size *without replacement* (finite population correction factor).

$$n = \frac{n'}{1 + (n'/N)}$$

Note: n is more efficient (i.e., smaller) than n' because of the finite population correction factor. However, n' must be calculated before n can be determined.

6. If n is greater than 30, randomly select the additional sample items using computer generation, random number table, or systematic selection. (See Chapter 2 for a discussion of sample selection techniques.)

7. Select the additional sample items and calculate the following sample results.

8. Calculate the standard deviation of the total sample (WORKSHEET 1 in Appendix A may be used to calculate the standard deviation.)

9. Calculate the standard error using the following equation:

$$SE = \frac{SD}{\sqrt{n}}$$

10. Calculate achieved precision A' based on the following equation (use SE from step $\boxed{9}$):

$$A' = U_R \cdot SE \cdot N \sqrt{1 - (n/N)}$$

11. If $A' \leq A$, go to step $\boxed{13}$; otherwise go to step $\boxed{12}$.

12. Increase the sample size according to the following equation (afterward, go back to step $\boxed{6}$):

$$\text{Adjusted } n = \left(\frac{U_R \cdot SD_{\text{step } \boxed{8}} \cdot N}{A} \right)^2$$

13. Calculate the mean $\bar{x}$ of the total sample.

$$\bar{x} = \frac{\text{sum of each audited sample}}{n}$$

14. Calculate estimated value EV.

$$EV = \bar{x} \cdot N$$

15. Conclude that you believe that at the reliability level specified in step $\boxed{1}$ that the true book value is within $EV \pm A'$. Your conclusion should also address the effectiveness of the procedures used to generate the projected amount and whether or not accounting personnel applied the procedures correctly.

16. State book value at EV (step $\boxed{14}$).

Caution

1. Do not use this approach if the client has a book value that you are trying to decide whether or not to accept. (It is not appropriate to make a statistical estimate of a population total and, finding the

book value somewhere within the precision interval, to accept the book value as materially correct. If this type of decision procedure is to be used, the audit hypothesis approach should be employed.)

2. Do not use this approach if you can stratify the population or use difference or ratio estimation.

DEMONSTRATION OF UNSTRATIFIED MEAN PER UNIT

To illustrate simple extension, let us assume Red Raider, Inc., is trying to estimate the total dollars in inventory for a particular subsidiary. The subsidiary does not have perpetual records or a book total for inventory. Red Raider, Inc., decides that a material misstatement would be $60,000. They desire 95 percent reliability and plan to use unrestricted random sampling (unstratified) without replacement. To estimate the standard deviation of the inventory population, a pilot sample of 30 items from the total population of 2000 items was selected. The pilot sample produced an arithmetic mean of $4000 and a standard deviation of $150.

1. Reliability is set equal to 95 percent. Red Raider, Inc., is willing to tolerate a 5 percent chance of sampling error. That is, 5 percent of the time, if they repeat this process over and over again, a projection would be produced plus and minus precision A' that would not include the true population total.

2. Based on 95 percent reliability, the reliability coefficient (U_R) is 1.96.

3. Precision (A) is judgmentally set equal to $60,000—the amount considered material for this application.

4. $n' = \left(\dfrac{1.96 \cdot \$150 \cdot 2000}{\$60,000} \right)^2$

   $n' = 96$ (rounded)

5. $n = \dfrac{96}{1 + (96/2000)}$

   $n = 92$ (rounded)

6. Sixty-two additional sample items are added to the pilot sample of 30 to yield the total sample of 92.

7. The 62 additional sample items are selected.

8. A standard deviation based on 92 items is calculated. Assume that the result is a standard deviation of $136.

9. $SE = \dfrac{\$136}{\sqrt{92}} = 14.18$ (rounded).

10. $A' = (1.96) \cdot (14.18) \cdot (2000) \cdot \sqrt{1 - \dfrac{92}{2000}} = \$54{,}292.$

11. Calculated precision A' is less than or equal to predefined precision A; therefore, go to step $\boxed{13}$.

12. It is not necessary to increase the sample size. Skip step $\boxed{12}$.

13. The mean of the 92 inventory items is calculated as follows, assuming the sample totals $370,977:

$$\bar{x} = \frac{\$370{,}977}{92} = \$4032.36$$

14. $EV = \$4032.36 \cdot 2000 = \$8{,}064{,}720.$

15. Red Raider, Inc., is 95 percent certain that the true inventory balance of all 2000 inventory items is within $8,064,720 $\pm$ $54,292.

16. Red Raider, Inc., should book $8,064,720 as their subsidiary's ending inventory.

STRATIFIED MEAN PER UNIT

When a population is highly variable (large standard deviation), unstratified MPU (unrestricted random sampling) may produce very large sample sizes. Stratification of the population produces an estimate having a desired level of precision with a reduced sample size. Such a sampling approach is more efficient than unstratified MPU. Stratified MPU may be applied to populations where no monetary errors are expected, or a moderate rate and amount of monetary errors are expected. Stratified MPU is widely used in practice.

Stratified sampling increases efficiency because the weighted sum of the stratum standard deviations is less than the standard deviation for the whole population. To illustrate, suppose a population consists of seven items—five have a value of $1 each and two have a value of $3 each. The standard deviation of this population is close to $1, but by forming two strata with the five items of value $1 and the remaining two items of value $3 in the other stratum, the standard deviation of each stratum is 0 and the weighted sum is also 0. By grouping sampling units with similar characteristics into the same strata, stratified MPU sampling reduces the variability among the items in a stratum.

To use stratified sampling, the accountant should adhere to three rules:

1. Every element must belong to one and only one stratum.

2. There must be a tangible, specifiable difference that defines and distinguishes the strata.

3. The *exact* number of elements in each stratum must be known.

The accountant can select the stratum boundaries as desired *if* all three of the above criteria are satisfied. If logical divisions exist in the population, they can be used (e.g., product line, type of item, location, and geographic areas). However, there must be some reason to expect the standard deviation of each stratum to be less than the standard deviation of the total population. As is explained below, the usual basis for stratification is the dollar amount of sample units.

In stratifying a population, one useful approach is to select stratum boundaries so that each stratum contains approximately the same total dollars [except the 100 percent (nonsampled) stratum]. To use dollar stratification, the total population amount is reduced by the 100 percent stratum and the remainder is divided by the number of strata desired. This yields a target dollar amount. The stratum boundaries then are selected so that each stratum has nearly the desired dollar amount. Usually three to five strata, including the 100 percent stratum is reasonable.[2]

In defining strata and their boundaries, consideration must be given to the cost (implementation expense) and benefit (efficiency in resulting sample size). From a cost perspective, recorded book amounts are widely used as a basis for population stratification. Likewise, if possible, manual stratification of a large population should be avoided, because it is time-consuming and expensive. One reason that accounts for the popularity of stratified MPU application in practice is that the method can be easily computerized. Because of the use of computer programs, most stratifying is done on a quantitative field (e.g., book recorded amount).

Most accountants, even in nonstatistical sampling, treat separately all population units that are individually significant. Statistically, there are two good reasons for this:

1. It reduces the variability of the population to be sampled, thus reducing the sample size.

2. It improves the stability of the standard error of the mean, thus maintaining the target risk levels of the sampling plan.

---

[2] According to Roberts, "In some limited empirical work, it was found that using up to about five strata can be expected to result in large savings in sample size. With more strata, the incremental saving persists but becomes appreciably smaller because a few differences of larger size than anticipated can adversely affect the sample evaluation." Donald M. Roberts, **Statistical Auditing** (New York: AICPA, 1978), p. 96.

A useful rule of thumb is to place all sampling units with amounts greater than four or five times the mean of the total sample into the 100 percent stratum. Some accounting populations, however, may not contain any of these key items.

Two methods are used to allocate a total sample to individual strata. One method is known as *proportional allocation*. In this method, the percentage of the sample allocated to each stratum is the same as the percentage of the total population accounted for by that stratum. That is,

$$n_i = n \cdot N_i/N$$

where n_i represents the sample size for the ith stratum, n the total sample size, N_i the number of population items in the ith stratum, and N the total population size.

A more precise method, however, is *optimal allocation*. Optimal allocation allocates the total sample to the individual stratum on the basis of the relative stratum size N and the stratum standard deviation SD.

$$n_i = n \cdot \frac{N_i SD_i}{\Sigma N_i SD_i}$$

where

$$
\begin{aligned}
n_i &= \text{sample size per stratum } i \\
n &= \text{total sample} \\
N_i &= \text{population size of stratum } i \\
SD_i &= \text{standard deviation of stratum } i
\end{aligned}
$$

WORKSHEET 2 in Appendix A is based on optimal allocation.

In summary, stratified sampling makes it feasible to sample a nonhomogeneous population without requiring an extremely large sample size. To ascertain whether or not stratified sampling should be used, consider the following:

1. The range of items in the population.
2. The shape of the population (compare with a normal curve).
3. The sample size produced via nonstratified sampling.

STEPS IN APPLYING STRATIFIED MEAN PER UNIT

1. Define reliability level. Generally, a high reliability level should be used (99–90%).

2. Based on the following table, convert step 1 into a U_R coefficient.

Reliability	U_R coefficient
.99	2.58
.95	1.96
.90	1.65

3. Set acceptable precision equal to an amount material for the application.

4. Define each straum.

   A. Every population element must belong to one and only one stratum.

   B. There must be a tangible, specifiable difference that defines and distinguishes the strata.

   C. The exact number of elements in each stratum must be known.

   D. One approach to use in stratifying a population is to select the stratum boundaries so that each stratum contains approximately the same total dollars

   E. The top stratum generally should be sampled 100 percent.

5. Calculate required sample size *without replacement* by using WORKSHEET 2 in Appendix A. If you cannot estimate the standard deviation of each stratum, draw a random sample of 30 items from each stratum (use sampling without replacement) and use WORKSHEET 1 in Appendix A to estimate the standard deviations. Instead of using WORKSHEET 2 and WORKSHEET 1, the following equations may be used for calculating stratum standard deviation and sample size:

$$SD = \sqrt{\frac{\sum_{j=1}^{n} x_j^2 - n\bar{x}^2}{n - 1}}$$

$$n_i = \frac{(N_i SD_i)(\Sigma N_i SD_i)}{(A/U_R)^2 + \Sigma N_i SD_i^2}$$

   If any n_i is greater than N_i, set that stratum sample size equal to its population size and recalculate the sample sizes for the remaining strata. The saturated stratum may be excluded from WORKSHEET 2.

6. Randomly select the additional sample elements (if pilot samples were used) using computer generation, the random number table, or systematic selection.

7. Select the additional sample items.

8. Calculate achieved precision A' by using WORKSHEET 3 in Appendix A or use the following equation:

$$A' = U_R \sqrt{\Sigma \frac{N_i SD_i^2 (N_i - n_i)}{n_i}}$$

Note that a 100 percent audited stratum (a saturated stratum) has no effect on A'. Thus, a saturated stratum should be omitted from the A' calculation.

9. If $A' \leq A$, go to step $\boxed{11}$; otherwise, go to step $\boxed{10}$.

10. Use WORKSHEET 2 in Appendix A to recalculate and reallocate sample size. Use the standard deviations of each stratum based on the total sample from each stratum. WORKSHEET 1 in Appendix A may be employed to calculate the standard deviation of each stratum. Go back to step $\boxed{6}$ after the recalculated (larger) sample size is determined.

11. Calculate the mean $\bar{x}$ of each stratum based on n_i for each stratum.

12. Calculate the *estimated population value* total according to the following.

$$\begin{aligned}
\bar{x}_1 \cdot N_1 &= \bar{x}_1 N_1 \\
\bar{x}_2 \cdot N_2 &= \bar{x}_2 N_2 \\
\bar{x}_3 \cdot N_3 &= \underline{\bar{x}_3 N_3} \\
& \underline{\underline{\Sigma \bar{x}_i N_i = EV \text{ for sampled stratum}}}
\end{aligned}$$

$EV = EV$ for sampled stratum PLUS total for any 100 percent nonsampled stratum

where

$$\begin{aligned}
\bar{x}_i &= \text{the mean of a defined stratum} \\
N_i &= \text{the total number of items per} \\
& \text{a defined stratum} \\
\Sigma \bar{x}_i N_i &= \text{sum of } (\bar{x}_i N_i)
\end{aligned}$$

13. Conclude that you believe that at the reliability level specified in step $\boxed{1}$ that the true book value is within $EV \pm A'$ (step $\boxed{8}$). Your conclusion should also address effectiveness of procedures used to generate the projected amount and whether or not accounting personnel applied the procedures correctly.

14. State book value at EV (step $\boxed{12}$).

Caution

Do not use this approach if the client has a book value that you are trying to decide whether or not to accept. (It is not appropriate to make a statistical estimate of a population total and, finding the book value somewhere within the precision interval, to accept the book value as materially correct. If this type of decision procedure is to be used, the audit hypothesis approach should be employed.)

If you understand the Red Raider, Inc., problem as is illustrated in applying simple extension, stratified simple extension should not be difficult to comprehend. The only additional reminder concerns step 12, where the estimated population total *EV* is calculated. For a 100 percent stratum, the estimated value is increased by the total of that stratum. Likewise, calculated precision *A'* is not affected by a 100 percent stratum.

DIFFERENCE ESTIMATION

Difference estimation is a model used to estimate dollar amounts, similar to unstratified and stratified MPU. Difference estimation, however, is sometimes more efficient (i.e., smaller sample size). Instead of computing the mean value and the standard deviation of the sample item values as in MPU, the mean value and standard deviation of the individual *differences* between each sample item's value and book value are computed. A difference is defined to be the sample item value minus book value and will be zero if these quantities are equal. Algebraically, a positive difference indicates an understated book value, but a negative difference indicates an overstated book value. As we discuss later, difference estimation can be used with or without stratification.

Difference estimation may be appropriate and advantageous when:

1. There is a book value for each population item.
2. The total book value is known and corresponds to the addition of all the individual book values. (Before using difference estimation the book values *must* be footed.)

For difference estimation to be efficient and effective, the sample size should be large enough for the distribution of sample mean differences to be approximately normal. Whether or not practical sample sizes that approximate normality are produced depends on: (1) the proportion of sample units with nonzero differences, and (2) the distribution of these differences in terms of their magnitude (dollar amount) and their algebraic sign (understated or overstated).

Unstratified difference estimation works effectively if the population and sample units contain a large proportion of nonzero differences. Also, the differences should be nearly equally divided between overstatement and understatement, and the misstatements should be fairly constant in amount. If differences are highly skewed, stratified difference estimation or ratio estimation should be considered.

[handwritten margin note: If all that the book value is pretty good.]

Before the standard deviation can be safely estimated, a minimum number of nonzero differences must be observed. What is the minimum number of differences? According to Roberts:

There is no simple answer to this question. A small number would suffice if all the non-zero differences are nearly equal whereas a large number would be necessary when the differences vary widely. Whatever the number, the auditor should be reasonably satisfied that the observed differences appear to be typical for the particular situation. In that case, recognizing that any numerical guideline has exceptions, the auditor might use 15 or 20 as a minimum number.[3]

One large CPA firm recommends a minimum of about 30 differences to ensure a good estimate of the standard deviation of differences. For illustration purposes, a minimum of 30 will be used in this text.

The mean of the differences for unstratified difference estimation is calculated as:

$$\bar{d} = \frac{\Sigma d_i}{n}$$

where

$$\bar{d} = \text{mean of the differences}$$
$$\Sigma d_i = \text{sum of observed differences considering signs}$$

After calculating the mean of the differences, the estimated population difference is obtained by

$$\hat{D} = N\bar{d}$$

where

$$\hat{D} = \text{estimated population difference}$$

An estimate of the total value is calculated as

$$EV = \text{book value} + \hat{D} \text{ (if net differences are positive) or}$$
$$- \hat{D} \text{ (if net differences are negative).}$$

The standard deviation of the differences then is used to compute the precision of the total observed value at some predetermined reliability level.

The approach to a difference estimation application is essentially the same as the approach used in unstratified MPU. The primary difference as depicted by the following model is that the mean of the differences $\bar{d}$ and the standard deviation of differences SD_d is used instead of $\bar{x}$ and SD. Thus, difference estimation improves the efficiency (smaller sample size) and precision (tighter precision) vis-à-vis other estimation techniques.

---

[3] Donald M. Roberts, **Statistical Auditing**, p 74. See also, J. H. McCray, "Ratio and Difference Estimation in Auditing," **Management Accounting** (December 1973), p. 47.

Stratified difference estimation may further enhance the efficiency of difference estimation. In fact, unless nonzero differences are reasonably small in dollar amount, unstratified difference estimation probably should not be used.

Three to five strata are commonly employed in stratified difference applications, with stratum boundaries selected so that each stratum contains nearly an equal dollar amount—except the top stratum, which is the 100 percent nonsampled stratum. The only change in the stratified MPU model is that d is substituted for $\bar{x}$ and SD_d for SD for each stratum. Also, if stratified difference estimation is used, several differences should be observed in each stratum. After the sample has been selected and sample item values established, the estimated total difference is calculated according to the following equation, assuming three strata:

$$\hat{D} = N_1\bar{d}_1 + N_2\bar{d}_2 + N_3\bar{d}_3$$

Because of the qualifying error conditions that are necessary before difference estimation can be used, its application is sometimes limited. For example, in large banks, savings and loan institutions, and public utilities characterized by strong internal control, differences between sample item values and book values may be rare. One widely used application is in the area of Lifo. If a company maintains Fifo records that are converted to Lifo at year-end, difference estimation, stratified or unstratified, is very useful in making this conversion.

STEPS IN APPLYING UNSTRATIFIED DIFFERENCE ESTIMATION

1. Define reliability level. Generally a high reliability level should be used (99–90%).
2. Based on the following table convert step $\boxed{1}$ into a U_R coefficient.

Reliability	U_R coefficient
.99	2.58
.95	1.96
.90	1.65

3. Set acceptable precision equal to an amount material for the application.
4. Calculate required sample size *with replacement*.

$$n' = \left(\frac{U_R \cdot SD_d \cdot N}{A}\right)^2$$

where

n' = sample size with replacement.

SD_d = standard deviation (based on prior knowledge or random sample). WORKSHEET 4 in Appendix A delineates the steps involved in calculating a standard deviation of differences from a sample. The size of the pilot sample must be large enough to contain several nonzero differences. Otherwise, SD_d would be zero and n' could not be computed. The pilot sample (if used) should be selected without replacement.

5. Adjust step $\boxed{4}$ to sample size *without replacement*.

$$n = \frac{n'}{1 + (n'/N)}$$

6. Randomly select additional samples (if pilot sample was used) by using computer generation, a random number table, or systematic selection.

7. Determine the difference between sample item values and book values. Examine the cause of observed errors to ascertain that any unobserved errors that might exist are likely to be in about the same range of values as observed errors.

8. Calculate the standard deviation of the sample differences. WORKSHEET 4 in Appendix A may be used to calculate the standard deviation of the differences, or the following equation may be used.

$$SD_d = \sqrt{\frac{\Sigma d_i^2 - n\bar{d}^2}{n - 1}}$$

9. Calculate the standard error of the differences by using the following equation:

$$SE_d = \frac{SD_d}{\sqrt{n}}$$

10. Calculate achieved precision A' based on the following equation. Use SE_d from step $\boxed{9}$.

$$A' = U_R \cdot SE_d \cdot N \sqrt{1 - \frac{n}{N}}$$

11. If $A' \leq A$, go to step $\boxed{13}$; otherwise, go to step $\boxed{12}$.

12. Increase the sample size according to the following equation. Afterward, go back to step $\boxed{6}$.

$$\text{Adjusted } n = \left(\frac{U_R \cdot SE_d \text{ (step } \boxed{8}) \cdot N}{A}\right)^2$$

13. Calculate the mean of the differences $\bar{d}$ of the total sample.

$$\bar{d} = \frac{\Sigma d_i}{n}$$

14. Calculate the estimated population difference $\hat{D}$.

$$\hat{D} = N \cdot \bar{d}$$

15. Calculate estimated value, EV.

$$EV = \text{book value (footed)} + \hat{D} \text{ (if net differences are positive) or} - \hat{D} \text{ (if net differences are negative)}.$$

16. Conclude that you believe that at the reliability level specified in step $\boxed{1}$ that the true book value is within $EV \pm A'$. Your conclusion should also address effectiveness of procedures used to generate the projected amount and whether or not accounting personnel applied the procedures correctly.

17. State book value at EV (step $\boxed{15}$).

Caution

1. Do not use this approach if the client has a book value that you are trying to decide whether or not to accept.

2. The *observed* error rate (sample item value minus book value) in the final sample must include at least a minimum of 30 differences. *Otherwise,* consider using stratified MPU or probability proportionate to size sampling.

RATIO ESTIMATION

Ratio estimation is applied in much the same fashion as difference estimation. Because of its close similarity to difference estimation and the complexity involved in manual calculations, only a brief introduction is presented here.

Like difference estimation, ratio estimation may be appropriate and efficient when a book value exists for each population item, and differences between sample item values and book values are not rare. Ratio estimation assumes that the book values are all positive.

To apply ratio estimation, a sample is selected from a population and the observed sample item value OV of each item is determined along with the corresponding book value BV. From the selected random sample, the estimated population ratio $\hat{R}$ is calculated as follows:

$$\hat{R} = \frac{\Sigma OV_i}{\Sigma BV_i}$$

The estimated value (point estimate) for the population total is

$$EV = \hat{R} \cdot \text{book value}$$

If $\hat{R}$ is less than one, the sample evidence indicates that book value is overstated; but, if $\hat{R}$ is greater than one, the book value appears to be understated.

Ratio estimation will be more efficient relative to unstratified MPU if the standard deviation of ratios SD_r is smaller than the SD of the sample item values. Likewise, ratio estimation may, in certain situations, be more efficient than difference estimation if SD_r is less than SD_d. Ratio estimation is favored relative to difference estimation when the absolute differences (sample item values—book values) are nearly a constant percentage of book values. That is, if each sample item value is nearly proportional to book value, ratio estimation produces a more efficient sample size. Recall that difference estimation tends to be more efficient when the absolute differences are nearly the same amount (without regard to book value). To illustrate, the following situation would favor ratio estimation:

Sample item value	Book value	Difference
$2,000	$1,800	$200
4,000	4,480	(480)
10,000	10,000	0
3,000	3,390	(390)
12,000	10,800	1,200
$31,000	$30,470	$530

Conversely, the next situation would favor difference estimation, relative to ratio estimation.

Sample item value	Book value	Difference
$2,000	$1.730	270
4,000	4,300	(300)
10,000	10,000	0
3,000	2,680	320
12,000	11,760	240
$31,000	$30,470	$530

The tedious manual calculations inherent in ratio estimation applications perhaps can best be appreciated by the equation for SD_r.

$$SD_r = \left[\frac{\Sigma OV^2 + R^2\Sigma BV^2 - 2R\Sigma(OV)(BV)}{n - 1}\right]^{1/2}$$

SUMMARY

When the accountant is faced with a situation requiring the projection of a total quantity or total dollars based on a mean of a sample, accounting estimation is the appropriate tool to use. By using estimation sampling, a projection can be made of the estimated population value that becomes the booked amount. The estimated population value plus and minus calculated precision is expected to contain the true but unknown value at a defined reliability level.

Four estimation models are discussed in this chapter. They are: (1) unstratified mean per unit, (2) stratified mean per unit, (3) difference estimation, and (4) ratio estimation. Ranked in order of efficiency (smallest sample size), stratified difference estimation or ratio estimation would most likely produce the most efficient sample size. Unstratified difference estimation would be next, followed by stratified mean per unit. Unstratified mean per unit is the most inefficient accounting estimation model; consequently, it is used only when necessary.

Stratified mean per unit is probably more widely used in practice than the other accounting estimation models discussed in this chapter. Extensive use of stratified mean per unit occurs primarily because qualifying error conditions that are necessary for using difference and ratio estimation are somewhat limiting.

GLOSSARY

Acceptable precision   A planned precision determined by considering materiality for a given account balance.

Accounting estimation   A statistical model used to estimate a dollar balance or quantity total when the point estimate is to be entered into the accounting records.

Achieved precision   A calculated precision A' determined by multiplying reliability (U_R) times the standard error SE times the population size N.

Audit hypothesis approach   A statistical model used to determine if an already existing book value or quantity is misstated by a material amount.

Central limit theorem   A theorem that states that if a large number of samples are drawn from a given population, the distribution of sample means tends to be normally distributed, almost independently of the shape of the original population distribution.

Difference   The sample item value minus the book value.

Difference estimation   See Chapter 1 glossary.

Estimated population difference   A positive or negative total determined by multiplying the difference mean $\bar{d}$ times the population size N yielding an estimated population difference $\hat{D}$.

Estimated value   A point estimate determined by multiplying the sample mean $\bar{x}$ times the population size N or adding/subtracting the estimated population difference $\hat{D}$ to a footed book value total.

Estimation   The projection (extrapolation) of a sample characteristic to a population.

Mean   The arithmetic average—the total of all items divided by the number of items.

Median   The midpoint of a population or sample.

Mode   The value that occurs most frequently in a distribution.

Normal distribution   A frequency distribution in which item values tend to congregate around the mean with no tendency for deviation toward one side rather than the other. A normal distribution is represented graphically by a bell-shaped curve.

Optimal allocation   A method to determine strata sample sizes based on the relative size of each stratum and its standard deviation.

Point estimate   The same as estimated value (EV).

Precision   A measure of closeness of a sample estimate to the corresponding population characteristic. A range of values around a point estimate within which the true value is expected to fall. It is a probabilistic measure in that the precision of an estimate A' can only be made for a specified reliability.

Precision interval If the precision of an estimate EV is A', the interval from $EV + A'$ to $EV - A'$ is the precision interval.

Proportional allocation A method to determine strata sample sizes based on only the relative size of each stratum.

Quantity The value of an item, usually in dollars.

Ratio estimation A variable sampling model whereby a ratio $\hat{R}$ of the sum of observed sample item values divided by the sum of book values is calculated from a sample. The ratio is multiplied by the total book value to yield a point estimate of the population total.

Skewness The degree of asymmetry or lopsidedness of a distribution. Typical accounting populations are skewed because there are many small to medium amounts and a few very large amounts.

Standard deviation A unit of measure of the variability of a frequency distribution. In a normal distribution, 68 percent of all item values fall within ± 1 standard deviation, 95 percent within ± 1.96 standard deviations, and 99 percent within ± 2.58 standard deviations.

Standard error of the mean The standard deviation of the distribution of sample means. The estimated standard error of a sample mean is equal to the standard deviation of the sample divided by the square root of the sample size.

Statistical efficiency A statistical model is said to be more efficient than another if it requires a smaller sample size to achieve the same precision and reliability.

Stratified mean per unit See Chapter 1 glossary.

True value An account balance determined by a complete examination of the account details (without the use of sampling).

Unstratified mean per unit See Chapter 1 glossary.

REVIEW QUESTIONS

4-1. Each of the following assumes the uses of unrestricted random sampling without replacement. State whether each one is true (T) or false (F).

A. If an accountant wishes to use a table of random digits to select a random sample, he or she must first find a table that conforms to the numbering employed by the items in the population the accountant wishes to sample.

B. If a usable number appears more than once in the table of random digits during the selection of the sample, the item should be included in the sample only once and another number should be selected from the table.

C. A random sample of at least 50 items would have to be discarded if it produced one item disproportionately large in relation to the other items selected.

D. The effect of the inclusion by chance of a very large or a very small item in a random sample can be lessened by increasing the size of the sample.

E. The reliability specified by the accountant for a sample estimate expresses the degree of confidence that the true value will be within the computed precision interval.

F. The standard deviation is a measure of variability of items in the population.

G. Variability of items in the population is a factor that usually causes the point estimate of the population and its true value to be different.

H. It is necessary to determine the true standard deviation for a population to determine the size of the sample to be drawn from that population.

I. The standard error of the mean generally will be less than the estimated standard deviation computed on the basis of a sample.

J. Precision and reliability have no meaning unless paired with each other.

K. Variable sampling is used primarily for compliance testing.

4-2. What is variable sampling?

4-3. What is the primary difference in accounting estimation versus audit hypothesis testing?

4-4. Calculate the standard deviation of the following sample items.

$$\frac{x}{}$$

8

15

2

34

16

4-5. Why is the unstratified mean per unit sometimes referred to as simple extension?

4-6. Is the standard error of the mean smaller or larger than the standard deviation? Explain.

4-7. If calculated precision A' is larger than predefined precision A, the sample size has to be increased. Why?

4-8. Prove that the mathematical definition of precision is equal to the sample size formula. That is,

$$A = U_R \cdot SE \cdot N \quad \text{equals} \quad n' = \left(\frac{U_R \cdot SD \cdot N}{A} \right)^2$$

4-9. List the three rules that must be followed if stratified mean per unit is to be used correctly.

4-10. What are two methods used to allocate a total sample to individual strata? Which one is recommended in the text?

4-11. The Clay Corporation is applying simple statistical sampling to estimate their receivable balance. They have four strata. The stratum containing the largest accounts was not sampled. It totals $88,900. The other three strata produced the following results:

Stratum	$\bar{x}$	N
1	238	250
2	154	600
3	53	1500

Calculated precision (A') is $20,000. What is the estimated value?

4-12. Determine the sample size for each stratum using (a) proportional allocation and (b) optimal allocation.

Stratum	Stratum boundaries	Size	Standard deviation
1	0–300	5500	80
2	301–800	2000	150
3	801–1600	500	200
4	1601–3000	300	400

4-13. Difference estimation often is more efficient than unstratified MPU. However, before difference estimation can be used, two conditions must be met. What are these conditions? What is the minimum number of observed differences that are recommended in the text before difference estimation can be safely used?

4-14. If a population of size N is footed and yields $10,000 and the mean of differences $\bar{d}$ is $+\$50$, what is the estimated population difference if $N = 100$?

4-15. If the estimated population difference $\hat{D}$ is $-\$500$, what is the estimated value if the footed book value is $\$10,000$?

4-16. What causes difference estimation to be more efficient than unstratified MPU? What could cause ratio estimation to be more efficient than difference estimation?

4-17. Calculate the mean of the following differences.

Sample item value	Book value
$20	18
40	40
36	38
21	36
15	15

ACCOUNTING ESTIMATION CASES

CASE 4-1 EMPRESS COSMETIQUE CASE*
(estimated time to complete: 4 hours)

Empress Cosmetique markets inexpensive, quality cosmetics for the mature woman. Well established in the state, Empress maintains five regional warehouses with approximately equal stock levels.

Until recently, Mrs. Naomi Van Diver, the company's founder and director, followed traditional management practices by insisting upon the pricing of all inventory items in each warehouse. Now under new management, Empress Cosmetique is considering the use of statistical sampling techniques for estimating its inventory for financial reporting purposes.

The company's inventory consists of 100 different beauty products in each of the five warehouses. For inventory control purposes, perpetual inventory counts for each product are maintained for each warehouse location.

The new plan will consist of randomly selecting inventory lots for count and comparison with the perpetual record. Using statistical sampling, an

---

* This case was prepared by Doyle Z. Williams, Dean, School of Accounting, University of Southern California, and Dale A. Stewart, BBA Accounting, Texas Tech University, and is copyrighted by Doyle Z. Williams. It is reproduced here with permission.

estimate of the inventory value will be made that provides 95 percent assurance that the estimated value is within ± $58,000 of the actual amount.

A list of perpetual inventory units by lot as of June 30 (pages 115–127) and a product price schedule page 128 are provided. Assume that there are no differences in physical and perpetual inventory counts.

REQUIREMENTS

For each of the following, prepare complete, well-organized, and documented work papers.

A. As the chief accountant for Empress Cosmetique, describe the sampling plan appropriate for estimating the June 30 inventory.
B. Using appropriate statistical sampling techniques, estimate the value of the June 30 inventory that will meet the $58,000 precision and 95 percent confidence level indicated. If you use a random number table, the illustration on page 25 may be employed. The price list for the inventory appears on page 128.
C. By using the data obtained from your preliminary sample of 30 items, calculate the required sample size (n'), assuming the desired levels of precision and reliability in each case are as follows:

Case	Reliability	Precision
(1)	95%	$60,000
(2)	90%	$30,000
(3)	90%	$14,000
(4)	85%	$60,000

D. If you were the independent auditor of Empress Cosmetique, could you accept the use of a statistical sampling model instead of a 100 percent inventory count? Consult your Statements on Auditing Standards for authoritative support.

Inventory

Empress Cosmetique			
Line Number	**Item Number**	**Quantity**	**Description**
	A001R	1103	Lipstick Red
	B001R	1250	
	C001R	1301	
	D001R	1012	
5	E001R	1212	
	A001P	1062	Lipstick Pink
	B001P	1013	
	C001P	1081	
	D001P	1039	
10	E001P	1072	
	A001M	1017	Lipstick Mocha
	B001M	1041	
	C001M	1101	
	D001M	1013	
15	E001M	1076	
	A001W	1001	Lipstick Wine
	B001W	1031	
	C001W	1114	
	D001W	1061	
20	E001W	1103	
	A101R	1143	Nail Polish Red
	B101R	1116	
	C101R	1189	
	D101R	1135	
25	E101R	1147	
	A101P	1481	Nail Polish Pink
	B101P	1414	
	C101P	1539	
	D101P	1564	
30	E101P	1491	
	A101M	1521	Nail Polish Mocha
	B101M	1416	
	C101M	1429	
	D101M	1497	
35	E101M	1465	
	A101W	1270	Nail Polish Wine
	B101W	1128	
	C101W	1252	
	D101W	1148	

Inventory (Continued)

	Empress Cosmetique		
Line Number	Item Number	Quantity	Description
40	E101W	1165	
	A002BK	1465	Eye Liner Black
	B002BK	1471	
	C002BK	1461	
	D002BK	1488	
45	E002BK	1450	
	A002BR	1273	Eye Liner Brown
	B002BR	1285	
	C002BR	1314	
	D002BR	1269	
50	E002BR	1298	
	A202BR	1199	Eye Brow Pencil Brown
	B202BR	1265	
	C202BR	1233	
	D202BR	1301	
55	E202BR	1277	
	A202BK	1414	Eye Brow Pencil Black
	B202BK	1459	
	C202BK	1504	
	D202BK	1499	
60	E202BK	1517	
	A202G	1777	Eye Brow Pencil Gray
	B202G	1711	
	C202G	1734	
	D202G	1741	
65	E202G	1768	
	A003B	1503	Eye Shadow Blue
	B003B	1507	
	C003B	1487	
	D003B	1475	
70	E003B	1496	
	A003G	1749	Eye Shadow Green
	B003G	1696	
	C003G	1765	
	D003G	1731	
75	E003G	1677	
	A003W	1916	Eye Shadow White
	B003W	1959	
	C003W	2001	
	D003W	1966	

Inventory (Continued)

Empress Cosmetique			
Line Number	**Item Number**	**Quantity**	**Description**
80	E003W	1940	
	A003CG	1633	Eye Shadow Charcoal Gray
	B003CG	1617	
	C003CG	1576	
	D003CG	1621	
85	E003CG	1588	
	A003T	1501	Eye Shadow Topaz
	B003T	1520	
	C003T	1511	
	D003T	1469	
90	E003T	1471	
	A003Y	1851	Eye Shadow Oyster
	B003Y	1913	
	C003Y	1857	
	D003Y	1901	
95	E003Y	1862	
	A003M	1702	Eye Shadow Mauve
	B003M	1727	
	C003M	1727	
	D003M	1714	
100	E003M	1682	
	A003L	1611	Eye Shadow Lavender
	B003L	1661	
	C003L	1587	
	D003L	1634	
105	E003L	1550	
	A303C	1299	Blusher Copper
	B303C	1324	
	C303C	1349	
	D303C	1377	
110	E303C	1409	
	A303LO	1439	Blusher Light Orange
	B303LO	1522	
	C303LO	1491	
	D303LO	1486	
115	E303LO	1500	
	A303R	1616	Blusher Rose
	B303R	1644	
	C303R	1677	
	D303R	1579	

Inventory (Continued)

Empress Cosmetique			
Line Number	**Item Number**	**Quantity**	**Description**
120	E303R	1663	
	A303P	1625	Blusher Pearlie Pink
	B303P	1721	
	C303P	1755	
	D303P	1760	
125	E303P	1641	
	A303DR	1193	Blusher Dawn Red
	B303DR	1212	
	C303DR	1206	
	D303DR	1187	
130	E303DR	1197	
	A303B	1076	Blusher Beige
	B303B	1111	
	C303B	1057	
	D303B	1082	
135	E303B	1124	
	A316P	1024	Hair Rinse Platinum
	B316P	1036	
	C316P	1048	
	D316P	1031	
140	E316P	1054	
	A316SM	1114	Hair Rinse Silver Mist
	B316SM	1196	
	C316SM	1174	
	D316SM	1165	
145	E316SM	1159	
	A316A	1117	Hair Rinse Auburn
	B316A	1124	
	C316A	1106	
	D316A	1131	
150	E316A	1119	
	A316BN	1227	Hair Rinse Brownette
	B316BN	1234	
	C316BN	1221	
	D316BN	1241	
155	E316BN	1236	
	A316BL	1179	Hair Rinse Blonde
	B316BL	1184	
	C316BL	1214	

Inventory (Continued)

	Empress Cosmetique		
Line Number	**Item Number**	**Quantity**	**Description**
	D316BL	1166	
160	E316BL	1193	
	A316BR	1634	Hair Rinse Brunette
	B316BR	1586	
	C316BR	1599	
	D316BR	1649	
165	E316BR	1651	
	A316SF	1786	Hair Rinse Silver Flake
	B316SF	1759	
	C316SF	1741	
	D316SF	1697	
170	E316SF	1681	
	A366	1083	Nail File
	B366	1076	
	C366	1074	
	D366	1085	
175	E366	1036	
	A367	1029	Nail File
	B367	1001	
	C367	1093	
	D367	1033	
180	E367	1097	
	A368	1032	Nail File
	B368	1003	
	C368	1005	
	D368	1059	
185	E368	1033	
	A369	1976	Nail File
	B369	2043	
	C369	1903	
	D369	2072	
190	E369	1968	
	A370	1321	Nail File
	B370	1383	
	C370	1391	
	D370	1395	
195	E370	1366	
	A410	1136	Emery Board Fine
	B410	1159	

Inventory (Continued)

Empress Cosmetique			
Line Number	Item Number	Quantity	Description
	C410	1127	
	D410	1147	
200	E410	1161	
	A411	1132	Emery Board Fine
	B411	1103	
	C411	1115	
	D411	1159	
205	E411	1330	
	A420	1377	Emery Board Medium
	B420	1405	
	C420	1411	
	D420	1389	
210	E420	1394	
	A421	1316	Emery Board Medium
	B421	1324	
	C421	1339	
	D421	1331	
215	E421	1306	
	A430	1387	Emery Board Coarse
	B430	1374	
	C430	1391	
	D430	1398	
220	E430	1377	
	A431	1283	Emery Board Coarse
	B431	1290	
	C431	1349	
	D431	1301	
225	E431	1297	
	A440	1314	Tweezers
	B440	1324	
	C440	1311	
	D440	1301	
230	E440	1332	
	A450	1214	Tweezers
	B450	1187	
	C450	1212	
	D450	1196	
235	E450	1210	
	A460	1354	Tweezers

Inventory (Continued)

	Empress Cosmetique		
Line Number	**Item Number**	Quantity	Description
	B460	1339	
	C460	1362	
	D460	1341	
240	E460	1350	
	A500	1080	Depilatory Unscented
	B500	1068	
	C500	1030	
	D500	1067	
245	E500	1070	
	A501	1021	Depilatory Scented
	B501	1062	
	C501	1001	
	D501	1079	
250	E501	1075	
	A520S	1018	Deodorant Spray
	B520S	1053	
	C520S	1029	
	D520S	1065	
255	E520S	1019	
	A520P	1085	Deodorant Powder
	B520P	1068	
	C520P	1011	
	D520P	1062	
260	E520P	1056	
	A520R	1063	Deodorant Roll-on
	B520R	1064	
	C520R	1039	
	D520R	1034	
265	E520R	1088	
	A530S	1025	Antiperspirant Spray
	B530S	1076	
	C530S	1042	
	D530S	1066	
270	E530S	1021	
	A530P	1082	Antiperspirant Powder
	B530P	1025	
	C530P	1011	
	D530P	1076	
275	E530P	1063	

Inventory (Continued)

	Empress Cosmetique		
Line Number	Item Number	Quantity	Description
	A530R	1467	Antiperspirant Roll-on
	B530R	1455	
	C530R	1301	
	D530R	1357	
280	E530R	1477	
	A601	1427	Hair Spray Mist
	B601	1314	
	C601	1260	
	D601	1276	
285	E601	1372	
	A602F	1925	Hair Spray Fine Hold
	B602F	1864	
	C602F	1862	
	D602F	1912	
290	E602F	1964	
	A602R	1311	Hair Spray Regular Hold
	B602R	1473	
	C602R	1360	
	D602R	1493	
295	E602R	1375	
	A602H	1407	Hair Spray Hard-to-Hold
	B602H	1305	
	C602H	1577	
	D602H	1442	
300	E602H	1457	
	A603	1878	Hair Spray Unscented
	B603	1961	
	C603	1896	
	D603	1929	
305	E603	1836	
	A650	1865	Shampoo Dandruff
	B650	1882	
	C650	1892	
	D650	1816	
310	E650	1828	
	A652D	1145	Shampoo Dry
	B652D	1192	
	C652D	1163	
	D652D	1101	

Inventory (Continued)

Empress Cosmetique			
Line Number	**Item Number**	Quantity	Description
315	E652D	1162	
	A652N	1295	Shampoo Normal
	B652N	1291	
	C652N	1292	
	D652N	1213	
320	E652N	1218	
	A652Y	1311	Shampoo Oily
	B652Y	1284	
	C652Y	1395	
	D652Y	1348	
325	E652Y	1273	
	A654	1795	Shampoo Color Treated
	B654	1549	
	C654	1784	
	D654	1634	
330	E654	1665	
	A660	1123	Creme Rinse Lemon
	B660	1076	
	C660	1077	
	D660	1114	
335	E660	1115	
	A662	1710	Creme Rinse Unscented
	B662	1712	
	C662	1758	
	D662	1679	
340	E662	1793	
	A670R	1936	Setting Gel Regular
	B670R	1895	
	C670R	1827	
	D670R	1843	
345	E670R	1937	
	A670H	1708	**Setting Gel Hard-to-Hold**
	B670H	1620	
	C670H	1763	
	D670H	1661	
350	E670H	1742	
	A672R	**1631**	Setting Lotion Regular
	B672R	**1635**	
	C672R	1636	

Inventory (Continued)

	Empress Cosmetique		
Line Number	**Item Number**	**Quantity**	**Description**
	D672R	1729	
355	E672R	1748	
	A672H	1021	Setting Lotion Hard-to-Hold
	B672H	1004	
	C672H	1062	
	D672H	1069	
360	E672H	1087	
	A701	1228	Hand Lotion
	B701	1121	
	C701	1197	
	D701	1137	
365	E701	1234	
	A702	1039	Hand Creme
	B702	1086	
	C702	1064	
	D702	1069	
370	E702	1017	
	A712	1017	Skin Moisturizer
	B712	1097	
	C712	1076	
	D712	1088	
375	E712	1087	
	A714	1358	Body Lotion
	B714	1399	
	C714	1345	
	D714	1224	
380	E714	1205	
	A750	1262	Bath Oil
	B750	1120	
	C750	1275	
	D750	1190	
385	E750	1180	
	A751	1474	Bath Oil
	B751	1439	
	C751	1362	
	D751	1426	
390	E751	1492	
	A752	1311	Bath Oil
	B752	1493	

Inventory (Continued)

	Empress Cosmetique		
Line Number	Item Number	Quantity	Description
	C752	1365	
	D752	1480	
395	E752	1456	
	A761	1651	Bubble Bath Beads
	B761	1694	
	C761	1572	
	D761	1681	
400	E761	1688	
	A762	1576	Bubble Bath Powder
	B762	1627	
	C762	1437	
	D762	1489	
405	E762	1578	
	A763	1859	Bubble Bath Liquid
	B763	1968	
	C763	1804	
	D763	1886	
410	E763	1998	
	A800	1946	Makeup Remover
	B800	1903	
	C800	1900	
	D800	1908	
415	E800	1951	
	A810	1623	Cold Creme
	B810	1732	
	C810	1632	
	D810	1722	
420	E810	1605	
	A814	1541	Medicated Lotion
	B814	1670	
	C814	1793	
	D814	1804	
425	E814	1908	
	A815	1534	Medicated Creme
	B815	1527	
	C815	1518	
	D815	1571	
430	E815	1563	
	A824	1770	Hair Texturizer

Inventory (Continued)

	Empress Cosmetique		
Line Number	Item Number	Quantity	Description
	B824	1765	
	C824	1773	
	D824	1745	
435	E824	1791	
	A830	1592	Nail Polish Remover
	B830	1526	
	C830	1588	
	D830	1565	
440	E830	1591	
	A831	1347	Nail Polish Remover
	B831	1395	
	C831	1393	
	D831	1356	
445	E831	1421	
	A860B	1456	Mascara Black
	B860B	1472	
	C860B	1476	
	D860B	1453	
450	E860B	1360	
	A860LB	1097	Mascara Light Brown
	B860LB	1026	
	C860LB	1074	
	D860LB	1037	
455	E860LB	1033	
	A860DB	1052	Mascara Dark Brown
	B860DB	1068	
	C860DB	1073	
	D860DB	1016	
460	E860DB	1098	
	A901	1372	Skin Be Gone
	B901	1370	
	C901	1361	
	D901	1331	
465	E901	1333	
	A911	1378	Nails Hard
	B911	1401	
	C911	1373	
	D911	1407	
470	E911	1466	

Inventory (Continued)

Line Number	Item Number	Quantity	Description
	A990B	1006	Eyelashes Black
	B990B	1024	
	C990B	1088	
	D990B	1017	
475	E990B	1083	
	A990LB	1024	Eyelashes Light Brown
	B990LB	1044	
	C990LB	1004	
	D990LB	1010	
480	E990LB	1067	
	A990MB	1038	Eyelashes Medium Brown
	B990MB	1176	
	C990MB	1119	
	D990MB	1050	
485	E990MB	1045	
	A990DB	1131	Eyelashes Dark Brown
	B990DB	1183	
	C990DB	1142	
	D990DB	1192	
490	E990DB	1132	
	A990A	1146	Eyelashes Auburn
	B990A	1198	
	C990A	1109	
	D990A	1076	
495	E990A	1182	
	A990S	1098	Eyelashes Strawberry
	B990S	1016	
	C990S	1022	
	D990S	1003	
500	E990S	1033	

Price List

			Empress Cosmetique		
Item Number	Price	Item Number	Price	Item Number	Price
001M	$1.35	316SM	$1.39	662	$1.32
001P	$1.39	366	$1.19	670H	$1.34
001R	$1.39	367	$1.29	670R	$1.31
001W	$1.35	368	$1.39	672H	$1.42
101M	$1.25	369	$1.41	672R	$1.41
101P	$1.29	370	$1.45	701	$1.39
101R	$1.29	410	$1.19	702	$1.38
101W	$1.25	411	$1.29	712	$1.50
002BK	$1.40	420	$1.19	714	$1.41
002BR	$1.40	421	$1.29	750	$1.36
202BK	$1.19	430	$1.19	751	$1.40
202BR	$1.19	431	$1.29	752	$1.38
202G	$1.19	440	$1.19	761	$1.41
003B	$1.31	450	$1.29	762	$1.38
003CG	$1.29	460	$1.39	763	$1.39
003G	$1.31	500	$1.40	800	$1.29
003L	$1.35	501	$1.44	810	$1.36
003M	$1.33	520P	$1.29	814	$1.44
003T	$1.33	520R	$1.35	815	$1.41
003W	$1.29	520S	$1.39	824	$1.51
003Y	$1.35	530P	$1.29	830	$1.39
303B	$1.45	530R	$1.35	831	$1.37
303C	$1.40	530S	$1.39	860B	$1.29
303DR	$1.45	601	$1.40	860DB	$1.29
303LO	$1.40	602F	$1.41	860LB	$1.29
303P	$1.38	602H	$1.42	901	$1.79
303R	$1.38	602R	$1.45	911	$1.61
316A	$1.37	603	$1.39	990A	$1.40
316BL	$1.40	650	$1.37	990B	$1.41
316BN	$1.37	652D	$1.39	990DB	$1.37
316BR	$1.40	652N	$1.38	990LB	$1.40
316P	$1.39	652Y	$1.40	990MB	$1.39
316SF	$1.45	654	$1.41	990S	$1.40
		660	$1.34		

CASE 4-2 STRATIFIED SAMPLING, INC.
(estimated time to complete: 45 minutes)

Population: 1600 job orders in process.

Objective: to estimate dollar value of work in process inventory.

Acceptable Precision: $7500.

Reliability: 95 percent.

By analyzing book-value data, the following additional data were obtained:

	N	Standard deviation
Stratum 1	100	$500
Stratum 2	500	40
Stratum 3	1000	10

A. What is the sample size for each stratum?
B. Assuming sample sizes of:
    100 for Stratum 1
    43 for Stratum 2
    22 for Stratum 3
    90 percent reliability, and standard deviations of $500, $40, and $10 for Stratum 1, 2, and 3, respectively, what is the achieved precision?
C. Is $A' \leq A$?
D. If $\bar{x}$ is $40 and $65 for Stratum 2 and 3 respectively, and the total of Stratum 1 is $200,000, what is EV?

CASE 4-3 FOOT, TICK, & TIE, CPAs
(estimated time to complete: 15 minutes)

An audit partner of Foot, Tick, & Tie, CPAs is developing an office training program to familiarize his professional staff with statistical models that are applicable to dollar-value balances. He wishes to demonstrate the relationship of sample sizes to population size and variability and to specifications as to precision and confidence level. The partner prepared the following table to show comparative population characteristics and specifications of two populations.

	Characteristics of Population 1 Relative to Population 2		Specifications as to a Sample from Population 1 Relative to a Sample from Population 2	
	Size	Variability	Acceptable Precision Interval	Specified Confidence Level
Case 1	Equal	Equal	Equal	Higher
Case 2	Equal	Larger	Wider	Equal
Case 3	Larger	Equal	Narrower	Lower
Case 4	Smaller	Smaller	Equal	Lower
Case 5	Larger	Equal	Equal	Higher

In items 1 to 5 below, indicate for the specific case from the above table the required sample size to be selected from population 1 relative to the sample from population 2.

Your answer choice should be selected from the following responses:

a. Larger than the required sample size from population 2.
b. Equal to the required sample size from population 2.
c. Smaller than the required sample size from population 2.
d. Indeterminate relative to the required sample size from population 2.

    (1) In case 1 the required sample size from population 1 is ___*a*___
    (2) In case 2 the required sample size from population 1 is ___*d*___
    (3) In case 3 the required sample size from population 1 is ___*d*___
    (4) In case 4 the required sample size from population 1 is ___*c*___
    (5) In case 5 the required sample size from population 1 is ___*a*___

(AICPA adapted)

CASE 4-4 ACE CORPORATION

(estimated time to complete: 20 minutes)

Ace Corporation does not conduct a complete annual physical count of purchased parts and supplies in its principal warehouse but instead uses statistical sampling to estimate the year-end inventory. Ace maintains a perpetual inventory record of parts and supplies and believes that statistical sampling is highly effective in determining inventory values and is sufficiently reliable to make a physical count of each item of inventory unnecessary.

REQUIRED

Identify the audit procedures that change, or are in addition to normally required audit procedures, that should be used by the independent auditor when a client uses statistical sampling to determine inventory value, and does not conduct a 100 percent annual physical count of inventory items.

(AICPA adapted)

USING VARIABLE SAMPLING FOR AUDIT HYPOTHESIS TESTING

Learning Objectives

After a careful study and discussion of this chapter, you will be able to:

1. Use unstratified mean per unit (MPU), stratified MPU, and difference estimation to test a client's book value for material misstatement.
2. Define the various audit risks inherent in sampling, understand the interrelationships among these risks, and be able to control risk in particular fact settings.
3. Describe what action(s) to take if a variable sampling application does not support a client's book value.
4. Identify areas of judgment involved in using the audit hypothesis model.

Substantive tests (as defined in Section 320.79 of SAS No. 1) are those in which the feature of audit interest is the amount of monetary errors that would affect the financial statements being audited, including errors and irregularities. By definition, therefore, substantive tests are concerned with reaching conclusions about whether financial amounts are materially correct. The variable sampling model is often used for substantive testing. Variable sampling is useful because conclusions are produced that are stated in monetary-unit terms and can be related directly to financial statement impact. Attribute sampling (see Chapter 3), on the other hand, is more readily applicable to compliance tests.

This chapter explains the audit hypothesis approach from a variable sampling perspective. To do so, we explain and demonstrate the concepts of audit risk and its component risks. Following the discussion of these risks, the audit hypothesis testing model is presented and illustrated.

SAMPLING RISK AND AUDIT SAMPLING

SAS No. 39 (AU350.12) is concerned with two aspects of sampling risk in performing a substantive test of details: the *risk of incorrect acceptance* and the *risk of incorrect rejection*. *Risk of incorrect acceptance* is the risk the auditor is willing to accept that the sample supports the conclusion that the recorded account balance is not materially misstated when it is. It is an aspect of sampling risk for a substantive test of details of an account balance using audit sampling.

In planning the sample, the risk of incorrect acceptance is the *detection risk* for that test. The risk of incorrect acceptance is established using a "risk model" presented later in this chapter.

There is another aspect of sampling risk for a substantive test of details of an account balance — the *risk of incorrect rejection*. This is the risk that the sample supports the conclusion that the account balance is materially misstated when it is not. This aspect of sampling risk relates to audit efficiency rather than effectiveness. If the auditor incorrectly concludes that an account balance is materially misstated, the auditor ordinarily expands substantive tests and eventually reaches the appropriate conclusions.

In statistics, the risk of incorrect rejection is called the *alpha risk* and the risk of incorrect acceptance is called the *beta risk*. The relationship between audit terms and statistical terms is summarized as follows:

SAS 39 *term*	*Statistical* *term*	*Relates* *to*
Risk of Incorrect Rejection	Alpha Risk	Audit Efficiency
Risk of Incorrect Acceptance	Beta Risk	Audit Effectiveness

Alpha risk is the chance that the statistical evidence might fail to support a materially correct book value. This type of error usually results in testing additional sample items. Alpha risk is the complement of reliability that is specified when calculating sample size.[1] Alpha risk is controlled by decreasing or increasing reliability.

Many practitioners believe alpha risk should be set at 5 percent or less ($U_R = 1.96$ reliability coefficient at 95 percent reliability). In audit practice, a 90 to 98 percent range is typical. A higher alpha risk (i.e., lower reliability) may be justified when the cost and effort of selecting additional samples is low and very few differences (audited value minus book value) are expected. Let us consider why this is so. Alpha risk becomes a concern when evaluating audit sample results only if the auditor rejects a client's book value. Consequently, if a rejection decision is made, based on a low reliability level, the auditor's first inclination is to extend the sample. This is especially true if the sample evidence already produced shows few differences (errors). A low reliability level may be tolerated if the cost of selecting additional items at a later date is relatively easy and involves low sampling set-up costs.

The second risk inherent in a variable-sampling audit-hypothesis model is beta risk. Beta risk is the probability that the statistical evidence might support a lack of material misstatement of a materially misstated book value. Beta risk is controlled by adjusting the ratio of precision A to materiality M. In Chapter 4, beta risk was not considered because we were not trying to decide if a book value was materially misstated. In accounting estimation, the statistical projection is used to determine the book value.

In audit hypothesis testing, the auditor's primary concern is controlling beta risk. A simple illustration explains why. If an auditor rejects the client's recorded inventory value, the client will generally insist on: (1) an increase in sample size, or (2) a search for additional evidence that the inventory balance is misstated. The combined evidence available after such additional work may indicate a need for the auditor to reverse his or her initial decision in a small percentage of cases (alpha percent). It is this risk of subsequent reversal or the potential for such a reversal that alpha is usually meant to control. Auditors sometimes refer to alpha as the red face or client's risk. Alpha risk relates to audit *efficiency*.

On the other hand, if the auditor accepts the client's recorded inventory when it is materially misstated (beta risk), the client will not demand an increase in sample size or a search for additional evidence. In fact, the auditor may have done exactly what the client wished. The risk in this

---

[1] Reliability can be related to beta risk (negative approach) and the quality of internal control, or associated with alpha risk (positive approach) and the cost of obtaining evidence. The latter approach is used here. Both approaches generate the same solution. For an excellent discussion of the negative versus the positive approach, see Donald M. Roberts, **Statistical Auditing** (New York: AICPA, 1978), pp. 45–48.

situation, of course, emanates from investors and other external financial statement users. The auditor may be sued and possibly could lose his or her right to practice. Beta risk relates to audit *effectiveness*.

The sample mean distribution (Figure 5.1) graphically depicts alpha risk at 95 percent reliability. At 95 percent reliability, alpha equals 5 percent. That is, sampling error will occur 5 times out of 100 causing an auditor to reject a *true* book value.

The following example will aid an understanding of alpha as is shown in Fig. 5.1. The true book value T and the amount recorded by the client BV are equal. The recorded amount is $1,000,000 and the population size N is 1000; thus, $\bar{X}$ times N is $1,000,000. The standard error of the distribution in Figure 5.1 is $100. Figure 5.1 was derived by taking repeat samples of the same size from the population of 1000 items and plotting the sample means times N. Achieved precision is 1.96 × $100 × 1000 equals $196,000. The decision interval is $1,000,000 ± $196,000.

If a sample mean is produced that is between $804 and $1196, the client's book value will be accepted. On the other hand, if a sample mean less than $804 (e.g., $750) or more than $1196 (e.g., $1200) is produced, the true client book value will be rejected. Given that the client's book value is fairly stated at $1,000,000, the distribution in Figure 5.1 shows that there is a 2.5 percent chance in each tail of the distribution where sample results will cause a rejection of a true value. This rejection probability is referred to as an alpha sampling error.

In an actual audit engagement, a distribution of sample means is not produced. Only one set of sample items and, hence, one mean is typically used in projecting the estimated audited value. Figure 5.1 demonstrates the

FIGURE 5.1 ALPHA RISK

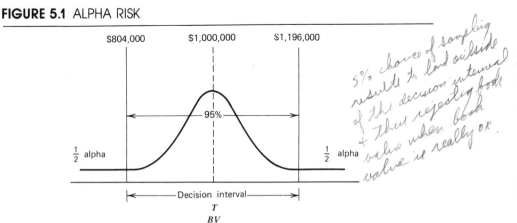

Note: Control alpha errors by varying confidence level (reliability)
Reliability = 95 percent
Alpha risk = 5 percent
True value, T = book value; BV = $1,000,000

probabilities associated with different possible estimated audited values coming up at different points on the distribution.

Figure 5.2 shows the beta risk of a projected sample mean distribution for an overstatement and an understatement exactly equal to a material amount. Case 1 of Figure 5.2 demonstrates that if precision A is set equal to

FIGURE 5.2 ILLUSTRATIONS OF BETA RISK

CASE 1

Book value overstated by exactly a material amount. Precision A equals materiality M. BV equals book value. T equals true value.

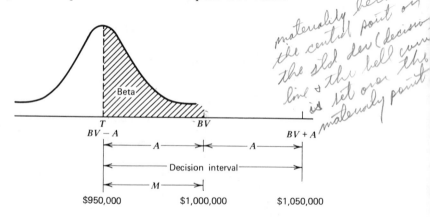

CASE 2

Book value understated by exactly a material amount. Precision A equals materiality M.

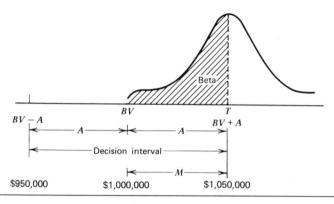

materiality ($50,000) in planning sample size and the true book value ($950,000) is overstated by exactly a material amount (recorded book value is $1,000,000), beta risk is 50 percent. That is, 50 samples out of 100 samples would lead to an acceptance of a materially overstated book value. Beta risk is depicted by the amount of the distribution that overlaps the decision interval. The decision interval is book value $1,000,000 ± $50,000. Projected sample means ($\bar{x} \cdot N$) falling between $950,000 and $1,050,000 would lead to acceptance, but projected sample means below $950,000 would indicate rejection of the client's book value.

Case 2 of Figure 5.2 indicates that if book value is understated by an amount exactly equal to materiality ($50,000), beta risk again is equal to 50 percent. The auditor would accept a materially understated book value if the projected sample mean falls between $950,000 and $1,050,000. In fact, where precision is set equal to materiality, the maximum beta risk is 50 percent. That is, there is a fifty-fifty chance of accepting a materially understated book value or a materially overstated book value when the correct decision would be to reject the book value (based on only the sample evidence).

Other beta risk situations are shown in Figure 5.3. Case 1 of Figure 5.3 demonstrates that beta risk is drastically reduced when precision is set equal to one-half of materiality. Precision in Case 1 is $25,000, because materiality is $50,000. The true book value in Case 1 is $950,000, and the recorded book value is $1,000,000. The decision interval is $1,000,000 ± $25,000. A smaller portion of the distribution overlaps the decision interval (above $975,000); thus, a mean projection below $975,000 will cause the book value to be rejected. Beta risk in Case 1 falls to 2½ percent.

Case 2 of Figure 5.3 shows that beta risk is reduced even further if the book value is overstated by 1½ times materiality. In Case 2 the book value is recorded at $1,025,000, but the true value is $950,000. For an acceptance decision to result, a sample mean projection of $1,000,000 or greater must be obtained. The probability of incurring beta in a Case 2 situation is very remote.

Beta risk is always measured and controlled in relation to materiality rather than precision. Consequently, beta risk is expressed as a maximum probability (in a conservative fashion). Figure 5.4 presents an alpha and beta risk matrix. The matrix demonstrates that if alpha occurs, beta cannot occur. Alpha and beta are mutually exclusive. However, in an actual audit the auditor does not know where the true value actually lies; thus, he or she has to control both beta and alpha. As the illustrations show, beta is controlled by varying precision in relation to materiality, but alpha is controlled by varying reliability or confidence. Note that beta risk is controlled with respect to a misstatement of precisely a material amount. In audit sampling, this amount is referred to as tolerable error. It is, conceptually, the maximum monetary error that can exist in a particular account balance without causing the financial statements to be materially misstated.

FIGURE 5.3 OTHER ILLUSTRATIONS OF BETA RISK

CASE 1

Book value *overstated* by exactly a material amount. Precision A equals one-half materiality, M. BV equals book value. T equals true value.

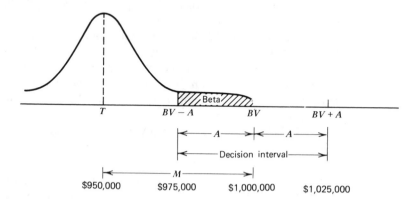

CASE 2

Book value overstated by 1½ materiality. Precision A equals one-half materiality M.

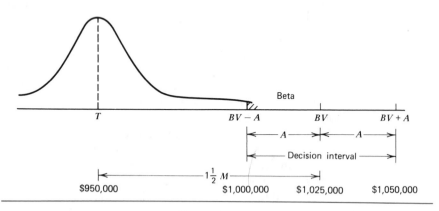

AUDIT RISK AND SUBSTANTIVE AUDIT TESTS

According to SAS No. 47 (AU 312), *Audit Risk and Materiality in Conducting an Audit*, audit risk is the risk that auditors incur if they express an unqualified opinion on materially misstated financial statements. Audit risk is actually a combination of four risks:

FIGURE 5.4 ALPHA AND BETA RISK MATRIX

Client's Book Value is:

Audit Evidence Indicates:	Not Materially Misstated	Materially Misstated
Accept	Correct Decision (1 − Alpha)	Beta Error
Reject	Alpha Error	Correct Decision (1 − Beta)

1. A material error occurs in the financial statements (i.e., inherent risk).
2. The internal control system fails to detect and correct the error (i.e., control risk).
3. The auditor's nonstatistical audit procedures (supplemental procedures) fail to detect the error (i.e., detection risk).
4. The auditor's statistical audit procedures fail to detect the error (i.e., the beta risk component of detection risk).

The underlying rationale of the audit risk model is that the combined risk of a material error remaining undetected is a product of the four independent component risks. This combined risk—the audit risk at the account balance level—should be relatively low; in quantitative terms that would be 5 or 10 percent. Audit risk is given the symbol UR in the risk model formula. (In the SAS No. 39 risk model formula UR is used for audit risk because it used to be called ultimate risk.)

The risk model, including component risks and their corresponding formula symbols, is as follows:

$$UR = IR \times IC \times AR \times TD$$

(audit risk) (inherent risk) (control risk) (other procedures risk) (test of details detection risk − beta)

The other procedures risk is the quantification of the detection risk for audit procedures that are relevant to achieving the same audit objective as the substantive test of details being planned. It has the symbol AR because these other procedures frequently are analytical review procedures.

To use the model, the auditor has to quantify as a percentage the inherent risk, control risk, and other procedures risk. This is a subjective professional judgment. An approach often used in practice is to associate a percentage with a qualitative level of assessment. Maximum is obviously 100 percent. Specification of the percentage associated with the minimum is a critical professional judgment. It quantifies the lowest degree of risk and, implicitly, the maximum degree of assurance ever attributed to the model component. For example, professional standards indicate that complete reliance should not be placed on accounting control. This provides a general guide in establishing the percentage for minimum control risk. In practice the percentages associated with qualitative levels often are established as a matter of CPA firm policy.

Separate assessment of inherent risk (*IR*) at levels below the maximum is a controversial issue. The risk model in SAS No. 39 is presented with inherent risk assumed to be at the maximum (100 percent or 1). SAS No. 47 indicates that if inherent risk is assessed at less than the maximum the auditor should have an "appropriate basis" for the assessment.

At the account balance level, inherent risk (*IR*) is defined as the susceptibility of an account balance to material error given inherent and environmental characteristics, but without regard to prescribed accounting control procedures. In this book inherent risk is assumed to be at the maximum (100 percent). Control risk (*IC*) is the risk that material error in an account balance may occur and not be prevented or detected on a timely basis by prescribed accounting control procedures. Detection risk is the risk that an auditor's procedures will lead to the conclusion that material error does not exist in an account balance when the account balance is actually materially misstated. It has two components in the model—*AR* and *TD* (beta risk).

The auditor's approach is to assess the level of control risk (*IC*) and other procedures risk (*AR*), and to adjust beta risk accordingly to restrict the audit risk (*UR*) for the account balance to a relatively low level.

The auditor calculates the desired beta risk by solving the risk model for *TD* as follows:

$$TD \text{ (beta)} = \frac{UR}{IC \times AR}$$

INTERNAL CONTROL RISK

Let us now turn to quantifying the internal control risk (*IC*). As we demonstrate later, the smaller the *IC*, the larger allowable beta risk becomes. The control risk (*IC*) is judgmentally determined in practice. *IC* must be determined separately for each transaction cycle (or account balance). Of course, weaknesses in one transaction cycle do not offset strengths in another.

Effectiveness of an internal control subsystem is judgmentally determined based on the auditor's inquiries, internal control questionnaires, transaction walk-throughs, attribute sampling models applied to test compliance, and compliance error analysis. One large CPA firm permits the risk percentage to vary from 20 to 100 percent. The 20 percent limit assumes that even the best system of internal control has inherent limitations. The following table depicts feasible *IC* risk ranges.

Auditor's qualitative level of reliance on internal control	Control risk percentage (IC)	Control procedure percentage effectiveness
Substantial	20	80
Moderate	50	50
Little	80	20
None	100	0

To illustrate, if an auditor concludes that control risk (*IC*) is 20 percent; the internal controls *over a particular transaction* class are such that there is a 20 percent chance that errors could occur on enough accounts or to such a degree that the cumulative effect would materially misstate the financial statements. This illustration gives some insight into a very complex judgmental decision process. *IC* should not be equated with the achieved upper precision limit as determined in an attribute sampling model (see Chapter 3).

Another factor to consider in judgmentally setting *IC* is the potential for management override of the system of internal control. Although it is impossible to determine with certainty those cases in which management has overridden the internal control system, it generally should be possible to evaluate this risk through consideration of factors such as the type of organization being audited, the susceptibility of the area being examined to misstatement, the requirement for management judgment in determining the amounts in the records, and prior experience in auditing the area being examined. If the *potential* for override is deemed significant, the auditor should limit reliance on internal control and assess *IC* as high (e.g., 80 or 100 percent).

OTHER PROCEDURES RISK (ANALYTICAL REVIEW)

Quantifying the risk associated with analytical review procedures or other relevant substantive tests also is rather difficult. Any substantive audit procedure that is not part of the variable-sampling statistical test falls into this category. For example, in the audit of accounts receivable an auditor may decide that the following procedures are to be performed at Dock Company's balance sheet date.

1. Obtaining and reviewing an aged trial balance of trade accounts receivable.
2. Confirming selected accounts with positive confirmations.
3. Confirming selected accounts with negative confirmations.
4. Determining whether shipments on consignment have been included in sales and receivables.
5. Entering in the working papers any collections of accounts receivable subsequent to the balance sheet date.
6. Reviewing the year-end cutoff of sales transactions.
7. Preparing a comparative analysis of receivable turnover.

If Dock's auditor decides to use variable sampling only for item 2, the other six substantive procedures are not part of the statistical test and would be assessed to establish AR.

Analytical review procedures usually involve trend analysis, gross margin reviews, comparisons of cost and selling prices of inventory items, review of variance accounts, and so on. Generally, AR should be conservatively estimated and probably should rarely be less than 50 percent. If, however, a CPA firm uses a very robust mathematical model for analytical reviews, AR may be less than 50 percent. For teaching purposes, we will permit AR to vary from 50 to 100 percent.

CALCULATING BETA RISK

As was explained earlier, rearranging the audit risk equation, we have

$$TD \text{ (beta)} = \frac{UR}{IC \times AR}$$

After the auditor has calculated the desired beta risk, he or she uses the beta risk to determine sample size by figuring out how much precision A has to be reduced in relation to materiality. Beta risk is controlled by reducing precision in the sample size equation relative to materiality.

To illustrate, let us assume UR = 5 percent, IC = 20 percent, and AR = 90 percent.

$$TD \text{ (beta)} = \frac{.05}{.20 \times .90}$$

$$TD \text{ (beta)} = 28.8 \text{ percent}$$

If beta computes to a value of 1.0 or greater (e.g., IC = .10 and AR = .50), the auditor may decide to omit the statistical test because UR has already

been achieved by reliance on the internal control system and other procedures. If beta computes to an amount between 1.0 and .50, auditors believe
that a statistical test should have at least an even chance of detecting a
material error. Accordingly, we adopt the policy that is prevalent in practice
that beta risk for all statistical tests should be set at 50 percent or less.

Rather than use the beta risk equation, another method of deriving beta
used in practice appears in Figure 5.5. The beta outcome resulting from
Figure 5.5 should be approximately equal to the previous equation.

The relationship of beta risk calculation to the sample size equation is as
follows:

1. Beta is calculated according to the previous equation.
2. Precision is adjusted in relation to materiality based on the calculated beta risk. (This calculation will be explained in the section
   that follows.)
3. Precision A is introduced in the sample size equation to calculate
   sample size.

$$n' = \left(\frac{U_R \cdot SD \cdot N}{A} \right)^2$$

THE AUDIT HYPOTHESIS MODEL

The audit hypothesis model is a series of mathematical–statistical equations.
We describe the model with a 22-step approach, beginning with a preliminary evaluation of internal control and ending with an accept or reject decision as to the material misstatement of an account balance. The audit hypothesis model can be categorized into four separate phases: phase I,
internal control analysis and evaluation; phase II, substantive test planning;
phase III, substantive test execution; and phase IV, substantive test evaluation. Before getting into the details of each distinct step, the objective of
each of the four phases is briefly reviewed.

The primary purpose of phase I (internal control analysis and evaluation) is to assign a risk percentage to IC for subsequent use in the beta risk
equation. As we discussed previously, to accomplish this the auditor uses
his or her preliminary evaluation of internal control, the results of detailed
compliance testing, compliance error analysis, and observation tests for
controls that do not leave an audit trail.

Phase II (substantive test planning) of the audit hypothesis model is
concerned primarily with the selection of the appropriate sampling model
and calculation of the needed sample size for the statistical test. The appropriate variable sampling model has to be selected based on audit objectives
and population characteristics. Model selection is discussed in Chapter 7.

FIGURE 5.5 SELECTION OF BETA FOR HYPOTHESIS TEST

Reliance assigned to internal control

- If there is a significant risk that management could override the controls in effect over the areas being examined, enter 0.

- Otherwise, evaluate the internal controls in effect over the area being examined. _____

If the controls are	Enter
Excellent	4
Good	3
Fair	2
Poor	1
Nonexistent	0

Reliance assigned to other procedures

- Evaluate the other audit procedures that might detect material errors of the type being tested for by the statistical tests.

- For each significantly effective additional test allow 2 points and for each moderately effective additional test allow 1 point. Enter the total (not to exceed 4 points).

Total _____

If the total above is	Use this beta
0	.05
1	.10
2	.15
3	.30
4	.50
5	.50[b]
6–8	.50[c]

[a] Adapted with permission from Robert K. Elliott and John R. Rogers, "Relating Statistical Sampling to Audit Objectives," **Journal of Accountancy** (July 1972), p. 50.

[b] In view of these conditions, the auditor may wish to consider increasing the effectiveness of other auditing procedures and omitting the statistical test.

[c] In view of these conditions, the auditor may wish to consider omitting the statistical test.

Assuming for illustrative purposes that unstratified MPU will be the sampling model used, we find that the sample size equation (with replacement) is

$$n' = \left(\frac{U_R \cdot SD \cdot N}{A}\right)^2$$

In phase II, U_R has to be determined based on acceptable alpha risk; SD may be estimated using a pilot sample of 30; N must be defined; precision A must be calculated based on desired or calculated beta risk. To calculate A, beta has to be determined by specifying UR, IC (from phase I), and AR. Also, materiality has to be predefined. The following figure illustrates the decisions that must be made before n' can be determined:

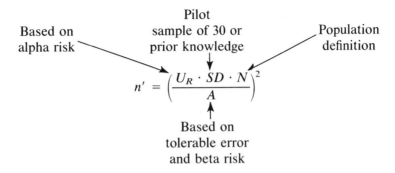

After calculating n', sample size without replacement is determined and phase III commences. Phase III (substantive test execution) has as its major objectives: (1) selecting the sample, (2) auditing the sample, and (3) calculating achieved precision A'. In addition, A'', which is "adjusted precision," will be calculated using the following equation:

$$A'' = A' + TE\,(1 - A'/A)$$

where

$$
\begin{aligned}
A'' &= \text{adjusted precision}\\
A' &= \text{achieved precision}\\
TE &= \text{tolerable error}\\
A &= \text{acceptable precision}
\end{aligned}
$$

The A'' calculation produces an achieved beta risk equal to planned beta. Roberts explains the rationale of A'' as follows:

. . . the auditor can adjust the precision whenever the achieved precision differs from the planned precision. This occurs when the achieved standard error differs from the standard error used in planning. Without an adjustment, the effective beta risk differs from the planned beta risk whenever the achieved precision is not equal to the planned precision. If the achieved precision is smaller than planned, the effective beta risk is smaller, while an achieved precision larger than planned results in a higher effective beta risk.[2]

In other words, A' will be larger than A whenever SE is larger than planned. A' will be smaller than A whenever SE is smaller than planned. The following computations illustrate the A'' concept.

Example 1

$$TE = \$100$$
$$A = TE = \$100$$
$$\text{Beta} = 50 \text{ percent}$$
$$A' = \$110$$

$$A'' = \$110 + \$100 \left(\frac{\$110}{\$100}\right)$$

$$A'' = \$100$$

Example 2

$$TE = \$100$$
$$A = TE = \$100$$
$$\text{Beta} = 50 \text{ percent}$$
$$A' = \$90$$

$$A'' = \$90 + \$100 \left(1 - \frac{\$90}{\$100}\right)$$

$$A'' = \$100$$

Finally, phase IV (substantive test evaluation) is reached. In phase IV, the auditor calculates estimated audit value, constructs a decision interval around the client's book value, and ascertains whether the sample evidence supports or rejects material correctness of that book value. If estimated audit value falls within the constructed decision interval, the auditor concludes that the book value is acceptable.

Before the auditor constructs the decision interval, it may be necessary to adjust the recorded book value for any systematic errors discovered. A systematic error is a nonrandom error. For example, an error in a computerized inventory program pertaining to the computation of factory overhead may produce an overstatement in inventory. If the audit sample procedure discloses several errors involving erroneous factory overhead compu-

---

[2] *Ibid.*, p. 43.

tations, the auditor's error analysis investigation may identify the occurrence as systematic. Thus, in looking at additional inventory cost extensions (extended tests of individually significant items), the total adjustment for factory overhead can be established and the recorded inventory corrected accordingly.

PHASE I: INTERNAL CONTROL ANALYSIS AND EVALUATION

1. Complete the internal control questionnaire, flowcharts, or related narrative memoranda for the relevant transaction classes. Make a preliminary evaluation of internal control effectiveness.

2. Decide which control procedures you want to place reliance on to limit substantive testing.

3. Set desired risk of overreliance (10 percent or less) and tolerable rate (e.g., 5 percent or less for substantial reliance) for compliance tests.

4. Perform compliance tests. There is no need for a compliance test when internal controls are evaluated as nonexistent or the cost of a compliance test exceeds potential savings from a restriction of the related substantive test.

5. Make final evaluation of internal control risk (IC) for each class of transaction and related assets. Concluding that internal controls over a particular transaction cycle permit an IC of .10 means that there is a 10 percent chance that errors could occur on enough accounts or to such a degree that the cumulative effect would be a material misstatement of the account balance.

PHASE II: SUBSTANTIVE TEST PLANNING

6. Evaluate (conservatively) the risk of other audit procedures (AR) failing to detect a material error ($AR \geqslant 50$ percent).

7. Select 5 or 10 percent audit risk (UR) and calculate maximum planned beta risk.

$$TD \text{ (beta)} = \frac{UR}{IC \times AR}$$

8. Set alpha risk at 5 percent or lower. Alpha risk is the complement of reliability. Reliability should be set between 95 and 99 percent.

9. Based on the following table, convert step $\boxed{8}$ into a U_R coefficient.

Reliability	U_R factor
.99	2.58
.95	1.96
.90	1.65

TABLE 12 Normal Curve Area Table

Standard Deviation	.00	.01	.02	.03	.04	.05	.06	.07	.08	.09
0.0	.0000	.0040	.0080	.0120	.0159	.0199	.0239	.0279	.0319	.0359
0.1	.0398	.0438	.0478	.0517	.0557	.0596	.0636	.0675	.0714	.0753
0.2	.0793	.0832	.0871	.0910	.0948	.0987	.1026	.1064	.1103	.1141
0.3	.1179	.1217	.1255	.1293	.1331	.1368	.1406	.1443	.1480	.1517
0.4	.1554	.1591	.1628	.1664	.1700	.1736	.1772	.1808	.1844	.1879
0.5	.1915	.1950	.1985	.2019	.2054	.2088	.2123	.2157	.2190	.2224
0.6	.2257	.2291	.2324	.2357	.2389	.2422	.2454	.2486	.2518	.2549
0.7	.2580	.2612	.2642	.2673	.2704	.2734	.2764	.2794	.2823	.2852
0.8	.2881	.2910	.2939	.2967	.2995	.3023	.3051	.3078	.3106	.3133
0.9	.3159	.3186	.3212	.3238	.3264	.3289	.3315	.3340	.3365	.3389
1.0	.3413	.3438	.3461	.3485	.3508	.3531	.3554	.3577	.3599	.3621
1.1	.3643	.3665	.3686	.3708	.3729	.3749	.3770	.3790	.3810	.3830
1.2	.3849	.3869	.3888	.3907	.3925	.3944	.3962	.3980	.3997	.4015
1.3	.4032	.4049	.4066	.4083	.4099	.4115	.4131	.4147	.4162	.4177
1.4	.4192	.4207	.4222	.4236	.4251	.4265	.4279	.4292	.4306	.4319
1.5	.4332	.4345	.4357	.4370	.4382	.4394	.4406	.4418	.4430	.4441
1.6	.4452	.4463	.4474	.4485	.4495	.4505	.4515	.4525	.4535	.4545
1.7	.4554	.4564	.4573	.4582	.4591	.4599	.4608	.4616	.4625	.4633
1.8	.4641	.4649	.4656	.4664	.4671	.4678	.4686	.4693	.4699	.4706
1.9	.4713	.4719	.4726	.4732	.4738	.4744	.4750	.4758	.4762	.4767
2.0	.4773	.4778	.4783	.4788	.4793	.4798	.4803	.4808	.4812	.4817
2.1	.4821	.4826	.4830	.4834	.4838	.4842	.4846	.4850	.4854	.4857
2.2	.4861	.4865	.4868	.4871	.4875	.4878	.4881	.4884	.4887	.4890
2.3	.4893	.4896	.4898	.4901	.4904	.4906	.4909	.4911	.4913	.4916
2.4	.4918	.4920	.4922	.4925	.4927	.4929	.4931	.4932	.4934	.4936
2.5	.4938	.4940	.4941	.4943	.4945	.4946	.4948	.4949	.4951	.4952
2.6	.4953	.4955	.4956	.4957	.4959	.4960	.4961	.4962	.4963	.4964
2.7	.4965	.4966	.4967	.4968	.4969	.4970	.4971	.4972	.4973	.4974
2.8	.4974	.4975	.4976	.4977	.4977	.4978	.4979	.4980	.4980	.4981
2.9	.4981	.4982	.4983	.4984	.4984	.4984	.4985	.4985	.4986	.4986
3.0	.4986	.4987	.4987	.4988	.4988	.4988	.4989	.4989	.4989	.4990
3.1	.4990	.4991	.4991	.4991	.4992	.4992	.4992	.4992	.4993	.4993

Other U_R coefficients can be calculated from the normal curve area table presented on this page. Table 12 can be used to determine additional U_R coefficients by multiplying the numbers in the body of the table by 2, since they are only for one-half of a normal curve starting from the center. For example, 1.96 standard deviations corresponds to an area of .4750; .4750 × 2 = 95 percent. Also, 90 percent reliability U_R is 1.65 (.90 ÷ 2 = .45); .45 in the table is located at 1.65 standard deviations. Likewise, 96 percent reliability U_R is 2.06.

10. Determine tolerable error (materiality for the account balance). Tolerable error is judgmentally determined, and it is dependent on factors such as net income, total assets, equity, as well as other considerations in relation to the account balance being audited.

11. Determine the amount of acceptable precision to introduce into the sample size equation. Acceptable precision is based on beta risk specified in step ⑦, alpha risk specified in step ⑧, and tolerable error specified in step ⑩. Use the following formula to calculate acceptable precision.

$$A = TE \cdot \frac{U_R}{U_R + Z_{\text{beta}}}$$

where

$$
\begin{aligned}
A &= \text{precision} \\
TE &= \text{tolerable error} \\
U_R &= \text{reliability factor} \\
Z_{\text{beta}} &= \text{beta risk coefficient}
\end{aligned}
$$

Table 12 (the normal curve area table) can be used in determining the beta risk coefficient (Z_{beta}). Z_{beta} is the normal curve value that includes an area of .5 − beta. If, for example, you want to find the Z_{beta} for a 1 percent beta risk, subtract 1 percent (.01) from .5, yielding .4900. From the table, .4900 corresponds to a Z_{beta} coefficient of 2.33. Next, substitute 2.33 in the equation as Z_{beta} and solve for A. Instead of using the equation for A, which is illustrated here, Table 13 may be consulted for the factor to multiply the tolerable error by to determine A.

(Acceptable precision)   (Consult Table 12)
↓   ↓

A equals TE times $\dfrac{U_R}{U_R + Z_{\text{beta}}}$

↑   ↑

(Tolerable error)   (Consult Table 12)

TABLE 13 Tolerable Error Adjustment for Common Alpha and Beta Risk Values

	Tolerable Error Adjustment Factor for:		
Beta Risk Percent	10 Percent Alpha Risk	5 Percent Alpha Risk	1 Percent Alpha Risk
1	.415	.457	.525
2.5	.457	.500	.568
5	.500	.543	.609
7.5	.534	.576	.641
10	.563	.605	.668
15	.613	.653	.712
20	.663	.700	.753
25	.708	.742	.791
30	.757	.787	.829
35	.809	.834	.868
40	.864	.883	.908
50	1.000	1.000	1.000

12. Calculate the required sample size.

A. If you are using *unstratified* mean per unit, the following equations are appropriate:

$$n' = \left(\frac{U_R \cdot SD \cdot N}{A} \right)^2$$

$$n = \frac{n'}{1 + n'/N}$$

WORKSHEET 1 (Appendix A) may be used to estimate the standard deviation based on a pilot sample.

B. If you are using *stratified* mean per unit, define each stratum and use WORKSHEET 2 (Appendix A) to calculate the sample size. If the standard deviation of each stratum is not estimable, draw a random sample of 30 items from each stratum (without replacement) and use WORKSHEET 1 (Appendix A) to estimate the standard deviation.

C. If you are using *difference* estimation, the following equations are appropriate:

$$n' = \left(\frac{U_R \cdot SD_d \cdot N}{A} \right)^2$$

$$n = \frac{n'}{1 + n'/N}$$

WORKSHEET 4 (Appendix A) may be used to estimate the standard deviation based on a pilot sample. The pilot sample must contain some differences (errors). Otherwise, the pilot sample must be larger.

PHASE III: SUBSTANTIVE TEST EXECUTION

13. Randomly select the additional sample items by using computer generation, random number table, or systematic selection.

14. Perform a test of sample representativeness. The sample mean of book values (i.e., sample book values ÷ n) and the population mean of book values (i.e., the client's book value ÷ N) should not be substantially different. For example, if the sample mean of book values is $100 but the population mean of book values is $800, barring an arithmetic mistake, the sample may not be representative. Consequently, the first sample should be discarded and a new one selected. The test of sample representativeness helps to control sampling error.

15. Perform audit procedures on sample items selected for substantive tests.

16. Analyze errors noted in the sample to determine their cause, nature, and whether a systematic pattern exists. A systematic error is a recurring error that does not occur randomly. For example, an employee pricing inventory may improperly price certain items based on an outdated price list.

17. Calculate achieved precision A'.

A. *For unstratified simple extension*

(1) The standard deviation of the sample (WORKSHEET 1).

(2) The standard error using the following equation:

$$SE = \frac{SD}{\sqrt{n}}$$

(3) A' (achieved precision) based on the following equation:

$$A' = U_R \cdot SE \cdot N \sqrt{1 - (n/N)}$$

B. *For stratified MPU*

    (1) The standard deviation of each stratum (WORKSHEET 1).

    (2) A' (achieved precision) by using WORKSHEET 3.

C. *For difference estimation*

    (1) The standard deviation of the differences (WORKSHEET 4).

    (2) The standard error of the differences by using the following equation:

$$SE_d = \frac{SD_d}{\sqrt{n}}$$

    (3) A' based on the following equation:

$$A' = U_R \cdot SE_d \cdot N \sqrt{1 - (n/N)}$$

only used without sampling with replacement.

18. If A' is not equal to A, calculate A'' according to the following equation:

$$A'' = A' + TE \left(1 - \frac{A'}{A}\right)$$

where

$$TE = \text{tolerable error from step } \boxed{10}.$$
$$A' = \text{achieved precision from step } \boxed{17}.$$
$$A = \text{acceptable precision from step } \boxed{11}.$$

This equation gives a new precision yielding a beta risk equal to the planned beta risk in step $\boxed{7}$. If $A = A'$, set $A'' = A'$.

19. Calculate estimated audited value, *EAV*.

For unstratified MPU

A. Calculate the $\bar{x}$ of the total sample.

$$\bar{x} = \frac{\Sigma \text{ of each audited value}}{n}$$

B. Calculate *EAV* as:

$$EAV = \bar{x} \cdot N$$

For stratified MPU

A. Calculate the mean $\bar{x}$ of each stratum based on n_i for each stratum.

B. Calculate *EAV* as:

$$
\begin{aligned}
\bar{x}_1 \cdot N_1 &= \bar{x}_1 N_1 \\
\bar{x}_2 \cdot N_2 &= \bar{x}_2 N_2 \\
\underline{\bar{x}_3 \cdot N_3} &= \underline{\bar{x}_3 N_3}
\end{aligned}
$$

$$EAV = \Sigma \bar{x}_i N_i + 100 \text{ percent audited stratum}$$

For difference estimation

A. Calculate the mean of the difference $\bar{d}$ of the total sample.

B. Calculate $\hat{D} = N \cdot \bar{d}$.

C. Calculate estimated audited value, *EAV*.

$$EAV = \text{book value (footed)} \pm \hat{D}$$

PHASE IV: SUBSTANTIVE TEST EVALUATION

20. Calculate a decision interval as follows:

$$
\begin{gathered}
\text{Book value adjusted for any systematic (nonrandom)} \\
\text{differences} \pm A''
\end{gathered}
$$

21. Determine whether sample evidence supports the material correctness of the client's book value. If *EAV* from step [19] falls within the decision interval in step [20], conclude that the statistical evidence supports the book value and stop. If the *EAV* does not fall within the decision interval in step [20], go to step [22].

22. If statistical evidence does not support the material correctness of the book value and the errors (audit values minus book values) do not show a systematic pattern, the client should be requested to perform an investigation of the account balance detail. The client's work, of course, should be tested by the auditor. If the client makes an adjustment after the investigation, the statistical evidence should support the material correctness of the *adjusted* book value. In the event that it does not, the auditor should have enough evidence to reach a judgment conclusion concerning the reasonableness of the adjusted book value.

DEMONSTRATION OF THE AUDIT HYPOTHESIS MODEL

In this section we discuss selected aspects of the audit hypothesis model. For the purpose of illustration, let us assume that John Alderman, CPA, is auditing Axline Corporation's physical inventory. The inventory is recorded on Axline's balance sheet at $1,000,000. It consists of 12,500 kinds of items of approximately equal value. There are no identifiable dollar-value strata. Axline does not use perpetual inventory unit records, but does have a well-planned inventory taking and counting operation. In fact, Axline uses two count teams with the supervision of counting in each department performed by a member of the internal audit department. Moreover, Axline shuts down plant operations for inventory taking purposes. Based on (1) compliance test counting, (2) observation to ascertain that inventory taking instructions are followed, and (3) evaluation of the competence and carefulness of client personnel taking inventory, John decides that internal control risk (IC) is no more than 20 percent.

John concludes that the inventory valuation of $1,000,000 will be acceptable if he can be 95 percent confident that the actual inventory is within ± $50,000. The statistical test will consist of recounting, repricing, and extending each sample item selected. Other audit procedures (AR) consist of inventory turnover calculations, comparison with prior years, and cutoff tests to ensure that purchases and sales are reflected in inventory in the proper accounting period. John's best guess is that these other procedures have an 80 percent risk. (Remember that AR represents the auditor's judgment concerning the risk that such procedures would fail to detect a material monetary error if it existed in the account.)

Having completed the internal control analysis and evaluation of Axline's inventory taking procedures, John begins his substantive test planning. The primary question to be resolved is what size sample should be selected. To determine sample size according to the sample size equation,

$$n' = \left(\frac{U_R \cdot SD \cdot N}{A}\right)^2$$

he must determine SD and A. U_R already has been defined as 1.96 (95 percent reliability), and N is given as 12,500 inventory lines. To estimate SD, he should take a pilot sample of 30 inventory lines. Let us assume that the standard deviation that results from the pilot sample is $25.

Next, John calculates A. To calculate A, he needs to know beta risk. Based on audit risk of 5 percent, internal control risk of 20 percent, and other procedure risk of 80 percent, beta is

$$TD \text{ (beta)} = \frac{.05}{.20 \times .80} = .3125$$

Given that planned beta is .3125, the beta risk coefficient is .5000 minus .3125 equals .1875. By using the normal curve area table (see p. 148), the appropriate beta risk coefficient of approximately .49 can be found in the last column of the fifth row of the table.

Beta is controlled by varying precision A in relation to tolerable error (*TE*). The formula is

$$A = TE \cdot \frac{U_R}{U_R + Z_{\text{beta}}}$$

Thus,

$$A = \$50,000 \cdot \frac{1.96}{1.96 + .49}$$

$$A = \$40,000$$

A, of course, is acceptable (planned) precision.

Now, John is ready to calculate sample size. The calculation is

$$n' = \left[\frac{(1.96)(\$25)(12,500)}{40,000} \right]^2 = 235$$

$$n = \frac{235}{1 + (235/12,500)} = 231$$

After the sample size without replacement is calculated, a random sample of 231 items from the 12,500 inventory lines should be selected. Following sample selection, a test of sample representativeness should be applied to control sampling error. This test is applied before any audit work is performed on the sample. If the sample selected appears representative (e.g., the client's book value $\div$ N is not substantially different from the sample book value $\div$ n), the sample is audited. That is, each sample item is recounted, repriced, and extended. All errors identified at this stage should be analyzed to determine their cause.

Following error anlysis, A' is calculated. Before A' can be determined, the standard deviation of the 231 sampled items must be calculated along with *SE*. For illustrative purposes, assume that the standard deviation of the 231 sampled items is \$28. Therefore, *SE* is $\$28/\sqrt{231}$, which equals 1.84 (rounded).

$$A' = (1.96)\,(1.84)\,(12,500) \sqrt{1 - \frac{231}{12,500}}$$

$$A' = \$44,662$$

If A' is not equal to A, A'' must be determined. A is \$40,000 and A' is \$44,662; thus, A'' is

$$A'' = \$44{,}662 + \$50{,}000 \left(1 - \frac{\$44{,}662}{\$40{,}000}\right)$$

$$A'' = \$38{,}834$$

Estimated audited value is calculated after determination of the value for A''. *EAV* is the mean of the 231 sampled items times N. Let us say that the mean of the 231 sampled items is \$81. Then, *EAV* is \$81 $\times$ 12,500 = \$1,012,500.

To determine whether the book value of \$1,000,000 of Axline's inventory is not materially misstated, a decision interval is constructed. The decision interval is \$1,000,000 $\pm$ \$38,834. Since *EAV* of \$1,012,500 falls within the decision interval, John can conclude that the statistical evidence supports material correctness.

PROPOSING A STATISTICAL ADJUSTMENT

In the event that the statistical evidence does not support material correctness of an *adjusted* client book value, *as a last resort,* a statistical adjustment *may* be proposed. To propose a statistical adjustment, the sample evidence should meet certain conclusiveness criteria. Conclusive is defined by one major CPA firm as at least 95 percent reliability and no more than 5 percent beta risk. To determine conclusiveness, proceed as follows:

A. Express tolerable error (*TE*) in dollars.
B. Divide A' by U_R.
C. Divide *TE* by the answer in *B*.
D. Ascertain whether the answer in *C* is equal to or greater than 3.61 (i.e., 1.96 + 1.65), where 1.96 is U_R and 1.65 is Z_{beta} for 5 percent.

If step D is not equal to or greater than 3.61, the sample size should be increased, the client should revalue the account balance, or additional audit procedures should be applied. If step D indicates that the sample evidence is conclusive enough to propose an adjustment to the client's book value, the dollar amount of the adjustment should be calculated. To perform this calculation, A''' should be calculated if the U_R of A' is different from 1.96. A''' is A' divided by its U_R times 1.96. If A was calculated using 1.96, set A''' equal to A'.

The minimum and maximum adjustments for an *overstated* book value are illustrated as follows:

$$\overline{\quad \cdot \qquad\qquad \cdot \qquad \cdot \qquad\qquad \cdot \quad}$$
$$EAV - A''' \qquad EAV \qquad EAV + A''' \qquad BV$$

The minimum adjustment is demonstrated by the distance between BV (book value) and $EAV + A'''$, and the maximum adjustment is the distance from $EAV - A'''$ to BV. If the book value is *decreased* anywhere within $EAV \pm A'''$, the statistical evidence will support of the adjusted book value at 95 percent reliability and at a beta risk not exceeding 5 percent. Note that a precision interval ($EAV \pm A'''$) approach is used instead of a decision interval ($BV + A''$) when the statistical evidence indicates that BV is materially misstated. By using a precision interval, the range of acceptable book adjustments is easier to determine.

For an *understated* book value, the minimum and maximum adjustments are illustrated as follows:

$$\overline{\quad \cdot \quad\quad \cdot \qquad\qquad \cdot \qquad \cdot \quad}$$
$$BV \quad EAV - A''' \qquad EAV \qquad EAV + A'''$$

The minimum adjustment is the distance from BV to $EAV - A'''$, and the maximum adjustment is the distance from $EAV + A'''$ to BV. Note that in this illustration the adjustment is *added* to BV, because it is understated.

SUMMARY

In Chapter 5 we present and illustrate three variable sampling models (unstratified MPU, stratified MPU, and difference estimation) that are used to test a client's book value for material correctness—audit hypothesis testing. Two risks are encountered when audit hypothesis testing is used—alpha risk and beta risk. Alpha risk is the chance that a true book value will be rejected by the auditor's statistical test. Beta risk is the chance that a materially misstated book value will be accepted by the auditor. Alpha risk is controlled by varying reliability, whereas beta risk is controlled by varying precision in relation to tolerable error.

The audit hypothesis model differs from the accounting estimation model introduced in Chapter 4 in the following ways. Risk percentages for audit risk (UR), internal control (IC), and other audit procedures (AR) must be predefined to calculate desired beta risk. After beta and alpha risk levels are defined, the variation in precision must be calculated. Once precision is determined, the substantive test sample size is then calculated.

After the sample items selected are audited, the auditor ascertains whether the statistical evidence supports material correctness of the client's book value. A number of alternate procedures are available to the auditor in situations where material correctness is not supported. They are to increase sample size, to request that the client revalue the account balance, to rely on additional audit procedures to determine material correctness or, as a last resort, to propose a statistical adjustment.

An important point to remember is that if the auditor accepts a client's book value, the conditions that correspond with alpha risk are no longer present. Likewise, if the auditor rejects the book value, the conditions that correspond with beta risk are not present. Alpha and beta are mutually exclusive after the final audit decision to accept or to reject the client's book value is made.

GLOSSARY

Adjusted precision, A″   The precision amount calculated to yield the same beta risk as expressed by planned precision, *A*.

Alpha risk   The chance that the sample evidence erroneously fails to support the material correctness of a client's account balance when the same audit procedures, if applied to the total population, would support the material correctness of the account balance. Also referred to as risk of incorrect rejection.

Audit risk   The chance that material errors will occur in the accounting process and will not be detected by the auditor's examination. Audit risk is the *product* of (1) the risk that the internal control system allows a material error to go undetected, (2) the risk that other audit procedures fail to detect a material error, and (3) the beta risk. In practice, risks (1) and (2) are quantified before the auditor applies statistical sampling in a substantive test. Likewise, audit risk is usually predefined to equal no more than 5 percent. Consequently, the aiditor solves for beta risk as follows:

$$\text{beta risk} = \frac{\text{audit risk}}{(\text{internal control risk})(\text{other audit procedure risk})}$$

Beta risk   The chance that the sample evidence erroneously supports the material correctness of the client's account balance when the same audit procedures, if applied to the total population, would reveal a material error. Also referred to as risk of incorrect acceptance.

Decision interval   The range from the recorded client book value (adjusted for systematic errors) plus and minus the precision.

Normal curve area table   A table that shows the relative area under a normal curve from one standard deviation to another. The table is used to determine the beta risk coefficient and can be used to determine the reliability coefficient.

Precision interval   The range described by the estimated audit value plus and minus the precision.

Risk of incorrect acceptance   The risk that the sample supports the conclusion that the recorded account balance is not materially misstated when it is. (An aspect of sampling risk for substantive test; in statistics, the equivalent term is beta risk.)

Risk of incorrect rejection   The risk that the sample supports the conclusion that the recorded account balance is materially misstated when it is not. (An aspect of sampling risk for substantive test; in statistics, the equivalent term is alpha risk.)

Sample mean projection   The sample mean $\times$ N yields the estimated audit value *EAV*.

Systematic error   A recurring error that is not random. The term "random error" is used to mean accidental, unintentional, or not occurring in any pattern. An example of a systematic error is a pricing error on invoices prepared by a particular employee.

Tolerable error   The maximum monetary error for an account balance or class of transactions that may exist without causing the financial statements to be materially misstated. (A planning concept. Tolerable error combined for the entire audit plan should not exceed preliminary estimates of materiality levels.)

REVIEW QUESTIONS

 5-1. Indicate whether each one of the following statements is true (T) or false (F).

A. The greater the tolerable error (amount considered material), the smaller the sample size.

B. One minus audit risk is equal to the confidence level.

C. A graph of most accounting populations generally will resemble a normal distribution.

D. Audit hypothesis testing cannot be used unless the actual value of the universe standard deviation is known.

E. Reliance placed on internal control varies inversely with beta risk.

F. A decision interval is constructed based on estimated audited value plus and minus precision.

G. One minus reliability is audit risk.

H. If a client account balance is overstated by an amount less than tolerable error, beta risk for the smaller amount is greater than beta risk for tolerable error.

I. Beta risk is usually measured in terms of a material misstatement.

J. A'' is always smaller than A' and A.

K. Any combination of IC and AR whose product equals .50 permits a tolerable beta risk of .10 for an audit risk of .05.

5-2. Define alpha risk and beta risk. Relate these terms to the risk of incorrect rejection and the risk of incorrect acceptance.

5-3. Explain how alpha risk and beta risk are controlled.

5-4. Why is beta risk not encountered if an accounting estimation approach is used instead of an audit hypothesis testing approach?

5-5. In an audit context, why is beta risk of greater concern to the auditor than alpha risk?

5-6. Identify each lettered item in the following illustration. For example, f = tolerable error.

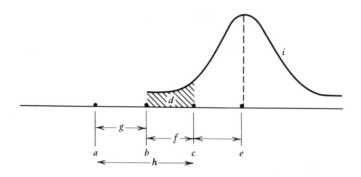

5-7. How does an auditor determine the amount of the desired beta risk?

5-8. In the beta risk formula, $\beta = UR/IC \times AR$, which factors are determined by professional judgment and which are guided by authoritative auditing literature?

5-9. What is a decision interval and how is it constructed?

5-10. Define audit risk. Define detection risk.

5-11. What is the relationship between audit risk and audit assurance?

5-12. What are other audit procedures in an audit sampling context?

5-13. What does it mean to say that internal control risk is 20 percent?

5-14. Identify the acceptable ranges (percentages) within which (a) internal control risk, (b) other audit procedure risk, (c) audit risk, and (d) beta risk should fall.

5-15. Calculate beta for each of the following situations:

	UR	IC	AR
A.	5%	0	0
B.	5%	50%	70%
C.	5%	10%	50%
D.	5%	20%	50%
E.	5%	10%	80%

5-16. Using the normal curve area table on page 148, determine U_R for each of the following reliability levels:

A. 92%

B. 89%

C. 95%

5-17. How does beta affect the sample size formula?

5-18. If tolerable error is $100,000, $U_R = 1.96$ (95 percent), calculate acceptable precision based on the following beta risks (use the normal curve area table on page 148):

A. Beta equals 20%

B. Beta equals 50%

C. Beta equals 5%

5-19. What is A'' and when should it be calculated?

5-20. If A' is greater than A, will A'' be larger or smaller than A'?

5-21. Error analysis is not as useful in variable sampling as it is in attribute sampling. Do you agree? Explain.

5-22. If a systematic error is discovered by an auditor in sampling from an accounts receivable population, should the decision interval be constructed around the original book value or the book value be adjusted for the discovered systematic error?

5-23. After a decision interval is constructed, how is it used to ascertain whether the client's book value is or is not materially misstated?

5-24. What should the auditor do if EAV does not fall within book value $\pm$ A''?

5-25. Given the following facts, could you conclude that the sample evidence supports material correctness of the client's book value based on planned beta risk?

Book value	$500,000
EAV	470,000
A	20,000
A'	17,000
U_R	1.96
Tolerable error	25,000

AUDIT DECISION CASES

CASE 5-1 BLUMENTHAL, INCORPORATED
(estimated time to complete: 20 minutes)

Assume that your CPA firm is auditing Blumenthal, Incorporated, and that, as senior accountant on the job, one of your first tasks is to supervise confirmation of accounts receivable. There are 1000 accounts, with no extreme values, and the control account balance is $225,000. You decide to choose the accounts to be confirmed by statistical sampling methods, and your objective is to obtain reasonable assurrance of the validity of the dollar amount of receivables. A pilot sample indicates an estimated population standard deviation of $15. In your judgment a 95 percent confidence level (5 percent alpha risk) is appropriate.

A. If you specify a required precision of ± $1500, what would be the required sample size?
B. If you specify a required precision of ± $2250, what would be the required sample size?
C. The staff accountant assisting you on the job does not understand the relationship between the required sample sizes in (A) and (B) above. How would you explain the magnitude and direction of the differences in required sample size to him?
D. What factors would you consider in specifying precision? In this situation, what do you think would be an appropriate precision figure?
E. If you specified a precision of ± $1500 and a confidence level of 99 percent rather than 95 percent, what would be the required sample size?
F. What criteria would you use for deciding whether a confidence level of 95 percent or 99 percent was more appropriate?
G. How would you explain to the inquiring staff accountant the magnitude and direction of the differences in the required sample size in (E) as compared with (A)?

CASE 5-2 STATISTICAL, INCORPORATED
(estimated time to complete: 25 minutes)

During the course of an audit engagement, a CPA attempts to obtain satisfaction that there are no material misstatements in the accounts receivable of a client. Statistical sampling is a tool that the auditor often uses to obtain representative evidence to achieve the desired satisfaction. On a particular engagement an auditor determined that a material misstatement in a population of accounts would be $35,000. The auditor specified a 95 percent confidence level (5% alpha risk). The auditor decided to use unrestricted random sampling with replacement* and took a preliminary random sample of 100 items (n) from a population of 1000 items (N). The sample produced the following data:

Arithmetic mean of sample items, $\bar{x}$	$4000
Standard deviation of sample items, SD	$ 200

The auditor also has available the following information:

Standard error of the mean, $SE = SD/\sqrt{n}$
Population precision $P = N \times R \times SE$

Partial List of Reliability Coefficients

If Reliability Coefficient (R) Is	Then Reliability Is
1.70	91.086%
1.75	91.988
1.80	92.814
1.85	93.568
1.90	94.256
1.95	94.882
1.96	95.000
2.00	95.450
2.05	95.964
2.10	96.428
2.15	96.844

* This problem is taken from the Uniform CPA Examination and uses sampling with replacement. Consequently, the finite population correction factor adjustment [$\sqrt{1 - (n/N)}$] to achieved precision can be ignored.

REQUIRED

A. Define the statistical terms "reliability" and "precision" as applied to auditing.
B. If all necessary audit work is performed on the preliminary sample items and no errors are detected,
   1. What can the auditor say about the total amount of accounts receivable at the 95 percent reliability level?
   2. At what confidence level can the auditor say that the population is not in error by $35,000?
C. Assume that the pilot sample was sufficient,
   1. Compute the auditor's estimate of the population total.
   2. Indicate how the auditor should relate this estimate to the client's recorded amount.

(AICPA adapted)

CASE 5-3 DRAPER, INC.
(estimated time to complete: 25 minutes)

You desire to evaluate the reasonableness of the book value of the inventory of your client, Draper, Inc. You satisfied yourself earlier as to inventory quantities. During the examination of the pricing and extension of the inventory, the following data were gathered using appropriate unrestricted random sampling with replacement procedures.*

Total items in the inventory, N	12,700
Total items in the sample, n	400
Total audited value of items in the sample	$38,400
$\sum_{j=1}^{400}(x_j - \bar{x})^2$	$312,816

Equation for estimated population standard deviation

$$SD = \sqrt{\frac{\sum_{j=1}^{n}(x_j - \bar{x})^2}{n - 1}}$$

Equation for estimated standard error of the mean

$$SE = \frac{SD}{\sqrt{n}}$$

---

* This problem is taken from the Uniform CPA Examination and uses sampling with replacement. Consequently, the finite population correction factor adjustment [$\sqrt{1 - (n/N)}$] to achieved precision can be ignored.

Confidence level coefficient
of the standard error of   ± 1.96
the mean at a 95 percent confidence
(reliability) level (5 percent alpha risk)

REQUIRED

A. Based on the sample results, what is the estimate of the total value of the inventory?
B. What statistical conclusion can be reached regarding the estimated total inventory value calculated in A at the confidence level of 95 percent? Present computations in good form where appropriate.
C. Independent of your answers to A and B, assume that the book value of Draper's inventory is $1,700,000 and based on the sample results the estimated total value of the inventory is $1,690,000. The auditor desires a confidence (reliability) level of 95 percent. Discuss the audit and the statistical considerations the auditor must evaluate before deciding whether the sampling results support acceptance of the book value of Draper's inventory.

(AICPA adapted)

CASE 5-4 FAIRVIEW PUBLISHING COMPANY
(estimated time to complete: 45 minutes)

Fairview Publishing Company has 1000 royalty contracts: one with each textbook author. Royalty percentages vary from 3 to 8 percent of net sales, and royalties are accrued semiannually at December 31 and June 30. The company does not accumulate sales, returns, and so on by titles. However, this information is necessary to make an accurate accrual for royalties payable on each textbook. Semiannually, the company makes an *educated guess* of royalties payable on each textbook. Subsequently, by analyzing sales invoices, return reports, and so on, it determines net sales by textbook and applies the contract royalty rate to determine actual royalties for each textbook. Adjustments resulting from this calculation are made at the time of the next semiannual accrual. The amount of the adjustment for each textbook will not necessarily be proportional to the educated guess.

The previous accountants selected a sample of 125 textbooks on a judgment basis, and by analyzing sales invoices, return reports, and so forth determined the actual royalties payable on those textbooks. They then compared the audited values for the textbooks to the company's estimate of royalties payable for those textbooks. If the company's estimate for royalties payable was reasonably close to the audited values for the textbooks sampled, they accepted the book value as stated.

We would like to test this year's accrual of $1,405,165 by statistical sampling. Use the sample of 80 royalties selected to *estimate the royalty accrual using difference estimation.* Then, *determine the precision* achieved at 90 percent reliability.

A. What is the mean (average) difference?
B. What is the estimated total difference?
C. What is the estimated audit value?
D. What is A' at 90 percent reliability?
E. If tolerable error is preset at $27,000 and zero reliance is placed on internal control and other audit procedures, what is acceptable precision? Given acceptable precision, is your sample size of 80 adequate?
F. Does the statistical evidence support material correctness of the $1,405,165 liability?

(Adapted from and used with permission of Ernst & Whinney)

Sample of 80 Items from Royalty Contracts (Difference Method)

Item Number	Population Number	Book Value	Audited Value	Difference	Difference Squared
1	113	$ 2,030	$ 2,030.00	$ 0	0
2	420	1,979	2,137.32	158.32	25,065.22
3	347	219	238.71	19.71	388.48
4	541	985	1,053.95	68.95	4,754.10
5	964	679	679.00	0	0
6	377	2,233	2,233.00	0	0
7	607	1,760	1,760.00	0	0
8	319	1,657	1,657.00	0	0
9	71	340	323.00	(17.00)	289.00
10	254	426	426.00	0	0
11	221	872	810.96	(61.04)	3,725.88
12	886	1,362	1,266.66	(95.34)	9,089.72
13	84	1,256	1,256.00	0	0
14	998	1,558	1,558.00	0	0
15	520	1,001	1,001.00	0	0
16	226	2,083	2,083.00	0	0
17	690	1,778	1,778.00	0	0
18	265	1,523	1,523.00	0	0
19	837	1,293	1,422.30	129.30	16,718.49

Sample of 80 Items from Royalty Contracts (Difference Method)

Item Number	Population Number	Book Value	Audited Value	Difference	Difference Squared
20	624	2,116	1,946.72	(169.28)	28,655.72
21	401	2,075	2,261.75	186.75	34,875.56
22	775	201	201.00	0	0
23	125	32	32.00	0	0
24	76	697	766.70	69.70	4,858.09
25	175	168	168.00	0	0
26	636	984	984.00	0	0
27	463	1,317	1,317.00	0	0
28	458	633	689.97	56.97	3,245.58
29	957	1,438	1,438.00	0	0
30	793	1,794	1,686.36	(107.64)	11,586.37
31	711	425	463.25	38.25	1,463.06
32	324	2,081	2,205.86	124.86	15,590.02
33	869	520	520.00	0	0
34	891	1,485	1,603.80	118.80	14,113.44
35	807	1,912	1,797.28	(114.72)	13,160.68
36	785	369	369.00	0	0
37	345	1,435	1,435.00	0	0
38	965	1,538	1,538.00	0	0
39	259	1,961	1,961.00	0	0
40	237	1,449	1,449.00	0	0
41	523	1,831	1,831.00	0	0
42	782	1,132	1,052.76	(79.24)	6,278.98
43	856	580	580.00	0	0
44	819	1,477	1,550.85	73.85	5,453.82
45	102	1,704	1,601.76	(102.24)	10,453.02
46	217	1,498	1,348.20	(149.80)	22,440.04
47	658	1,238	1,238.00	0	0
48	655	1,154	1,084.76	(69.24)	4,794.18
49	591	2,041	2,041.00	0	0
50	285	2,411	2,652.10	241.10	58,129.21
51	38	577	577.00	0	0
52	590	1,291	1,291.00	0	0
53	540	1,915	1,915.00	0	0
54	471	1,489	1,489.00	0	0

Sample of 80 Items from Royalty Contracts (Difference Method)

Item Number	Population Number	Book Value	Audited Value	Difference	Difference Squared
55	350	828	770.04	(57.96)	3,359.36
56	264	2,080	1,934.40	(145.60)	21,199.36
57	665	855	855.00	0	0
58	473	1,475	1,548.75	73.75	5,439.06
59	483	2,147	2,254.35	107.35	11,524.02
60	475	1,369	1,369.00	0	0
61	786	419	419.00	0	0
62	847	1,726	1,726.00	0	0
63	176	448	416.64	(31.36)	983.45
64	920	1,365	1,365.00	0	0
65	133	2,403	2,403.00	0	0
66	943	1,752	1,752.00	0	0
67	616	1,797	1,940.76	143.76	20,666.94
68	912	750	750.00	0	0
69	550	1,156	1,156.00	0	0
70	368	1,005	1,075.35	0	4,949.12
71	416	2,409	2,409.00	0	0
72	668	2,063	2,063.00	0	0
73	138	881	969.10	88.10	7,761.61
74	393	907	907.00	0	0
75	234	972	972.00	0	0
76	799	1,531	1,531.00	0	0
77	495	1,359	1,494.90	135.90	18,468.81
78	161	1,544	1,544.00	0	0
79	921	1,885	2,054.65	169.65	28,781.12
80	349	818	818.00	0	0
TOTALS		$105,946	$106,820.96	$874.96	418,261.51

CASE 5-5 ACCOUNTS RECEIVABLE, INC.
(estimated time to complete: 20 minutes)

Audit hypothesis testing is applied to an accounts receivable total consisting of 1000 accounts. The sample size is 100. The client's book total is $850,000. A 95 percent reliability is needed (U_R of 1.96). The desired precision and tolerable error is $6000. The audit total of the sample is $80,000. The sum of the squared deviations is $89,100.

Answer the following questions:

A. Achieved precision A' is $ _____5,586_____

B. Estimated audit value is $ _____800,000_____

C. Assume that $A' = A$, show whether the client's book total is acceptable.

D. In planning sample size, what beta risk was used? _____50%_____

E. What actions would you recommend if the sample evidence indicates that the book value is *not* materially correct?

6 PROBABILITY PROPORTIONATE TO SIZE SAMPLING*

Learning Objectives

After a careful study and discussion of this chapter, you will be able to:

1. Define the objective and assumptions of probability proportionate to size sampling (pps sampling).
2. Identify when pps sampling is appropriate.
3. Apply pps sampling in an auditing context involving both overstatement and understatement errors.
4. List advantages and disadvantages of using pps sampling.
5. Define pps sampling concepts such as "upper bound," "lower bound," "most likely overstatement (or understatement) error," and "tainting."

* The authors are indebted to Donna C. McNeil, CPA, Peat, Marwick, Mitchell, and Co., Honolulu, Hawaii, for assistance with this chapter based on her extensive research of the pps sampling literature.

Several statistical sampling models are available to the auditor. Most of the models we have discussed, are derivations of two classical statistical sampling methods—attribute sampling, which is used primarily for compliance testing, and variable sampling, which is used primarily for substantive testing. Probability proportionate to size sampling (pps sampling) is a modified form of attribute sampling that can be used for both substantive and compliance testing. The discussion in this chapter is limited primarily to substantive testing. This chapter explains the application and evaluation technique of the basic pps sampling model and the circumstances under which the use of pps sampling is appropriate.[1]

OBJECTIVES AND ASSUMPTIONS OF PPS SAMPLING

The selection of a particular statistical sampling model requires that: (1) conclusions that can be drawn from the sample meet the test objectives of the auditor, and (2) assumptions of the model match the characteristics of the population being sampled. PPS sampling is designed to allow the auditor to make a statement about the dollar amount of error (both overstatement and understatement error) in the audited population. Substantive testing using pps sampling is a popular alternative to the variable sampling methods explained in Chapter 5. PPS sampling is designed to generate a conclusion similar to the following:

> Based on the sample's evidence, I am $X\%$ confident that the dollar amount of error in the account does not exceed $\$Y$ (where $\$Y$ depends on the sampling results).

The auditor will then compare the value obtained for $\$Y$ with the tolerable error to make a decision about the acceptability of the reported book value of the account.

Before the auditor decides to use the pps sampling model, he or she should ascertain whether the assumptions of the model are valid for the population being tested. Two assumptions incorporated in the pps sampling model are:

1. The error rate in the population should be small (less than 10 percent) and the population should contain 2000 or more items. (The *each $ is an item.*

---

[1] Probability proportionate to size sampling is frequently referred to as dollar-unit sampling. In the United States pps sampling was first applied in an auditing context by K. Stringer of Deloitte, Haskins & Sells. The Stringer method is referred to as cumulative monetary sampling.

use of the Poisson probability distribution for evaluation of the sample requires this feature.[2])

2. The amount of error in any item of the population cannot be more than the reported book value of the item. That is, if the book value of a customer's balance is $100, the amount of error in the balance cannot exceed $100.

If the assumptions of the pps sampling model are valid for the population being tested and the conclusions derived from using the model coincide with the audit test objectives, the auditor should consider applying pps sampling.

BASIC DESCRIPTION OF PPS SAMPLING

PPS sampling is a modified form of attribute sampling that permits dollar conclusions about the total dollar amount of error in the population. Unlike classical attribute sampling techniques, which focus on the physical units (e.g., invoices and vouchers) of the population, pps sampling focuses on the dollar units of the population. Suppose the auditor is sampling a population of $100,000 accounts receivable that contain 5000 individual customer balances. Instead of viewing the population as 5000 different physical units from which to draw a sample, the auditor would think of the population as 100,000 individual dollar units from which to draw a sample.

When an individual dollar is selected for examination, the dollar is not tested by itself. Instead, it acts as a hook and drags a whole item (physical unit) with it. As we discussed in Chapter 2, to find the item associated with the particular dollar unit being sampled, the auditor must add progressively through the population. For an illustration of this method, consider the partial listing of accounts below:

Item Number	Book Value	Cumulative Total	Associated Dollar units
1	$ 50	$ 50	1–50
2	100	150	51–150
3	80	230	151–230
4	200	430	231–430
5	300	730	431–730
.	.	.	.
.	.	.	.
.	.	.	.

---

[2] Roberts presents a pps sampling model useful for high error rate population situations. See Donald M. Roberts, **Statistical Auditing** (New York: AICPA, 1978), pp. 116–119.

If dollar unit 250 were selected, for example, the auditor would pull for examination account number 4, because 250 falls in the range 231–430. This method of selection results in selecting items with a probability directly proportional to their size. That is, a $100 item has a 10 times greater chance of being selected than a $10 item because it contains 10 times as many dollar units that could be selected for sampling. Ultimately, samples will contain a higher percentage of large items than small items. In this respect, pps sampling is similar to stratified sampling in that both give greater weight to items with larger recorded amounts.

Once the physical units have been found that correspond to the selected dollar units, the auditor examines the physical units for error. If an error is found in a physical unit, the unit is said to be tainted. Tainting t (or relative error) is the amount of error in the unit divided by the reported book value of the unit.

$$t = \frac{\text{amount of error}}{\text{reported book value of unit}}$$

The value for t tells the auditor the amount of error in each dollar unit contained in the physical unit. Specifically, t gives the auditor a value for the error in the dollar unit selected for sampling. For example, if a customer's account balance is reported at $100 and is overstated by $50 (audited value = $50)

$$t = \frac{\$50}{\$100} = .50$$

The auditor can state that each dollar unit in the customer's balance is in error by $0.50. Tainting t for each dollar unit found in error in the sample is used to determine the test results. Errors are classified as either understatement or overstatement error and, within each group, tainting values are ranked in descending order. For example, if two errors produce taintings of .37 and .42, then irrespective of the dollar amounts of the errors, .42 is designated t_1 and .37 is designated t_2.

After the ranking procedure is completed, the Poisson probability distribution is used to evaluate the results of the dollar units sampled at a specified risk level, SR. The evaluation produces an estimate of the maximum amount of dollar error in the population for both understatement and overstatement possibilities with a given degree of reliability. (The calculations involved are presented in the next section.) The auditor can then decide whether the population should be accepted as not materially misstated or rejected as being in error by a material amount.

EVALUATION BASED ON THE POISSON PROBABILITY DISTRIBUTION

Poisson probabilities are obtained from an equation that represents an idealized mathematical process generating occasional random events. Applied to an accounting population, the events are errors and the process is the accounting system and related controls. The Poisson distribution allows the auditor to state with a specified risk (SR), the upper error limit UEL_x per sample size n of the population, given the sample contains x errors. When the auditor specifies a risk level for the test, he or she determines which UEL_x to use for evaluation. Values for UEL_x are found in Table 8 (see Chapter 3). At a specified risk (SR), UEL_x divided by sample size n gives the maximum error rate that is projected to the population.

Maximum error rate for the population at the specified risk of incorrect acceptance (beta risk)[3] is

$$\frac{UEL_x}{n}$$

A portion of Table 8, which is used to determine UEL_x values, is reproduced below. UEL_x's are read from the body of the table.

Number of	*Risk Levels*		
Occurrences	**10%**	**5%**	**2.5%**
0	2.4	3.0	3.7
1	3.9	4.8	5.6
2	5.4	6.3	7.3
3	6.7	7.8	8.8

The following table contains examples of maximum error rates at different SR levels and a sample size of 50 with a defined number of errors.

Numbers of Errors Found	Risk Level, SR	Maximum Error Rate $UEL_x/50$
0	5%	6.0% (3.0 ÷ 50)
0	10	4.8 (2.4 ÷ 50)
1	5	9.6 (4.8 ÷ 50)
1	10	7.8 (3.9 ÷ 50)

[3] Note that with pps sampling the specified risk level is the risk of incorrect acceptance (SAS No. 39; AU 350) or, statistically, the *beta* risk. As is explained later in this chapter, the auditor does not consider alpha risk in estimating the sample size, but may incorporate an adjustment to control alpha risk in the evaluation of the sample results.

The maximum error rate does not generate information concerning the dollar magnitude of possible error in the population. The pps sampling approach in auditing was developed to convert error rates into dollars. Goodfellow, Loebbecke, and Neter outline the methodology for pps sampling evaluation of the maximum error rates found with the Poisson distribution.[4] The following discussion is an elaboration of this methodology. The evaluation technique is first developed when overstatement errors are found. Then, an example is presented illustrating both understatement and overstatement errors.

Consider a population that contains N physical units with total book value of the population equal to BV. The maximum error rate from a sample of size n at a specified risk level SR is UEL_x/n when x overstatement errors are found. The projection of the maximum number of physical units in error for the population is

$$\text{Maximum number of overstated physical units} = N \cdot \frac{UEL_x}{n}$$

If the maximum amount of overstatement of each of these units is X, then an estimate of the maximum dollar amount of overstatement in the population is

$$\text{Maximum dollar amount of overstatement} = N \cdot \frac{UEL_x}{n} \cdot X$$

If a pps sample were taken, BV is the total number of units (dollars) in the population, and the maximum dollar amount of overstatement each dollar may contain is \$1 (recall assumption number 2 of pps sampling). Since $BV = N$ and $X = 1$, the estimate of the maximum dollar overstatement in the population Max equals

$$\text{Maximum dollar amount of overstatement, } Max = BV \cdot \frac{UEL_x}{n} \cdot 1$$

This estimate of the maximum amount of overstatement in the population can be refined by using additional information found in the sample and by recognizing the cumulative nature of the Poisson UEL values.

First, if no errors are found in a sample, the auditor will estimate the maximum dollar amount of overstatement (referred to as the basic bound when there are no errors) as

$$\text{Basic bound} = BV \cdot \frac{UEL_0}{n} \cdot 1$$

---

[4] James L. Goodfellow, James K. Loebbecke, and John Neter, "Some Perspectives on CAV Sampling Plans," **CA Magazine** (October and November 1974). The notation, CAV, refers to combined attribute and variable sampling.

The "basic bound" tells the auditor that no matter what the results of the sample are, he or she will always estimate the maximum dollar amount of overstatement to be at least the basic bound for the given risk level. When one error is found in the sample, the estimate of the maximum dollar amount of overstatement will be larger than the basic bound. In fact, the increase in the estimate caused by finding an error is

$$\text{Addition to basic bound of one error found} = BV \cdot \frac{UEL_1 - UEL_0}{n} \cdot 1$$

Then the estimate of maximum dollar amount of overstatement in the population is equivalent to basic bound plus the additional effect of finding one overstatement error in the sample. That is,

$$Max = BV \cdot \frac{UEL_1}{n} \cdot 1$$

$$= \left(BV \cdot \frac{UEL_0}{n} \cdot 1 \right) + \left(BV \cdot \frac{UEL_1 - UEL_0}{n} \cdot 1 \right)$$

If two overstatement errors were observed, the estimate of the maximum dollar amount of overstatement would be equivalent to basic bound plus the additional effect of finding the first error and the additional effect of finding the second error. That is:

$$Max = BV \frac{UEL_2}{n} \cdot 1 = \left(BV \cdot \frac{UEL_0}{n} \cdot 1 \right)$$

$$+ \left(BV \cdot \frac{UEL_1 - UEL_0}{n} \cdot 1 \right) + \left(BV \cdot \frac{UEL_2 - UEL_1}{n} \cdot 1 \right)$$

In general, the cumulative nature of the Poisson *UEL* values can be broken down into parts to be used to find the estimate of the maximum dollar amount of overstatement. These parts then can be used to find the basic bound and the effect of finding each additional overstatement error.

The cumulative nature of the Poisson *UEL* values is not important when the maximum dollar amount of overstatement is considered to be $1 for each addition to the basic bound. However, the cumulative property is very useful if *additional information found in the pps sample is also used.* The tainting values of overstatement errors along with their relative rankings can be used to make an estimate of the maximum dollar amount of overstatement in the population. The basic bound will remain the same as before because the amount of overstatement error is considered to be maximal ($1). However, if one error is found with tainting *t*, then the additional effect of finding this error in the sample will be

$$\text{Addition to basic bound of one error} = BV \cdot \frac{UEL_1 - UEL_0}{n} \cdot t_1$$

If two overstatement errors are found, their rankings will determine their additional effect on the estimate of the maximum dollar amount of overstatement in the population. Let t_1 represent the error ranking number 1 and t_2 represent the error ranking number 2, then

$$\text{Effect of finding the first error} = BV \cdot \frac{UEL_1 - UEL_0}{n} \cdot t_1$$

and

$$\text{Effect of finding the second error} = BV \cdot \frac{UEL_2 - UEL_1}{n} \cdot t_2$$

The resulting value for the estimate of the maximum dollar amount of overstatement in the population at the specified reliability will be the most conservative (pessimistic) estimate when tainting values are used.

To illustrate the evaluation technique, consider an accounts receivable of $100,000. If a sample of size 100 contains two overstatement errors with $t_1 = .8$ and $t_2 = .5$, the estimate of the maximum dollar amount of overstatement at 5 percent risk of incorrect acceptance (using Table 8) is

$$Max = \left(\$100,000 \cdot \frac{3.0}{100} \cdot 1\right) + \left(\$100,000 \cdot \frac{4.8 - 3.0}{100} \cdot .8\right)$$
$$+ \left(\$100,000 \cdot \frac{6.3 - 4.8}{100} \cdot .5\right) = \$5,190$$

The calculation for the effect of finding the first error for t_1 is ($100,000 · 1.8/100 · .8). Likewise, the effect of finding the second error for t_2 is ($100,000 · 1.5/100 · .5).

PPS SAMPLING FOR OVERSTATEMENTS

The steps of the pps sampling model used for overtatements are outlined here. Following the model's outline, a typical application is presented.

Step Number	Action
1	State the objectives of the test and establish the parameters of the particular test. Define:

BV = book value of the population

TE = tolerable error

SR = risk level

N = number of physical units in the population

2   Select the sample.

Use: Systematic pps sampling if the population is in random order with respect to the audited characteristic.

$$n = \text{sample size} = \frac{UEL_0 \cdot BV}{TE}$$

$$I = \text{sampling interval} = \frac{BV}{n}$$

RS = random start between 0 and I

UEL_0 = value from Table 8, based on zero expected errors.

Dollar units selected will be $RS, RS + I, RS + 2I, RS + 3I, \ldots, RS + (n - 1)I$.

3   Audit the physical units associated with the selected dollar units.

4   Evaluate the sample and determine tainting t for each physical unit in error. Let

t_1 = tainting of largest relative error

t_2 = tainting of second largest relative error, and so on.

5   Determine the basic bound and additions to the basic bound as discussed earlier (*Max*).

6   Make decision about acceptability of reported book value by comparing *Max* with *TE*.

Instead of using systematic pps sampling as illustrated in Step 2, the sample could be selected by using a random number table or a random number generator as discussed in Chapter 2. Also, systematic sampling with multiple starts could be used as an additional safeguard against biased selection. To use multiple starts, the sampling interval from Step 2 would be multiplied by the desired number of starts. Recall that this was illustrated in Chapter 2.

To illustrate steps 1 to 6, assume that the auditor is trying to determine if a client's inventory balance of $3,000,000 is not materially misstated. Figure 6.1 presents an illustrative application.

One of the facts stated in Figure 6.1 is that all inventory records ($N = 50,000$ physical units) are less than $20,000. That is, no physical unit exceeded the sampling interval. In instances where physical units in the population are greater than the sampling interval, they are examined 100 percent. Consequently, the sample size is equal to n minus all 100 percent-examined units. This is important because in calculating *Max the reduced sample size and the reduced book value should be used*.

Another very important point also is illustrated in Figure 6.1. When a

FIGURE 6.1 ILLUSTRATIVE PPS SAMPLING APPLICATION—OVERSTATE-MENTS

Parameters

$BV = \$3{,}000{,}000$

$N = 50{,}000$ perpetual inventory records

$TE = \$60{,}000$

$SR = 5$ percent

Sample Size Equation

$$n = \frac{3.0 \cdot 3{,}000{,}000}{60{,}000} = 150$$

Sampling Interval and Sample Selection

$$I = \frac{3{,}000{,}000}{150} = 20{,}000$$

$RS = 1795$ (from a random number table)

Select dollar units: 1795; 21,795; 41,795; etc. All inventory records in the population are less than $20,000 and greater than zero. *If physical item had a value? sampling interval it shd be checked 100%.*

Sample Evaluation

Two errors observed, No. 1 had a book value of $1000 with overstatement of $500 and No. 2 had a book value of $2000 with overstatement of $1600. (Remember t_1 is the highest relative error, not the highest dollar error.)

$$t_1 = \frac{1600}{2000} = .8 \qquad t_2 = \frac{500}{1000} = .5$$

$$Max = \left(\$3{,}000{,}000 \cdot \frac{3.0}{150} \cdot 1\right) + \text{*tolerable error so any errors would lower theorm at once*}$$

$$\left(\$3{,}000{,}000 \cdot \frac{1.8}{150} \cdot .8\right) +$$

$$\left(\$3{,}000{,}000 \cdot \frac{1.5}{150} \cdot .5\right) = \$103{,}800$$

Auditor's Conclusion

Based on the sample evidence, the auditor is 95 percent confident that the dollar amount of overstatement in the inventory account does not exceed $103,800. Because $103,800 is greater than tolerable error ($60,000), the auditor may decide to reject the book value of the population and increase the sample size.

monetary overstatement is observed, the maximum dollar amount of overstatement exceeds the tolerable error. When this happens, Robert states:

As a result the auditor must obtain additional information to be able to decide whether or not there is a material amount of error. When, in fact, there is not a material amount of error, the result is overauditing. Stringer and others have recognized this and suggest determining the sample size so that the upper bound [max] with no observed errors is below the material amount [tolerable error].[5]

This can be accomplished by first estimating tolerable error (*TE*) and then calculating an adjusted tolerable error (*TE'*) as a fraction of tolerable error. In practice, several different approaches are used to estimate adjusted tolerable error (*TE'*). One conservative approach is to make *TE'* one-half of *TE*. This is the approach adopted in this chapter. Another approach is illustrated in the explanation of nonstatistical sampling in Chapter 7.

SAMPLING RISK AND PPS SAMPLING

Statistical sampling models are designed to give the auditor a method for making quantitative statements about the risks that result from conclusions based on a sample rather than application of an audit procedure to all items in a population. As in variable-sampling audit-hypothesis testing, two types of sampling risks are inherent in pps sampling when sample results are projected to the population—alpha risk and beta risk.

Recall from Chapter 5 that beta risk is the chance that the auditor will accept a population as materially correct when, in fact, it is materially in error. In pps sampling, the auditor controls beta risk when he or she specifies the risk level *SR* for the sampling plan. Beta risk is the risk level specified for pps sampling.

The auditor establishes the desired beta risk for pps sampling in the same manner as that used in Chapter 5 for variable sampling. The audit risk model for establishing beta risk is

$$TD \text{ (beta)} = \frac{UR}{IC \times AR}$$

However, for convenience, this chapter uses beta risk levels of 5 or 10 percent for illustrations of pps sampling.

---

[5] Roberts, **Statistical Auditing**, p. 122. For additional discussion of how to handle this problem, see R. Kaplan, "Sample Size Computations for Dollar-unit Sampling," **Studies on Statistical Methodology in Auditing: Journal of Accounting Research** (Supplement, 1975), pp. 126–133.

Recall, also, that alpha risk is the chance of concluding that the population is materially in error when, in fact, it is materially correct. When pps sampling is used, the auditor does not specifically control alpha risk. However, simulation studies have helped to establish a revision of the evaluation technique used in pps sampling that confines alpha risk to 5 percent. To limit alpha risk to 5 percent, the auditor determines the most likely estimate for both overstatement and understatement errors. That is,

$$MLE_{o/s} = \text{most likely error for overstatements}$$

$$= \frac{\text{sum of overstatement taintings}}{n} \cdot BV$$

$$MLE_{u/s} = \text{most likely error for understatements}$$

$$= \frac{\text{sum of understatement taintings}}{n} \cdot BV$$

Then the auditor determines the estimates for maximum dollar amount of overstatement and understatement error. That is,

$Max_{o/s}$ = maximum dollar amount of overstatement

= basic bound plus effect of finding each additional overstatement error found in the sample

$Max_{u/s}$ = maximum dollar amount of understatement

= basic bound plus effect of finding each additional understatement error found in the sample (same technique as $Max_{o/s}$)

Finally, the auditor nets the $Max_{o/s}$ with $MLE_{u/s}$ and the $Max_{u/s}$ with $MLE_{o/s}$ to yield:

$$Net\ Max_{o/s} = Max_{o/s} - MLE_{u/s}$$
$$Net\ Max_{u/s} = Max_{u/s} - MLE_{o/s}$$

The *Net Max*$_{o/s}$ and *Net Max*$_{u/s}$ are the values the auditor uses to determine the acceptability of the total book value of the population. The $MLE_{o/s}$ and $MLE_{u/s}$ are the auditor's best estimates of the actual errors of understatement and overstatement in the population. These two values can be netted to give an adjusting entry for the population if the auditor believes the sample size is sufficiently large.

PPS SAMPLING FOR OVERSTATEMENTS AND UNDERSTATEMENTS

The pps sampling approach that is used when both overstatement and understatement errors are observed follows the same procedure as that used only for overstatements. There are minor changes that are discussed and illustrated below.

Overstatement and understatement errors must be placed into separate groups. Then, tainting values for each item in the overstatement and the understatement group must be determined. After tainting values are calculated, they are ranked in descending order for each group. Next, the effect of finding each additional overstatement error and each additional understatement error is calculated. Finally, the most likely error for overstatements and the most likely error for understatements are calculated to arrive at net maximum overstatement and net maximum understatement.

Figure 6.2 illustrates the calculations involved when a pps sampling application produces both overstatement errors and understatement errors. Some auditors avoid calculating the most likely overstatement error and the most likely understatement error by simply subtracting the $Max_{o/s}$ from the $Max_{u/s}$ to arrive at a *Net Max* overstatement or understatement. According to Roberts, caution must be used when using this shortcut. The resulting reliability is less than that used for calculating $Max_{o/s}$ and $Max_{u/s}$.[6]

FIGURE 6.2 ILLUSTRATIVE PPS SAMPLING APPLICATION—OVERSTATEMENTS AND UNDERSTATEMENTS

Parameters

$$BV = \$4,000,000$$
$$N = 100,000 \text{ fixed-asset records}$$
$$TE = \$80,000$$
$$SR = 10 \text{ percent}$$

Sample Size Equation

$$n = \frac{2.4 \cdot 4,000,000}{80,000} = 120$$

Sampling Interval and Sample Selection

$$I = \frac{4,000,000}{120} = 33,333$$
$$RS = 15,700$$

[6] Ibid., p. 125.

FIGURE 6.2 (CONTINUED)

Select dollar units: 15,700; 49,033; 64,733; and so on. All fixed-assets records in the population are less than $15,700.

Sample Evaluation

One overstatement error is observed; it has a book value of $15,000 with overstatement of $9000.

$$t_1 = \frac{9,000}{15,000} = .600$$

Two understatement errors are observed; one has a book value of $30,000 with understatement of $25,000, and the second has a book value of $10,000 with understatement of $7,000.

$$t_1 = \frac{25,000}{30,000} = .833 \qquad t_2 = \frac{7,000}{10,000} = .700$$

$$\text{Basic bound} = \$4,000,000 \cdot \frac{2.4}{120} \cdot 1 = \$80,000$$

$$Max_{o/s} = \$80,000 + \left(\$4,000,000 \cdot \frac{1.5}{120} \cdot .600 \right) = \$110,000$$

$$Max_{u/s} = \$80,000 + \left(\$4,000,000 \cdot \frac{1.5}{120} \cdot .833 \right)$$

$$+ \left(\$4,000,000 \cdot \frac{1.5}{120} \cdot .700 \right) = \$156,650$$

$$MLE_{o/s} = \frac{.600}{120} \cdot \$4,000,000 = \$20,000$$

$$MLE_{u/s} = \frac{.833 + .700}{120} \cdot \$4,000,000 = \$51,000$$

$$Net\ Max_{o/s} = \$110,000 - \$51,100 = \$58,900$$
$$Net\ Max_{u/s} = \$156,650 - \$20,000 = \$136,650$$

Auditor's Conclusion

Based on the sample evidence, the auditor is 90 percent confident that the dollar amount of overstatement in the fixed-asset account does not exceed $58,900 and that the dollar amount of understatement in the fixed-asset account does not exceed $136,650. The auditor may decide to reject the book value of the population because of the materiality of the possible understatement errors.

ADVANTAGES AND DISADVANTAGES OF USING PPS SAMPLING

Pps sampling has several attractive features aside from the general advantages of using statistical sampling. A discussion of the advantages and disadvantages of the pps sampling model should allow the auditor to determine the applicability of the model for a particular test. Some of the advantages of pps sampling are:

1. PPS sampling satisfies the objectives of SAS No. 39 (AU 350) and can easily be used within the conceptual framework of audit sampling.

2. PPS sampling solves the problem of detecting a very small number of large errors (needles in the haystack) by giving the big items a much greater chance of being included in the audit sample. This is achieved by breaking up the big, but infrequent physical units into small but frequent monetary units.

3. PPS sampling allows the auditor to quantify the beta risk that he or she is assuming by making conclusions about the population based on a sample.

4. PPS sampling can be applied to a combination of several account balances. Accounts can be tested together because the sampling units (dollars) are homogeneous.

5. PPS sampling is relatively easy to use and understand, and requires only one table based on the Poisson probability distribution for evaluation.

6. PPS sampling does not depend on the sampling distribution being closely approximated by the normal distribution.

7. PPS sampling provides an alternative to using variable sampling to stratify a population. (Both pps sampling and stratified sampling give greater weight to items with large book values.)

Some of the disadvantages of pps sampling are:

1. The pps sampling evaluation technique requires the amount of error in each physical unit of the population not to exceed the book value of the unit.

2. Physical units that are understated have a lower probability of selection because they contain a smaller number of dollars to be selected for sampling. Furthermore, pps sampling cannot find errors in physical units with a book value of zero; however, many sampling plans suffer from this problem.

PPS SAMPLING FOR ATTRIBUTES

If the auditor selects a compliance test sample using pps sampling, the incidence of compliance deviations may be related to an upper bound of monetary error. Assume that a pps sample is selected from a population of sales invoices to ascertain whether credit was properly authorized. The population of sales invoices for the entire year has a recorded value of $789,000. Based on a preliminary review of the credit sales system and past experience, the auditor believes that the internal control is very good. By using a risk level of 5 percent and a predefined upper precision limit of 5 percent, the auditor selected a sample of 60 sales invoices.

Using Table 8 to evaluate the sample observation, if zero occurrences are noted, the auditor may concude that unauthorized sales dollars do not exceed $39,450 at a 5 percent risk level. The upper bound of monetary (dollar) compliance deviation is calculated as follows:

$$\text{Upper bound of monetary compliance deviation}$$
$$= \frac{3.0 \text{ from Table 8 (5\% risk)}}{60 \text{ sample size}} \times \$789,000 \, BV$$
$$= \$39,450$$

Similarly, if one occurrence is discovered, the auditor may conclude: I am 95 percent confident that no more than $63,120 of the sales invoice dollars were not properly approved.

$$\$63,120 = \frac{4.8}{60} \times \$789,000$$

As is demonstrated above, adapting pps sampling to compliance testing is easily accomplished. The auditor defines the attribute just as he or she would when attribute sampling is used (see Chapter 3). The primary difference between the pps sampling and attribute sampling concerns sample selection. Attribute sampling is based on physical unit sampling, but pps sampling is based on dollar sampling units.

SUMMARY

PPS sampling is a statistical sampling model that can be used for substantive or compliance testing. When the auditor wishes to estimate the maximum amount of monetary error contained in a population, he or she should consider using pps sampling. To determine if pps sampling is appropriate for a particular circumstance, the assumptions of the model are very important.

The pps sampling model is based on the Poisson probability distribution. The chapter explains and illustrates evaluation techniques by using the Poisson distribution. Advantages and disadvantages of the model are discussed to allow an enlightened decision by the auditor contemplating using pps sampling.

Although this chapter is not an exhaustive discussion of pps sampling, it gives the reader a good idea of what the model involves and how audit conclusions are derived from it. The conclusions generated from a pps sampling application are particularly well-suited to auditing applications.

GLOSSARY

Basic bound   The maximum dollar amount of error in a population, given that no errors were observed. The calculation of the basic bound is dependent on the risk of incorrect acceptance and the sample size.

Maximum dollar amount of overstatement (or understatement) error, Max   The basic bound plus the additional effects of finding errors in a sample, if any. It is also referred to as upper bound (overstatement) and lower bound (understatement).

Most likely error for overstatements (or understatements), MLE   The sum of overstatement (or understatement) taintings × book value divided by sample size.

Net Max   *Max* overstatement minus *MLE* understatements. *Max* understatement minus *MLE* overstatement equals *Net Max* understatement. The *Net Max* calculation is used to confine alpha risk to approximately 5 percent.

PPS sampling   A statistical model known as probability proportionate to size. The model is used for both substantive and compliance testing. In the pps sampling model, each sampling unit has a probability of being selected that is approximately proportionate to its reported book value.

Systematic pps sampling   A pps sampling method in which selected sample items are based on every BV/nth item and a defined random start(s).

Tainting   An account balance or other physical unit containing an error. Tainting t is the amount of error in the physical unit divided by the reported book value of the unit.

REVIEW QUESTIONS

6-1. Indicate whether each of the following is true (T) or false (F).

A. Sampling units with zero or negative book values must be treated separately when pps sampling is used.

B. In a pps substantive sampling application the risk level specified is beta risk.

C. PPS sampling is a modified form of discovery sampling.

D. A pps sample may be selected via a random number table (unrestricted random sampling) or systematic sampling.

E. Physical units (account items) that are overstated have a lower probability of selection in a pps sampling application.

F. To use pps sampling for compliance testing, the auditor defines attributes just as he or she would when using attribute sampling.

G. PPS sampling is actually a form of stratified sampling.

H. If a pps sample indicates that the proportion of dollar transactions associated with a compliance deviation is greater than was planned, internal control can be relied on from a quantitative perspective.

I. When systematic pps sampling is used, all accounts exceeding the total book value divided by the sample size are examined on a 100 percent basis.

J. The best way to calculate $Net\ Max_{o/s}$ is to substract $Max_{u/s}$ from $Max_{o/s}$.

6-2. What is the general form of conclusion that is generated by a pps sampling application?

6-3. List the two underlying assumptions of the pps sampling model.

6-4. Contrast sample selection by using classical sampling with sample selection using pps selection.

6-5. PPS sampling is similar to stratified sampling in some respects. Do you agree?

6-6. What is tainting and how is it calculated?

6-7. Calculate the maximum error *rate* at 97.5 percent reliability for a sample size of 100 assuming 0 errors, 2 errors, and 3 errors.

6-8. Calculate the basic bound, tainting, addition to basic bound, and the maximum dollar amount of overstatement in the population for the following situations:

Situation A

$$N = \$250,000$$
$$n = 100$$

Overstatement error = \$5000 book and \$4000 audit

$$SR = 5 \text{ percent}$$

Situation B

$$N = \$250,000$$
$$n = 100$$

First overstatement error = \$5000 book and \$4000 audit

Second overstatement error = \$2000 book and \$1000 audit

$$SR = 10 \text{ percent}$$

6-9. Assume that the errors in 6-8 situation A and situation B are understatements of the same dollar amount. What would the maximum dollar amount of understatement in the population be for each situation?

6-10. What is the pps sample size equation?

6-11. Describe how a pps sample would be selected by using systematic sampling (use one random start) and by using a random number table.

6-12. How is beta risk controlled in a pps sampling application? Contrast your response with controlling beta risk in a variable sampling application as presented in Chapter 5.

6-13. How is alpha risk controlled in a pps sampling application?

6-14. Calculate the most likely error (overstatement and understatement) for the following situation.

$$BV = \$100,000$$
$$n = 100$$

Overstatement taintings = .20, .30, .40

Understatement taintings = .60, .22, .08

6-15. Determine the pps sample size for the audit of an accounts receivable balance of \$175,000. Use a 10 percent beta risk and assume tolerable error is set equal to \$5000. The receivable balance contains \$2000 of credit balance accounts.

6-16. What are the primary advantages of pps sampling relative to variable sampling models presented in Chapter 5? What are the primary disadvantages?

6-17. Contrast pps substantive sampling with pps compliance sampling.

PPS SAMPLING CASE

CASE 6-1 CLIP JOINT, INC.
(estimated time to complete: 45 minutes)

Donna Marsh, senior internal auditor of Clip Joint, Inc., is concerned about the accuracy of the firm's inventory balance for the June 30 fiscal year-end. The inventory was counted without internal audit supervision. Donna wants to design a pps sampling application that will give her 5 percent risk that inventory errors do not exceed $50,000. Clip Joint's final inventory summary shows a balance of $1,000,000. Because she expects a few errors in her recount work, Donna sets the adjusted tolerable error for sample size determination at $25,000.

A. What is the needed sample size?

B. Calculate *Max* given that she observed the following errors:

	Book	Audit
No. 1	$2000	$500 - over
No. 2	1000	1200 - under
No. 3	3000	3350 - under

C. Calculate the most likely overstatement and the most likely understatement error.

D. Calculate *Net Max* overstatement and *Net Max* understatement.

E. Write a suitable conclusion for Donna's workpapers.

7

AUDIT SAMPLING POLICIES

Learning Objectives

After a careful study and discussion of this chapter, you will be able to:

1. Describe what additional audit work should be performed when an attribute compliance test is selected from less than 12 months of the fiscal year.
2. Construct a decision model to aid you in relating various variable sampling methods (unstratified simple extension or difference estimation) to various accounting population conditions.
3. Explain the audit logic involved in deciding whether a given asset account balance should be sampled or reviewed analytically.
4. Use a formal approach to the planning and evaluation of a nonstatistical audit sample.

Tests of compliance are often performed at an interim date before year-end. Consequently, if attribute sampling is used, the sample selected might not encompass the entire year. In the first section of this chapter we discuss various alternatives that should be considered when a compliance sample is selected from less than 12 months of the fiscal year. Then, guidelines for using variable sampling and pps sampling for accounting estimation and audit hypothesis testing are presented. Finally, the chapter concludes with a discussion of sampling logic as applied to asset account balances and an explanation of a formal approach to nonstatistical sampling.

COMPLIANCE SAMPLING POLICIES

SAS No. 1 (AU 320.70) states:

. . . tests of compliance . . . ideally should be applied to transactions executed throughout the period under audit because of the general sampling concept that the items to be examined should be selected from the entire set of data to which the resulting conclusions are to be applied.

AU 320.70 recognizes that tests of compliance are usually performed for a portion of the year at an interim date.

At year-end, preferably before related substantive tests are completed, the internal control reviews performed at interim periods should be updated. If the internal control has not changed in any significant way, additional compliance tests are not necessary. If the internal control system has changed significantly, the auditor should either test for compliance with the new procedures or consider the desirability of increasing substantive tests, or both.

In conducting post-interim interviews, the auditor should:

1. Ask appropriate client personnel about significant internal control or accounting system changes implemented since the interim date.

2. Determine from the client response and other evidence whether additional compliance or substantive tests may be desirable.

3. Document in the audit work papers conclusions about the need for additional tests and the related reasons.

Inquiries about changes in internal control should address areas such as reassignment of client employee duties, changes in key personnel, system modifications, and introduction of new equipment or procedures.

In assessing the need for additional tests of compliance, SAS No. 1 (AU 320.70) lists the following factors that should be considered:

- The results of interim compliance tests.

- Client responses to inquiries concerning the remaining period.

- The length of the remaining period.
- The nature and amount of transactions or balances involved.
- The nature and amount of substantive procedures to be applied at year-end.
- Evidence of compliance provided by substantive tests (dual-purpose tests).
- Other matters the auditor considers relevant (e.g., an understaffed condition, a dominating personality in a sensitive position, and so on).

In selecting a representative compliance sample, three sampling policies should be observed. They are:

Policy No. 1. If compliance tests of accounting controls were not selected from the full fiscal year, an internal control update memorandum is essential before placing reliance on internal control. The update memorandum should be responsive to SAS No. 1 (AU 320.70), as discussed above.

Policy No. 2. The compliance test usually should encompass the first nine or ten months of the year. (The rationale for this is explained in Chapter 3.) However, by estimating the year-end document count, it is often possible to select the sample from the entire fiscal period.

Policy No. 3. Compliance tests should not be extended into a period prior to the beginning of the one under audit in an attempt to maintain a continuous frame. For example, let us say that *last* year's compliance sample was selected from January 19X1 through September 20, 19X1 for a December 31 year-end audit. *This* year's compliance sample should not be selected from September 2, 19X1 to an interim test date in 19X2.

SUBSTANTIVE SAMPLING GUIDELINES AND POLICIES

Auditing Research Monograph No. 2, *Behavior of Major Statistical Estimators in Sampling Accounting Populations,* indicates that different statistical sampling methods seem to suit different audit objectives.[1] Furthermore, different statistical sampling methods perform well or poorly under different population conditions (e.g., skewness in the population, rate of errors, magnitude of errors, and direction of errors). The following guidelines are useful in relating various sampling methods (unstratified MPU, stratified MPU, difference or ratio estimation, pps sampling) to various population conditions. The guidelines are summarized in Figure 7.1.

---

[1] John Neter and James K. Loebbecke, "Behavior of Major Statistical Estimators in Sampling Accounting Populations," **Auditing Research Monograph No. 2** (New York: AICPA, 1975).

FIGURE 7.1 SELECTION OF SAMPLING METHOD

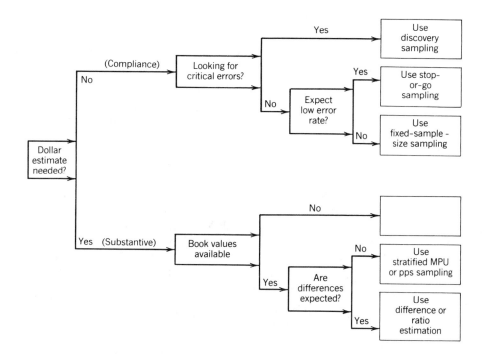

Guideline 1.   When performing substantive tests, always stratify high dollar items and other items of special interest, and audit 100 percent, regardless of the evaluation method used. When skewness (lopsidedness) is a concern, the cut-off point should generally be no higher than 10 times the population-mean book amount. When outliers (i.e., large infrequent errors that could invalidate the statistical tests) are a concern, the cut-off should be no higher than an amount equal to ⅓ of tolerable error. When both skewness and outliers are of concern, use the lower of the two cut-off points.

Guideline 2.   If a dollar estimate is not needed to satisfy the audit objective of the test, use attribute estimation (e.g., discovery sampling). If a dollar estimate is needed, apply guidelines 3 to 5 as appropriate.

Guideline 3.   If a frequency distribution of book values is not available for stratification prior to selection, pps sampling should be used. Difference or ratio estimation cannot be used. As a fallback method, unstratified MPU may be used. MPU may not be economical, but if individual book values are unavailable there is no alternative.

Guideline 4. If differences are expected, consider using difference or ratio estimation. As is discussed in Chapter 4, a minimum number of nonzero differences must be observed before difference or ratio estimation can be used.

Guideline 5. If the expected error rate does not qualify by Guideline 4, stratified MPU or pps sampling should be used.

Guideline 6. If the expected error results are less than the actual error findings, do not rely on the statistical conclusions. Instead, consider using another sampling model or applying other audit procedures responsive to specific types of errors found.

Underlying substantive sampling guidelines 1 to 6 is the idea that before auditors actually proceed with auditing sample results, they know what they expect to occur. If what they expect does not occur, they plan for the action that they will take. A key point to remember is that difference or ratio estimation cannot be used with low error-rate populations. However, pps sampling is well-suited to no or very low error-rate populations.

In addition to the six guidelines listed, the following policies, which were discussed in Chapter 5, also should be followed when using sampling to determine the acceptability of a client's book value.

Policy 1. In the formula for calculating beta,

$$TD \text{ (beta)} = \frac{UR}{IC \times AR}$$

a. Audit risk (*UR*) should be 5 or 10 percent.

b. Internal control risk *IC* should not be less than approximately 20 percent.

c. Other procedure risk *AR* normally should not be less than 50 percent.

d. Beta should not be higher than 50 percent.

Policy No. 2. Alpha risk generally should be set at 5 percent or lower. If the cost of selecting additional sample items is not significant, alpha risk may be set higher than 5 percent, or as in pps sampling, not considered directly.

Policy No. 3. If sampling is used to propose a statistical book adjustment, alpha risk should be set at 5 percent and beta risk at 5 percent. A statistical book adjustment should be proposed only as a last resort.

TIMING AND EXTENT OF ASSET ACCOUNT BALANCE TESTING

When should an asset account balance be sampled? Figure 7.2 illustrates, via a flowchart, the audit logic involved in deciding whether or not a particular asset account balance should be sampled randomly, using either *statistical* or *nonstatistical* sampling. The flowchart pertains to testing for asset account balance overstatement.

Figure 7.2 can best be illustrated with an example. Assume that the Green Eye Shade Company has an accounts receivable balance of $632,000, consisting of 600 individual accounts (records). The Green Eye Shade Company also has $1,000,000 of total assets and $200,000 of net income. The CPA firm of Foot, Tick, & Tie has decided that $8500 is the tolerable error for the audit of receivables. Foot, Tick, & Tie also has concluded that the account balance should be tested at year-end, because internal control over credit sales is weak.

According to Figure 7.2, the receivable balance of $632,000 is material. The third decision, as depicted in the flowchart, indicates that all individual accounts in excess of $2,800 (⅓ tolerable error rounded) should be audited 100 percent. Of the 600 individual accounts comprising receivables, assume that 38 are $2800 or larger. These 38 accounts total $408,000. The remaining receivable total of $224,000 is still material; therefore, a sample of the remaining 562 individual account balances should be selected. Figure 7.2 indicates that the sample selected from the 562 individual accounts should be representative. Moreover, the sample may be a statistical or nonstatistical sample. That is, the sample size may be determined according to statistical sample size equation or by auditor judgment. In either situation, the auditor should select a representative sample.

Using the sample size equation for unstratified MPU sampling and assuming that alpha risk is 5 percent, beta risk is 10 percent and the standard deviation is $58.13. Sample size with replacement is[2]

$$n' = \left(\frac{(1.96)\ (\$58)\ (562)}{\$5143} \right)^2$$

$$n' = 155$$

Sample size without replacement is

$$n = \frac{155}{1 + \dfrac{155}{562}}$$

$$n = 121$$

---

[2] Adjusted precision is determined by multiplying .605 times $8500 (tolerable error). The .605 factor is determined as follows:

$$.605 = \frac{1.96}{1.96 + 1.28}$$

FIGURE 7.2 TIMING AND EXTENT OF ASSET ACCOUNT BALANCE TESTING

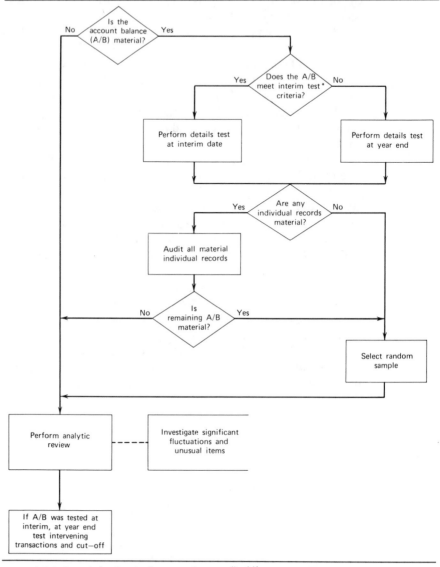

* Interim substantive testing may be applied if

No abnormal audit risks are present that impact the account balance.
The internal control procedures pertaining to the account balance are effective.
The account balance represents a large volume of transactions.
Transactions cut-off at year-end is not a major problem.
The account balance is susceptible to interim examination.
The year-end account balance can be tested satisfactorily by analytic review and
tests of intervening transactions.

These criteria were adapted from material presented by Deloitte, Haskins & Sells at an
Audit SCOPE Seminar held at Vail, Colorado, August 14–19, 1978.

The receivable balance should be reviewed analytically if (1) the balance before removing any individual accounts for 100 percent audit is *not* material, or (2) the remaining balance after audit of large dollar accounts is *not* material. Analytical review procedures are used to evaluate financial information through a process of study and comparison of interrelationships among data. A basic premise underlying the application of analytical review procedures is that known relationships may reasonably be expected to exist and continue in the absence of known conditions to the contrary. When significant unexpected fluctuations occur, the auditor should investigate them.

A FORMAL APPROACH TO NONSTATISTICAL SAMPLING[3]

Nonstatistical sampling plans can be formal or informal. The nonstatistical plan explained here is considered formal because it uses structured decision aids. The essential difference between statistical and nonstatistical sampling is that statistical sampling measures all evaluation characteristics (notably sampling risk) strictly according to probability theory.

All audit samples, statistical and nonstatistical, must meet the following critical requirements:

- Selection of a representative sample.
- Determination of sample size for substantive tests based on a consideration of materiality, risk, and population characteristics.
- Projection of error based on sample results with a consideration of the acceptability of sampling risk.

PRELIMINARY JUDGMENT ABOUT MATERIALITY

An essential first step in planning substantive tests is to make a preliminary judgment about the amount that will be considered material to the financial statements taken as a whole. The auditor's goal is to establish an amount that will serve as an approximate dividing line for a material misstatement of financial statements. The auditor wants to be able to conclude, with reasonable assurance, that the financial statements are not misstated by more than this amount.

---

[3] Adapted from W. Wade Gafford and D. R. Carmichael, "Materiality, Audit Risk and Sampling: A Nuts-and-Bolts Approach," **Journal of Accountancy,** October 1984 and November 1984.

MATERIALITY AS A PLANNING CONCEPT

In planning an audit, materiality is viewed as an allowance for known, likely, and potential undetected error in the financial statements taken as a whole. This notion uses materiality as a measure of how extensive and effective auditing procedures must be.

This does not mean that detected errors that, individually or combined, are below this amount automatically will be waived at the conclusion of the engagement. In evaluating the presentation of the financial statements, qualitative considerations or additional information may cause the auditor to change the threshold for materiality.

DEVELOPING A RULE OF THUMB

A usable rule of thumb for making a preliminary judgment about materiality requires specification of a base and a related percentage. Common bases used in practice are income before taxes, total revenue, and total assets. Total revenue and total assets generally are considered more stable and predictable. Obtaining the base amount from the financial statements is, of course, preferable, but if these amounts are unavailable or if significant audit adjustments are expected, estimating annual data from interim information or historical averages may be appropriate.

Common percentages applied to these bases are 5 to 10 percent of income before taxes and .5 to 2 percent of total revenue or total assets. Factors that influence the choice of the percentage include, but are not limited to, the size of the company (generally, the smaller the company, the larger the percentage) and the use that will be made of the financial statements. For example, 15 or 20 percent of income before taxes may be an appropriate measure of materiality of a small nonpublic company that is closely held and has no outstanding debt.

ILLUSTRATION OF PLANNING MATERIALITY

The auditor is planning the audit of the financial statements of EZS Company with the following selected financial data:

Total revenue	$11,675,000
Total assets	9,850,000
Income before taxes	910,000

The auditor is using a flexible rule of thumb that permits choice of a base dependent on the auditor's judgment in the circumstances. Total revenue is selected as the base, and the auditor uses approximately 1 percent of that base. In this instance, the auditor's judgment about materiality for planning purposes is $115,000.

RELATING THE PRELIMINARY JUDGMENT TO SPECIFIC SUBSTANTIVE TESTS

Once the auditor has made a preliminary judgment about the amount considered material to the financial statements taken as a whole (planning materiality) that amount needs to be related to specific substantive tests. The amount to be used in planning audit procedures for sampling applications is the basic allowance for potential undetected error. It is obtained by making initial and additional reductions from planning materiality.

INITIAL REDUCTION FROM PLANNING MATERIALITY

Planning materiality should be reduced for an estimate of errors that the auditor (1) expects to detect through audit procedures other than sampling applications, and (2) anticipates the client will not correct. If the auditor knows that, at the conclusion of the engagement, the financial statements will be affected by detected error that the client will not agree to correct, this reduces the allowance available for undetected error. Planning materiality reduced by this amount may be called adjusted planning materiality.

ADDITIONAL REDUCTIONS FROM PLANNING MATERIALITY

This sampling approach requires additional reductions from adjusted planning materiality. The auditor's objective is to estimate an amount that will be the basic allowance for potential undetected error that stems from an imprecision resulting from sampling. This basic allowance is essentially the equivalent of the basic bound—that is, the upper limit on monetary error achieved when no errors are detected—in a statistical pps sampling plan. In Chapter 6, the basic allowance is referred to as adjusted tolerable error.

To estimate this basic allowance, adjusted planning materiality is reduced by

- Projected errors in all populations sampled.
- The anticipated increase in imprecision.

Some auditors introduce additional conservatism by also reducing adjusted planning materiality for a judgmentally determined cushion to allow for the fact that reductions made in the planning stage are estimates.

Often, projected errors in sampled populations are not corrected; only the actual errors detected in sampled items are adjusted. Thus, to determine the basic allowance, adjusted planning materiality should be reduced by the projected error that is anticipated for all populations sampled.

Also, when errors are detected in sample items, part of the adjusted planning materiality is, in effect, used up by the additional imprecision. Detected errors are extrapolated to the population to determine projected error; however, because the projection is based on a sample, it cannot be a precise estimate of the amount of error. Thus, when determining the basic allowance, an allowance for additional imprecision is estimated and deducted from adjusted planning materiality.

ILLUSTRATION OF ALLOWANCE FOR UNDETECTED ERROR

Based on his knowledge of the nature and amount of errors detected in previous audits of EZS Company, the auditor anticipates $15,000 of known error to be detected in the current examination that the client will resist correcting. (The auditor expects $10,000 of error in accounting estimates and $5000 of error in items that will be examined 100 percent.) Adjusted planning materiality is, thus, $100,000 ($115,000 − $15,000).

The auditor has concluded that sampling will be used in two areas in the current audit: inventories, and property and equipment. The recorded amounts of the relevant accounting populations are:

Inventories	$1,140,000
Additions to property and equipment	$1,030,000

Based on past experience, the auditor expects a projected error of $10,000 of overstatement in the two accounting populations. The additional reduction for imprecision is estimated at an additional $10,000. The auditor decides to allow for an additional cushion of $5000 because of the difficulty of estimating errors. The auditor next establishes a basic allowance of $75,000, computed as follows:

Planning materiality	$115,000
Reduction for anticipated uncorrected known error from nonsampling tests	(15,000)
Adjusted planning materiality	$100,000
Reduction for expected projected error in sampling applications	(10,000)
Reduction for additional imprecision	(10,000)
Cushion for above estimates	(5,000)
Basic allowance (basic bound)	$75,000

USING THE BASIC ALLOWANCE

The basic allowance is used in essentially two ways in planning the extent of substantive tests:

1. To determine a dollar-amount cut-off for items that are individually significant because of their size.
2. To calculate sample size for sampling applications.

INDIVIDUALLY SIGNIFICANT AMOUNTS

In examining a specific population, the auditor will want to apply the planned audit procedure to all items that are individually significant. The auditor is unwilling to accept any risk of failing to detect error for these items. An item may be individually significant because of its nature or its amount. Examples of items that may be individually significant because of their nature are unusual or unexpected names of suppliers or customers for items recorded in a particular account.

To determine the cut-off amount for individually significant items, the general rule of thumb is to divide the basic allowance by 3. All items equal to or larger than this amount are examined. Dividing by 3 is based on the sampling theory of a pps statistical plan. Essentially, if all items in the financial statements equal to this amount are considered a single population, the use of the pps sample size formula (at a 5 percent risk level) indicates a sample size equal to the number of items in that population.

ILLUSTRATION OF INDIVIDUALLY SIGNIFICANT AMOUNTS

The auditor uses the $75,000 basic allowance to establish a cut-off amount of $25,000 ($75,000/3) for individually significant amounts. The auditor will examine all inventory items (price testing and extensions) and all property additions that are $25,000 or more.

Scanning the lists for these two populations, the auditor selects items that are greater than the $25,000 cut-off. These items total $140,000 for inventory and $130,000 for property and equipment. All selected items will be examined. The remaining populations, computed below, will be sampled.

Inventories	$1,140,000
Individually significant items	(140,000)
Remaining population	$1,000,000
Property and equipment additions	$1,030,000

Individually significant items	(130,000)
Remaining population	$900,000

CALCULATING SAMPLE SIZE

The basic allowance is used to calculate sample size in all sampling applications. It should be noted that the basic allowance does not have to be allocated to account balances. The only time allocation is required is when a classical statistical sampling plan is used; these are the variable sampling methods explained in Chapter 5. A pps statistical plan or a nonstatistical plan based on pps theory allows use of the same basic allowance for all sampling applications. The financial statements may be viewed as one population and the basic allowance for undetected error applies to the financial statements taken as a whole.

Sample size for a specific substantive test is calculated as follows:

$$\frac{\text{Sample}}{\text{size}} = \frac{\text{Remaining population recorded amount}}{\text{Basic allowance}} \cdot \frac{\text{Risk}}{\text{factor}}$$

ILLUSTRATION OF SAMPLE SIZE DETERMINATION

The basic allowance is $75,000 and the remaining population recorded amount for inventory is $1,000,000. Solely for the purpose of illustration, a risk factor of 3 is used to determine sample size. Determining the appropriate risk factor is explained in the next section. Risk factors in the approach under discussion may vary from 3 to 0.7, depending on the auditor's assessment of matters explained in the next section. Sample size for inventory, assuming a maximum risk factor of 3, is determined as follows:

$$\frac{\text{Sample}}{\text{size}} = \frac{\$1,000,000 \cdot 3}{\$75,000} = 40$$

Note: This is the same formula used for a pps plan explained in Chapter 6. In symbols, it is:

$$n = \frac{BV \cdot UEL_0}{TE'}$$

ESTABLISHING DETECTION RISK FOR A SPECIFIC SUBSTANTIVE TEST

For a specific substantive test, detection risk is the risk of failing to detect an amount of error that would be material to the financial statements for that test. It may be established by assessing the following risks:

1. Inherent risk—the risk of material error occurring considered independent of accounting controls.

2. Control risk—the risk that accounting control procedures will fail to prevent or detect material error.

3. Detection risk for related procedures—the risk that other related audit procedures such as analytical review procedures will fail to detect material error.

OBJECTIVE OF RISK ASSESSMENT

The auditor's objective in assessing these risks is to establish a detection risk for a specific substantive test that will hold the audit, or overall, risk for reaching a conclusion that the population is not materially misstated when it is materially misstated at a relatively low level. Audit risk is the result of combining inherent, control, and detection risk. Quantified, the desired audit risk may be 5 percent.

One approach to determining the detection risk for a substantive sample is introduced in the appendix to Statement on Auditing Standards No. 39, *Audit Sampling,* as is explained in Chapter 5. Another approach to the audit risk model is presented here in a table that relates qualitative categories for component risks to a factor used in the sample size formula. For example, the auditor may decide that control risk permits substantial, moderate, little, or no reliance on accounting control.

After similar qualitative categories are established for the other risks, the appropriate risk factors are assigned to these qualitative assessments. For example, if inherent risk is at the maximum no reliance is placed on accounting control and no other releant auditing procedures are applied, the appropriate risk factor is 3. This means that the auditor's sole source of evidence for reaching a conclusion on the account balance is the substantive test being applied using sampling. Of course, the detection risk in this case is the sole determinant of audit risk and should be relatively low or, in quantitative terms, say, 5 percent.

The risk factors to be used in determining sample size appear in the rows and columns of the body of the table:

Reliance on accounting control procedures	*Reliance on other relevant audit procedures**			
	None	**Little**	**Moderate**	**Substantial**
None	3.0	3.0	2.6	2.1
Little	3.0	2.6	2.3	1.9
Moderate	2.6	2.3	2.1	1.6
Substantial	2.1	1.9	1.6	1.2

* Other relevant auditing procedures include analytical review procedures or other tests of details directed to the same audit objective as the substantive test being applied using sampling.

Using this table, for example, if moderate reliance is placed on both accounting control and other relevant procedures, the sample size factor to be used in the formula is 2.1. If no reliance can be placed on accounting control, moderate reliance on other procedures indicates a factor of 2.6.

ILLUSTRATION OF RISK ASSESSMENT

The auditor believes that moderate reliance on control procedures is appropriate for inventory pricing and extension, and believes that other relevant auditing procedures, including comparison of gross margin by product and location on a month-by-month basis, are moderately effective. Using the preceding table, the auditor identifies a risk factor of 2.1 to determine sample size for the inventory sampling application as follows:

$$\text{Sample size} = \frac{\$1,000,000 \cdot 2.1}{\$75,000} = 28$$

The auditor concludes that substantial reliance is possible on control procedures and other relevant audit procedures for property and equipment additions. Thus, the appropriate risk factor is 1.2, and sample size is determined as follows:

$$\text{Sample size} = \frac{\$900,000 \cdot 1.2}{\$75,000} = 15$$

SAMPLE SELECTION

Because sample size determination is based on pps sampling theory, the auditor may use the pps selection method explained in Chapters 2 and 6 or a method that approximates pps selection. If a less rigorous selection technique is used the auditor should compensate by increasing the sample size computed. There is no specific percentage of increase that can be considered "correct." Practice among accounting firms varies from 0 to 20 to 100 percent. We believe 20 percent normally is adequate, but the auditor may choose to vary the increase according to the circumstances.

EVALUATING SAMPLE RESULTS

When the auditor detects errors in selected items, two separate evaluations should be made: qualitative and quantitative. The qualitative evaluation involves investigating the cause of errors. Investigation of the cause of errors may lead the auditor to (1) apply additional procedures; (2) revise his or her judgments about internal accounting control or the effectiveness of analytical review procedures; or (3) take other actions as the circumstances dictate.

The quantitative evaluation involves projecting the errors to determine how much error the remaining population is likely to contain. The projection method recommended here is based on pps sampling theory and recognizes that larger items are selected more often than smaller items. Each error is evaluated using the percentage of error occurring—the so-called error proportion.

The error proportion is calculated by dividing the error amount by the recorded amount. For example, if a $100 item (recorded amount) is misstated by $10 (audit value $90), the error proportion is 10 percent. The projected error is calculated by summing the error proportions, multiplying by the dollar amount of the remaining population, and dividing by the sample size, as shown in the following formula:

$$\text{Projected error} = \frac{\text{Sum of error proportions} \cdot \text{Remaining population recorded amount}}{\text{Sample size}}$$

After the auditor has determined the projected error for the remaining population, it is compared to the estimate of projected error for the entire engagement. If this amount exceeds the projected error used in planning or is a greater portion of it than the auditor will be able to tolerate when the results of all audit tests are combined, an alternative strategy should be developed.

ILLUSTRATION OF ERROR EVALUATION

In testing inventory prices and extensions, the auditor detects the following errors and computes the sum of error proportions as follows:

Sample items that contain errors			
Recorded amount	Audited amount	Error amount	Error proportion
10,530	10,310	220	.02
5,740	4,018	1,722	.30
3,114	3,425	(311)	(.10)
			.22

Using the previously stated formula, the auditor calculates projected error for inventory pricing as follows:

$$\text{Projected error} = \frac{.22 \times \$1,000,000}{28} = \$7858$$

The auditor finds no errors in testing the property and equipment additions. (If errors had been detected, the auditor would need to project the errors, make a qualitative assessment of their nature and cause, and reevaluate whether substantial reliance on controls and other relevant procedures is appropriate.) A qualitative assessment of inventory pricing errors was made that did not cause the auditor to reevaluate the risk assessments made in planning.

The auditor should consider the sample results in combination with the other information obtained in the remainder of the audit and combine the results of all audit tests.

SUMMARY

Whenever an interim compliance test sample is selected (from less than the 12 months fiscal period under audit), the auditor can either (1) extend compliance testing to cover the entire period, (2) prepare an internal control update memorandum explaining why it is not necessary to extend the compliance sample, or (3) elect to not rely on compliance testing and extend substantive testing.

Three compliance sampling policies are presented in this chapter. They are (1) an internal control update memorandum is essential if a compliance sample is selected from less than the full year and reliance is to be placed on internal control; (2) compliance tests should normally be selected from the first nine or ten months of a fiscal year; (3) compliance tests should not be extended into a prior audit period.

Guidelines are presented concerning the desirability of using unstratified MPU, stratified MPU, difference and ratio estimation, and pps sampling with different population conditions. The guidelines illustrate that sampling methods perform differently under varying population conditions.

A sampling logic flowchart also is presented and illustrated. The flowchart indicates that without regard to whether statistical or nonstatistical sampling is used, key items making up an asset account balance should be audited 100 percent. In addition, a random sample of an account balance is only needed for account balances that are material in total, excluding key records that are audited 100 percent. Finally, an explanation is provided of a formal approach to nonstatistical sampling, which is based on the pps sampling theory.

GLOSSARY

Analytical review procedures   Procedures used to evaluate financial information (e.g., account balances) through a process of study and comparison of interrelationships among data.

Internal control update memorandum   A memorandum that is prepared at year-end that explains why additional compliance tests during the period between the interim testing date and the balance sheet date are not needed. An update memorandum would only be needed when compliance samples were taken from less than 12 months and the auditor plans to rely on internal control to limit substantive tests.

Post-interim review   A study of an internal control system after interim compliance testing to ascertain if additional compliance tests are needed.

Qualifying errors   A necessary condition that must be achieved before ratio estimation can be used. Before difference estimation can be used, approximately 30 differences must be observed to ensure a good estimate of the error magnitude and standard deviation.

REVIEW QUESTIONS

7-1. Indicate whether each of the following is true (T) or false (F).

A. According to SAS No. 1 (AU 320), tests of compliance must encompass the entire fiscal year being audited.

B. If an internal control system that was tested at an interim date has not changed in any significant way, additional compliance testing is not necessary.

C. Compliance tests should not be extended into a period prior to the beginning of the period under audit.

D. Compliance tests should ideally encompass the entire fiscal year.

E. In evaluating the sampling models presented in this book, it becomes apparent that no single model is clearly superior in every audit situaton.

F. If individual book values are not available for selected samples, pps sampling cannot be used.

G. In auditing an account balance, high dollar items that equal or exceed one-third tolerable error should be audited 100 percent.

H. Difference or ratio estimation may be used in low error-rate populations.

I. According to sampling logic, a random sample should be selected if the asset account balance, reduced for 100 percent audited items, is not material.

J. An account balance may be audited analytically at year-end when it is not material.

7-2. Charles Cole, CPA, is restudying his substantive audit plan for the calendar year-end of Foreign Exchange, Inc. Charles performed detailed compliance tests as of 10/13/X1. The compliance tests confirmed his belief that Foreign Exchange, Inc., has an excellent system of internal control. Charles, in studying the substantive test plan based on the interim compliance tests, believes that things still look good and concludes that no additional internal control work need be performed. Do you agree?

7-3. What factors should be considered by a CPA in deciding whether additional compliance tests are needed to update interim compliance tests?

7-4. Why should compliance tests not be extended into the prior year to maintain a continuous frame?

7-5. Indicate which variable sampling model (unstratified MPU, stratified MPU, difference estimation, or pps sampling) would be used in each of the following situations:

A. Book values are not available and natural strata do not exist.

B. Qualifying errors are not expected, but book values are available.

C. A dollar estimate is not needed to satisfy the audit objectives.

D. Qualifying errors are expected and book values are available.

7-6. Compare and contrast the formal approach to nonstatistical sampling explained in this chapter with statistical pps sampling. How do the approaches differ? In what respects are they the same?

7-7. An auditor has analyzed additions to property and equipment for the year as follows:

Number of Additions	Range	Dollar Amount
5	Above $20,000	$190,000
20	1000 to 19,999	60,000
25		$250,000

The auditor plans to substantiate all the additions above $20,000 and rely on analytical review procedures for the remaining amount.

Required

A. Is this audit approach acceptable?

B. Is there any detection risk associated with this approach?

C. Is there any sampling risk associated with this approach?

7-8. You are planning an audit sample for confirmation of accounts receivable. The aged trial balance of receivables after removal of individually significant items has a remaining population of $1,000,000.

Assume that you have concluded that a tolerable error of $50,000 is appropriate in the circumstances and that you believe moderate reliance on relevant control procedures and moderate reliance on analytical review procedures is appropriate.

Required

A. What sample size would you use for confirmation of accounts receivable?

B. How would you decide the degree of reliance that was appropriate for internal accounting control or other relevant auditing procedures such as analytical review procedures?

NONSTATISTICAL SAMPLING CASE

CASE 7-1 NONSTATISTICAL INCORPORATED
(estimated time to complete: 25 minutes)

You are examining additions to property and equipment for the year using a formal nonstatistical approximation of the pps statistical method. The popu-

lation recorded amount is $1,000,000 and you believe a tolerable error of
$25,000 is appropriate. You have concluded that "little" reliance on ac-
counting control is appropriate, but that "moderate" reliance on other related substantive procedures is justified.

A. In determining the remaining population recorded amount, what dollar
   cut-off would be a reasonable amount for identifying individually significant additions?
B. Assume that there are ten additions above the cut-off amount that total
   $200,000. What sample size is appropriate?
C. Assume that after vouching the additions, you found errors in two items
   as follows:

Recorded Amount	Audited Amount
$5,000	$4,000
2,000	3,000

What is the projected monetary error based on your sample?

APPENDIX A:
CALCULATION
WORKSHEETS

WORKSHEET 1   Calculation of the Estimated Standard Deviation

$$\text{Standard deviation} = \sqrt{\frac{\sum_{j=1}^{n} x_j^2 - n\bar{x}^2}{n - 1}}$$

Step No.	Operation	Computation
1	Sample size	
2	Sum of each sample value	
3	Sum of squares of each sample value	
4	② ÷ ①	
5	① × ④ × ④	
6	③ − ⑤	
7	① − 1.0	
8	⑥ ÷ ⑦	
9	$\sqrt{⑧}$ (standard deviation)	

WORKSHEET 2 Stratified Simple Extension—Determination of Sample Size by the Optimal Allocation Method

$$n_i = \frac{(N_i SD_i)(\Sigma N_i SD_i)}{(A/U_R)^2 + \Sigma N_i SD_i^2}$$

Step No.	Operation	Computation Stratum 1	Stratum 2	Stratum 3	Total
1	Size of stratum				
2	Estimated standard deviation of each stratum (see WORKSHEET 1)				
3	Acceptable precision				
4	Reliability				
5	U_R based on ④				
6	③ ÷ ⑤				
7	⑥ × ⑥				
8	① × ②				
9	Crossfoot step ⑧				
10	⑨ × ⑧				
11	② × ⑧				
12	Crossfoot step ⑪				
13	⑦ + ⑫				
14	⑩ ÷ ⑬				

CAUTION:

If any stratum sample size (Step 14) is greater than the size of stratum (Step 1), set that stratum sample size equal to Step 1 and recalculate the sample sizes for the remaining strata using this worksheet, after eliminating the "saturated" stratum. The saturated stratum is audited 100 percent.

WORKSHEET 3 Stratified Simple Extension—Determination of Achieved Precision

$$A' = U_R \sqrt{\Sigma \frac{N_i SD_i^2 (N_i - n_i)}{n_i}}$$

Step No.	Operation	Computation Stratum 1	Stratum 2	Stratum 3	Total
1	Stratum size	500	750		
2	Stratum sample size	18	17		
3	Reliability				
4	Reliability factor (U_R)				1.96
5	Stratum standard deviation (see WORKSHEET 1)	370	303		
6	① × ⑤	185,000	227250		
7	⑤ × ⑥	68450000	68856750		
8	Crossfoot step ⑦				137306750
9	⑦ ÷ ②	7628153	8076868		
10	⑨ × ①		6		
11	Crossfoot step ⑩				
12	⑪ − ⑧				
13	√⑫				
14	Achieved precision ④ × ⑬				

WORKSHEET 4 Calculation of the Estimated Standard Deviation of Differences

$$SD_d = \sqrt{\frac{\Sigma d_i^2 - n\overline{d}}{n - 1}}$$

Step No.	Operation	Computation
1	Sample size	
2	Sum of differences	
3	Sum of squares of each difference	
4	② ÷ ①	
5	① × ④ × ④	
6	③ − ⑤	
7	① − 1.0	
8	⑥ ÷ ⑦	
9	√⑧	

B

APPENDIX B: LIST
OF EQUATIONS

1. Mean of a sample (see page 85)

$$\bar{x} = \frac{\Sigma x_j}{n}$$

2. Standard deviation of a sample (see page 86)

$$SD = \sqrt{\frac{\Sigma(x_j - \bar{x})^2}{n - 1}} \quad \text{or} \quad SD = \sqrt{\frac{\Sigma x_j^2 - n\bar{x}^2}{n - 1}}$$

3. Achieved precision—unstratified simple extension (see page 95)

$$A' = U_R \cdot SE \cdot N \sqrt{1 - (n/N)}$$

4. Achieved precision—stratified simple extension (see page 101)

$$A' = U_R \sqrt{\Sigma \frac{N_i SD_i^2 (N_i - n_i)}{n_i}}$$

5. Acceptable precision for audit hypothesis test (see page 149)

$$A = TE \cdot \frac{U_R}{U_R + Z_{\text{beta}}}$$

6. Adjusted precision (A'') (see page 145)

$$A'' = A' + TE (1 - A'/A)$$

7. Precision for proposing an adjustment (see page 156)

$$A''' = A'/U_R \times (1.96)$$

8. Standard error of the mean (see page 89)

$$SE = \frac{SD}{\sqrt{n}}$$

9. Unstratified MPU sample size with replacement (see page 92)

$$n' = \left(\frac{U_R \cdot SD \cdot N}{A} \right)^2$$

10. Unstratified MPU sample size without replacement (see page 92)

$$n = \frac{n'}{1 + (n'/N)}$$

11. Stratified MPU sample size (see page 100)

$$n_i = \frac{(N_i SD_i)(\Sigma N_i SD_i)}{(A/U_R)^2 + \Sigma N_i SD_i^2}$$

12. Estimated audit value (see page 152)

$$EAV = \bar{x} \cdot N$$

13. Mean of sample differences (see page 103)

$$\bar{d} = \frac{\Sigma d_i}{n}$$

14. Estimated population differences (see page 103)

$$\hat{D} = N \cdot \bar{d}$$

15. Standard deviation of differences (see page 105)

$$SD_d = \sqrt{\frac{\Sigma d_i^2 - n\bar{d}^2}{n - 1}}$$

16. Audit risk (see page 139)

$$UR = IC \times AR \times TD_{\text{beta}}$$

17. Beta risk (see page 140)

$$TD\,(\text{beta}) = \frac{UR}{IC \times AR}$$

18. PPS sample size (see page 178)

$$n = \frac{UEL_0 \cdot BV}{TE}$$

19. Tainting (see page 173)

$$t = \frac{\text{amount of error}}{\text{reported book value of unit}}$$

20. Basic bound (see page 175)

$$\text{Basic bound} = BV \cdot \frac{UEL_0}{n} \cdot 1$$

21. Most likely error for overstatements (see page 181)

$$MLE_{o/s} = \frac{\text{sum of overstatement taintings}}{n} \cdot BV$$

22. Most likely error for understatements (see page 181)

$$MLE_{u/s} = \frac{\text{sum of understatement taintings}}{n} \cdot BV$$

23. Net max overstatement (see page 181)

$$\text{Net Max}_{o/s} = \text{Max}_{o/s} - MLE_{u/s}$$

24. Net max understatement (see page 181)

$$\text{Net Max}_{u/s} = \text{Max}_{u/s} - MLE_{o/s}$$

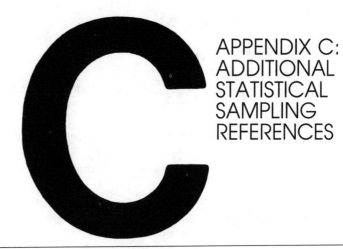

APPENDIX C:
ADDITIONAL
STATISTICAL
SAMPLING
REFERENCES

INTRODUCTORY

AICPA Statistical Sampling Subcommittee. "Audit Sampling," Audit and Accounting Guide, AICPA, New York, 1983.

Anderson, Rod, and A. D. Teitlebaum. "Dollar-Unit Sampling. A Solution to the Audit Sampling Dilemma." *CPA Magazine* (April 1973), pp. 30–38.

Arkin, Herbert. "Statistical Sampling and Internal Control." *CPA Journal* (January 1976), pp. 15–18.

Bedingfield, James P. "The Current State of Statistical Sampling and Auditing." *Journal of Accountancy* (December 1975), pp. 48–55.

Boatsman, James R., and Michael G. Crooch. "An Example of Controlling the Risk of a Type II Error for Substantive Tests in Auditing." *Accounting Review* (July 1975), pp. 610–615.

Copeland, Ronald M., and Ted D. Englebreecht. "Statistical Sampling: An Uncertain Defense Against Legal Liability." *CPA Journal* (November 1975), pp. 23–27.

Elliott, Robert K., and John R. Rogers. "Relating Statistical Sampling to Audit Objectives." *Journal of Accountancy* (July 1972), pp. 46–55.

Gafford, W. Wade and D. R. Carmichael. "Materiality, Audit Risk and Sampling: A Nuts-and-Bolts Approach." *Journal of Accountancy* (October 1984 and November 1984) pp 109–118, 125–138.

Goodfellow, James L., James K. Loebbecke, and John Neter. "Some Perspectives on CAV Sampling Plans." *CA Magazine* (October and November 1974), pp. 46–53.

Ijiri, Yuji, and Robert S. Kaplan. "The Four Objectives of Sampling in Auditing: Representative, Corrective, Protective, and Preventive." *Management Accounting* (December 1970), pp. 42–44.

Janell, Paul A. "Stop-or-Go Sampling: A Tool for Reducing Audit Costs." *Practical Accountant* (July–August 1978), pp. 53–59.

Kinney, William R. "Judgment Error in Evaluating Sample Results." *CPA Journal* (March 1977), pp. 61–62.

McCray, J. H. "Ratio and Difference Estimation in Auditing." *Management Accounting* (December 1973), pp. 45–48.

Naus, James H. "Effective Uses of Statistical Sampling in the Audit of a Small Company." *Practical Accountant* (March–April 1978), pp. 33–45.

Rittenberg, Larry Eugene, and Bradley J. Schwieger. "The Use of Statistical

Sampling Tools—Parts I and II.'' *Internal Auditor* (August 1978), pp. 27–44.

Taylor, Robert G. ''Error Analysis in Audit Tests.'' *Journal of Accountancy* (May 1974), pp. 78, 80–82.

Warren, Carl S. ''Audit Risk.'' *Journal of Accountancy* (August 1979), pp. 66–74.

Wilburn, Arthur J. ''Stop-or-Go Sampling and How it Works.'' *Internal Auditor* (May–June 1968), pp. 10–20.

ADVANCED

Felix, W. L., Jr., and R. A. Grimlund. ''A Sampling Model for Audit Tests of Composite Accounts.'' *Journal of Accounting Research* (Spring 1977), pp. 23–41.

Hansen, Don R., and Timothy L. Schaftel. ''Sampling for Integrated Objectives in Auditing.'' *Accounting Review* (January 1977), pp. 109–123.

Kaplan, Robert. ''Statistical Sampling in Auditing with Auxiliary Information Estimators.'' *Journal of Accounting Research* (Autumn 1973), pp. 238–258.

———. ''Sampling Size Computations for Dollar-Unit Sampling.'' *Journal of Accounting Research* (Supplement 1975), pp. 126–133.

Loebbecke, James K., and John Neter. ''Statistical Sampling in Confirming Receivables.'' *Journal of Accountancy* (June 1973), pp. 44–50.

———. ''Considerations in Choosing Statistical Sampling Procedures in Auditing.'' *Journal of Accounting Research* (Supplement 1975), pp. 38–69.

Neter, J., R. A. Leitch, and S. E. Fienberg. ''Dollar Unit Sampling: Multinominal Bounds for Total Overstatement and Understatement Errors.'' *Accounting Review* (January 1978), pp. 77–93.

Neter, J., and J. K. Loebbecke. *Behavior of Major Statistical Estimators in Sampling Accounting Populations.* Auditing Research Monograph No. 2 (New York: AICPA, 1975).

Roberts, Donald M. ''A Statistical Interpretation of SAP No. 54.'' *Journal of Accountancy* (March 1974), pp. 47–53.

APPENDIX D:
STATISTICAL
SAMPLING ON
THE CPA
EXAMINATION

Thirty-six multiple-choice questions pertaining to statistical or audit sampling were presented in CPA examinations from May 1979 through November 1983. This comprises approximately 6 percent of the 600 multiple-choice questions presented during this period. The number of multiple-choice questions that appeared on each of the examinations during this period is:

	May	November
1979	2	2
1980	3	4
1981	4	5
1982	4	1
1983	5	6

Total 36

Interestingly, only one essay question on statistical sampling was presented from May 1979 through November 1983.

If you understand the material discussed in Chapters 1 to 5 of this book, statistical sampling questions appearing on the Uniform CPA Examination should be easy for you to solve. The material given in Chapter 6 on pps sampling was not tested via any form of question on the examination during the period covered by this analysis.

Twenty-three illustrative multiple-choice questions selected from recent CPA examinations are presented next. *Annotated solutions follow the last question.*

MULTIPLE CHOICE
QUESTIONS
ADAPTED FROM
THE CPA
EXAMINATION

.01 For a large population of cash disbursement transactions, Smith, CPA, is testing compliance with internal control by using attribute sampling techniques. Anticipating a population deviation rate of 3 percent, Smith found from a table that the required sample size is 400 with a tolerable rate of 5 percent and a risk of overreliance of 5 percent. If Smith anticipated a population deviation rate of only 2 percent but wanted to maintain the same tolerable rate and risk, the sample size would be closest to:

a. 200.

b. 400.

c. 533.

d. 800.

.02 There are many kinds of statistical estimates that an auditor may find useful, but basically every accounting estimate is either of a quantity or an error rate. The statistical terms that roughly correspond to "quantities" and "error rate," respectively, are:

a. Attribute and variables.

b. Variables and attributes.

c. Constants and attributes.

d. Constants and variables.

.03 Auditors often use sampling methods when performing tests of compliance. Which of the following sampling methods is most useful when testing for compliance?

a. Attribute sampling.

b. Variable sampling.

c. Unrestricted random sampling with replacement.

d. Stratified random sampling.

.04 Which of the following *best* describes the distinguishing feature of statistical sampling?

a. It provides a means for measuring mathematically the degree of uncertainty that results from examining only part of a population.

b. It reduces the problems associated with the auditor's judgment concerning materiality.

c. It requires the examination of a smaller number of supporting documents.

d. It is evaluated in terms of two parameters: statistical mean and random selection.

.05 When using statistical sampling for tests of compliance, an auditor's evaluation of compliance would include a statistical conclusion about whether:

a. Procedural deviations in the population were within an acceptable range.

b. Population characteristics occur at least once in the population.

c. Monetary precision is in excess of a certain predetermined amount.

d. The population total is not in error by more than a fixed amount.

.06 A CPA's test of the accuracy of inventory counts involves two storehouses. Storehouse A contains 10,000 inventory items and Storehouse B contains 5000 items. The CPA plans to use sampling without replacement to test for an estimated 5 percent error rate. If the CPA's sampling plan calls for a specified reliability of 95 percent and a tolerable rate of 7.5 percent for both storehouses, the ratio of the size of the CPA's sample for Storehouse A to the size of the sample from Storehouse B should be:

a. More than 1:1 but less than 2:1.

b. 2:1.

c. 1:1.

d. More than 5:1 but less than 1:1.

.07 The statement, ''A CPA tests disbursement vouchers to determine whether or not compliance deviations exceed 0.2 percent,'' omits which of the following necessary elements of a discovery sampling plan?

a. Definition of the population.

b. Specified reliability.

c. Characteristic being evaluated.

d. Maximum tolerable rate.

.08 From prior experience, a CPA is aware of the fact that cash disbursements contain a few unusually large disbursements. In using statistical sampling, the CPa's best course of action is to:

a. Eliminate any unusually large disbursements that appear in the sample.

b. Continue to draw new samples until no unusually large disbursements appear in the sample.

c. Stratify the cash-disbursements population so that the unusually large disbursements are reviewed separately.

d. Increase the sample size to lessen the effect of the unusually large disbursements.

.09 The CPA's client wishes to determine inventory shrinkage by weighing a sample of inventory items. If a stratified random sample is to be drawn, the strata should be identified in such a way that:

a. The overall population is divided into subpopulations of equal size so that each subpopulation can be given equal weight when estimates are made.

b. Each stratum differs as much as possible with respect to expected shrinkage but the shrinkages expected for items within each stratum are as close as possible.

c. The sample mean and standard deviation of each individual stratum will be equal to the means and standard deviations of all other strata.

d. The items in each stratum will follow a normal distribution so that probability theory can be used in making inferences from the sample data.

.10 An auditor selects a preliminary sample of 100 items out of a population of 1000 items. The sample statistics generate an arithmetic mean of $120, a standard deviation of $12, and a standard error of the mean of $1.20. If the sample was adequate for the auditor's purposes and the auditor's desired precision was plus or minus $2000, the minimum acceptable dollar value of the population would be:

a. $122,000.

b. $120,000.

c. $118,000.

d. $117,600.

.11 How should an auditor determine the precision required in establishing a statistical sampling plan?

a. By the materiality of an allowable margin or error the auditor is willing to accept.

b. By the amount of reliance the auditor will place on the results of the sample.

c. By reliance on a table of random numbers.

d. By the amount of risk the auditor is willing to take that material errors will occur in the accounting process.

.12 Statement on Auditing Standards No. 1 suggests a formula for determining the risk level for substantive tests TD, based on the reliance assigned to internal accounting control and other relevant factors, *IC* and *AR*, and the overall audit risk level desired from both internal control and the substantive tests, *UR*. This formula is:

a. $TD = 1 - \dfrac{IC \times AR}{UR}$

b. $TD = UR - (IC \times AR)$

c. $TD = \dfrac{UR}{IC \times AR}$

d. $TD = UR - \dfrac{1}{IC \times AR}$

.13 An important statistic to consider when using a statistical sampling audit plan is the population variability. The population variability is measured by the:

a. Sample mean.

b. Standard deviation.

c. Standard error of the sample mean.

d. Estimated population total minus the actual population total.

Items .14 to .18 apply to an examination by Robert Lambert, CPA, of the financial statements of Rainbow Manufacturing Corporation for the year ended December 31, 198B. Rainbow manufactures two products: Product A and Product B. Product A requires raw materials that have a very high per-item cost. Raw materials for both products are stored in a single warehouse. In 198A Rainbow established the total value of the raw materials stored in the warehouse by physically inventorying an unrestricted random sample of items selected without replacement.

Mr. Lambert is evaluating the statistical validity of alternative sampling plans that Rainbow is considering for 198B. Lambert knows the size of the 198A sample and that Rainbow did not use stratified sampling in 198A. Assumptions about the population, variability, specified precision (confidence interval), and specified reliability (confidence level) for a possible 198B sample are given in each of the following five items. You should indicate in each case the effect on the size of the 198B sample compared with the 198A sample. Each of the five cases is independent of the other four and should be considered separately. Your answer choice for each item, .14 to .18 should be selected from the following responses:

a. Larger than the 198A sample size.

b. Equal to the 198A sample size.

c. Smaller than the 198A sample size.

d. Of a size that is indeterminate based on the information given.

.14 Rainbow wants to use stratified sampling in 198B (the total population will be divided into two strata, one each for the raw materials for Product A and Product B). Compared with 198A, the population size of the raw-materials inventory is approximately the same, and the variability of the items in the inventory is approximately the same. The specified precision and specified reliability are to remain the same. Under these assumptions, the required sample size for 198B should be:

a. Larger than the 198A sample size.

b. Equal to the 198A sample size.

c. Smaller than the 198A sample size.

d. Of a size that is indeterminate based on the information given.

.15 Rainbow wants to use stratified sampling in 198B. Compared with 198A, the population size of the raw-materials inventory is approximately the same, and the variability of the items in the inventory is approximately the same. Rainbow specified the same precision but desires to change the specified reliability from 90 to 95 percent.

According to these assumptions, the required sample size for 198B should be:

a. Larger than the 198A sample size.

b. Equal to the 198A sample size.

c. Smaller than the 198A sample size.

d. Of a size that is indeterminate based on the information given.

.16 Rainbow wants to use unrestricted random sampling without replacement in 198B. Compared with 198A, the population size of the raw-materials inventory is approximately the same, and the variability of the items in the inventory is approximately the same. Rainbow specifies the same precision but desires to change the specified reliability from 90 to 95 percent.

Under these assumptions, the required sample size for 198B should be:

a. Larger than the 198A sample size.

b. Equal to the 198A sample size.

c. Smaller than the 198A sample size.

d. Of a size that is indeterminate based on the information given.

.17 Rainbow wants to use unrestricted random sampling without replacement in 198B. Compared with 198A, the population size of the raw-materials inventory has increased, and the variability of the items in the inventory has increased. The specified precision and specified reliability are to remain the same.

Under these assumptions, the required sample size for 198B should be:

a. Larger than the 198A sample size.

b. Equal to the 198A sample size.

c. Smaller than the 198A sample size.

d. Of a size that is indeterminate based on the information given.

.18 Rainbow wants to use unrestricted random sampling without replacement in 198B. Compared with 198A, the population size of the raw-materials inventory has increased, but the variability of the items in the inventory has decreased. The specified precision and specified reliability are to remain the same.

Under these assumptions, the required sample size for 198B should be:

a. Larger than the 198A sample size.

b. Equal to the 198A sample size.

c. Smaller than the 198A sample size.

d. Of a size that is indeterminate based on the information given.

.19 The auditor faces a risk that the examination will not detect material errors in the financial statements. In regard to minimizing this risk, the auditor primarily relies on

a. Substantive tests.

b. Compliance tests.

c. Internal control.

d. Statistical analysis.

.20 Statistical sampling provides a technique for

a. Exactly defining materiality.

b. Greatly reducing the amount of substantive testing.

c. Eliminating judgment in testing.

d. Measuring the sufficiency of evidential matter.

.21 At times a sample may indicate that the auditor's planned degree of reliance on a given control is reasonable when, in fact, the true compliance rate does not justify such reliance. This situation illustrates the risk of

a. Overreliance.

b. Underreliance.

c. Incorrect precision.

d. Incorrect rejection.

.22 The theoretical distribution of means from all possible samples of a given size is a normal distribution and this distribution is the basis for statistical sampling. Which of the following statements is *not* true with respect to the sampling distribution of sample means?

a. Approximately 68 percent of the sample means will be within one standard deviation of the mean for the normal distribution.

b. The distribution is defined in terms of its mean and its standard error of the mean.

c. An auditor can be approximately 95 percent confident that the mean for a sample is within two standard deviations of the population mean.

d. The items drawn in an auditor's sample will have a normal distribution.

.23 In examining cash disbursements, an auditor plans to choose a sample using systematic selection with a random start. The primary advantage of such a systematic selection is that population items

a. that include irregularities will *not* be overlooked when the auditor exercises compatible reciprocal options.

b. May occur in a systematic pattern, thus making the sample more representative.

c. May occur more than once in a sample.

d. Do *not* have to be prenumbered in order for the auditor to use the technique.

ANNOTATED
ANSWERS

S.01 [a]

As the anticipated population deviation rate declines from 3 to 2 percent, the sample size must be less than 400. Answer (a) is the only response that meets this requirement.

S.02 [b]

If the auditor wishes to project a quantity from a sample, variable sampling is used; but, if an error rate is to be projected, attribute sampling is employed.

S.03 [a]

The term "attribute sampling" is usually associated with compliance testing.

S.04 [a]

Statistical sampling does not eliminate the need for professional judgment to gauge materiality; thus, (b) is incorrect. Response (c) may not always be correct. Statistical sampling may increase sample size. Response (d) is incorrect because statistical sampling uses two parameters: statistical mean and *standard deviation*, not random selection.

S.05 [a]

Response (b) is a discovery sample concept. Responses (c) and (d) are incorrect because attribute sampling does not generate monetary information.

S.06 [c]

The AICPA attribute sampling tables are not impacted by population size changes.

S.07 [b]

Response (a) is incorrect because the fact situation defines the population as "disbursement vouchers." Response (c) is incorrect because the statement generally identifies the characteristic being evaluated as "compliance deviations." The tolerable rate (d) is identified as "0.2 percent."

S.08 [c]

Items of special audit interest (e.g., large cash disbursements) are sometimes stratified and reviewed 100 percent. Responses (a), (b), and (d) are not logical solutions.

S.09 [b]

The primary purpose of stratified sampling is to decrease sample size. To bring this about, strata are defined to minimize stratum standard deviations. The population is not divided as suggested by response (a), (c), or (d).

S.10 [c]

120×1000 items $= \$120,000$

$120,000$ (point estimate) $- \$2000 = \$118,000$

S.11 [a]

For an accounting estimation problem, precision is determined by judgmentally defining materiality. Response (d) would be acceptable for an audit hypothesis problem, because precision is then dependent on materiality and tolerable beta risk. However, (a) is the best, most general answer.

S.12 [c]

TD = risk level for substantive tests.

UR = audit risk

$IC \times AR$ = risk assigned to internal control and other procedures

S.13 [b]

Response (a) is incorrect because it measures the average value of a population. Response (c) is a variability measure of a distribution of sample means. Response (d) is incorrect because the actual (true) population total is not known.

S-14 [c]

By stratifying the population, the sample size should *decrease*.

S.15 [d]

An increase in reliability from 90 to 95 percent causes sample size to *increase*. Stratification causes sample size to *decrease*. The net effect is indeterminable.

S.16 [a]

An increase in reliability causes sample size to *increase*.

S.17 [a]

An increase in population causes sample size to *increase*. An increase in variability (standard deviation) causes sample size to *increase*.

S.18 [d]

The population increase causes sample size to *increase*. However, variability has decreased causing sample size to *decrease*; therefore, the net effect is indeterminable.

S.19 [a]

Responses (b) and (c) do not provide direct information about whether financial statements are materially correct. Response (d) is a technique that may be used in quantifying risk at the account balance level.

S.20 [d]

The primary benefit of statistical sampling is that it permits determination of the adequacy of the sample size (i.e., evidential matter).

S.21 a

The risk of overreliance is encountered when the auditor's sample indicates that a control procedure is acceptable when the true compliance rate is not.

S.22 d

The distribution of the sample means will tend to be normally distributed, but the sample selected by the auditor will not generally be normally distributed.

S.23 d

Systematic selection is based on a selection of every nth item; thus, the items do not have to be prenumbered.

APPENDIX E:
SAS NO. 39—
AUDIT
SAMPLING

1. Audit sampling is the application of an audit procedure to less than 100 percent of the items within an account balance or class of transactions for the purpose of evaluating some characteristic of the balance or class.[1] This Statement provides guidance for planning, performing, and evaluating audit samples.

2. The auditor often is aware of account balances and transactions that may be more likely to contain errors.[2] He considers this knowledge in planning his procedures, including audit sampling. The auditor usually will have no special knowledge about other account balances and transactions that, in his judgment, will need to be tested to fulfill his audit objectives. Audit sampling is especially useful in these cases.

3. There are two general approaches to audit sampling: nonstatistical and statistical. Both approaches require that the auditor use professional judgment in planning, performing, and evaluating a sample and in relating the evidential matter produced by the sample to other evidential matter when forming a conclusion about the related account balance or class of transactions. The guidance in this Statement applies equally to nonstatistical and statistical sampling.

4. The third standard of field work states, "Sufficient competent evidential matter is to be obtained through inspection, observation, inquiries, and confirmations to afford a reasonable basis for an opinion regarding the financial statements under examination." Either approach to audit sampling, when properly applied, can provide sufficient evidential matter.

5. The sufficiency of evidential matter is related to the design and size of an audit sample, among other factors. The size of a sample necessary to provide sufficient evidential matter depends on both the objectives and the efficiency of the sample. For a given objective, the efficiency of the sample relates to its design; one sample is more efficient than another if it can achieve the same objectives with a smaller sample size. In general, careful design can produce more efficient samples.

6. Evaluating the competence of evidential matter is solely a matter of auditing judgment and is not determined by the design and evaluation of

---

[1] There may be other reasons for an auditor to examine less than 100 percent of the items comprising an account balance or class of transactions. For example, an auditor may examine only a few transactions from an account balance or class of transactions to (a) gain an understanding of the nature of an entity's operations or (b) clarify his understanding of the design of the entity's internal accounting control system. In such cases, the guidance in this statement is not applicable.

[2] For purposes of this statement, **errors** includes both errors and irregularities as defined in SAS No. 16, **The Independent Auditor's Responsibility for the Detection of Errors or Irregularities.**

an audit sample. In a strict sense, the sample evaluation relates only to the likelihood that existing monetary errors or deviations from prescribed procedures are proportionately included in the sample, not to the auditor's treatment of such items. Thus, the choice of nonstatistical or statistical sampling does not directly affect the auditor's decisions about the auditing procedures to be applied, the competence of the evidential matter obtained with respect to individual items in the sample, or the actions that might be taken in light of the nature and cause of particular errors.

UNCERTAINTY AND AUDIT SAMPLING

7. Some degree of uncertainty is implicit in the concept of "a reasonable basis for an opinion" referred to in the third standard of field work. The justification for accepting some uncertainty arises from the relationship between such factors as the cost and time required to examine all of the data and the adverse consequences of possible erroneous decisions based on the conclusions resulting from examining only a sample of the data. If these factors do not justify the acceptance of some uncertainty, the only alternative is to examine all of the data. Since this is seldom the case, the basic concept of sampling is well established in auditing practice.

8. For purposes of this Statement, the uncertainty inherent in applying auditing procedures will be referred to as *audit risk*. Audit risk is a combination of the risk that material errors will occur in the accounting process used to develop the financial statements and the risk that any material errors that occur will not be detected by the auditor. The risk of these adverse events occurring jointly can be viewed as the product of the respective individual risks. The auditor may rely on internal accounting control to reduce the first risk and on substantive tests (tests of details of transactions and balances and analytical review procedures) to reduce the second risk.

9. Audit risk includes both uncertainties due to sampling and uncertainties due to factors other than sampling. These aspects of audit risk are sampling risk and nonsampling risk, respectively.

10. Sampling risk arises from the possibility that, when a compliance or a substantive test is restricted to a sample, the auditor's conclusions may be different from the conclusions he would reach if the test were applied in the same way to all items in the account balance or class of transactions. That is, a particular sample may contain proportionately more or less monetary errors or compliance deviations than exist in the balance or class as a whole. For a sample of a specific design, sampling risk

varies inversely with sample size: the smaller the sample size, the greater the sampling risk.

11. Nonsampling risk includes all the aspects of audit risk that are not due to sampling. An auditor may apply a procedure to all transactions or balances and still fail to detect a material misstatement or a material internal accounting control weakness. Nonsampling risk includes the possibility of selecting audit procedures that are not appropriate to achieve the specific objective. For example, confirming recorded receivables cannot be relied on to reveal unrecorded receivables. Nonsampling risk also arises because the auditor may fail to recognize errors included in documents that he examines, which would make that procedure ineffective even if he were to examine *all* items. The risk of nonsampling error can be reduced to a negligible level through such factors as adequate planning and supervision (see SAS No. 22, *Planning and Supervision*) and proper conduct of a firm's audit practice (see SAS No. 25, *The Relationship of Generally Accepted Auditing Standards to Quality Control Standards*).

SAMPLING RISK

12. The auditor should apply professional judgment in assessing sampling risk. In performing substantive tests of details the auditor is concerned with two aspects of sampling risk:

- *The risk of incorrect acceptance* is the risk that the sample supports the conclusion that the recorded account balance is not materially misstated when it is materially misstated.

- *The risk of incorrect rejection* is the risk that the sample supports the conclusion that the recorded account balance is materially misstated when it is not materially misstated.

The auditor is also concerned with two aspects of sampling risk in performing compliance tests of internal accounting control:

- *The risk of overreliance* on internal accounting control is the risk that the sample supports the auditor's planned degree of reliance on the control when the true compliance rate does not justify such reliance.

- *The risk of underreliance* on internal accounting control is the risk that the sample does not support the auditor's planned degree of reliance on the control when the true compliance rate supports such reliance.

13. The risk of incorrect rejection and the risk of underreliance on internal accounting control relate to the efficiency of the audit. For example, if

the auditor's evaluation of an audit sample leads him to the initial erroneous conclusion that a balance is materially misstated when it is not, the application of additional audit procedures and consideration of other audit evidence would ordinarily lead the auditor to the correct conclusion. Similarly, if the auditor's evaluation of a sample leads him to unnecessarily reduce his planned degree of reliance on internal accounting control, he would ordinarily increase the scope of substantive tests to compensate for the perceived inability to rely on internal accounting control to the extent originally planned. Although the audit may be less efficient in these circumstances, the audit is, nevertheless, effective.

14. The risk of incorrect acceptance and the risk of overreliance on internal accounting control relate to the effectiveness of an audit in detecting an existing material misstatement. These risks are discussed in the following paragraphs.

SAMPLING IN SUBSTANTIVE TESTS OF DETAILS

PLANNING SAMPLES

15. Planning involves developing a strategy for conducting an audit of financial statements. For general guidance on planning, see SAS No. 22, *Planning and Supervision.*

16. When planning a particular sample for a substantive test of details, the auditor should consider

   - The relationship of the sample to the relevant audit objective (see SAS No. 31, *Evidential Matter*).
   - Preliminary estimates of materiality levels.
   - The auditor's allowable risk of incorrect acceptance.
   - Characteristics of the population, that is, the items comprising the account balance or class of transactions of interest.

17. When planning a particular sample, the auditor should consider the specific audit objective to be achieved and should determine that the audit procedure, or combination of procedures, to be applied will achieve that objective. The auditor should determine that the population from which he draws the sample is appropriate for the specific audit objective. For example, an auditor would not be able to detect understatements of an account due to omitted items by sampling the recorded items. An appropriate sampling plan for detecting such understatements would involve selecting from a source in which the omitted items are included. To illustrate, subsequent cash disbursements might be sampled to test recorded accounts payable for understatement because

of omitted purchases, or shipping documents might be sampled for understatement of sales due to shipments made but not recorded as sales.

18. Evaluation in monetary terms of the results of a sample for a substantive test of details contributes directly to the auditor's purpose, since such an evaluation can be related to his judgment of the monetary amount of errors that would be material. When planning a sample for a substantive test of details, the auditor should consider how much monetary error in the related account balance or class of transactions may exist without causing the financial statements to be materially misstated. This maximum monetary error for the balance or class is called *tolerable error* for the sample. Tolerable error is a planning concept and is related to the auditor's preliminary estimates of materiality levels in such a way that tolerable error, combined for the entire audit plan, does not exceed those estimates.

19. The second standard of field work states, "There is to be a proper study and evaluation of the existing internal control as a basis for reliance thereon and for the determination of the resultant extent of the tests to which auditing procedures are to be restricted." The second standard of field work recognizes that the extent of substantive tests required to obtain sufficient evidential matter under the third standard should vary inversely with the auditor's reliance on internal accounting control. These standards taken together imply that the combination of the auditor's reliance on internal accounting control and his reliance on his substantive tests should provide a reasonable basis for his opinion, although the portion of reliance derived from the respective sources may vary. The greater the reliance on internal accounting control or on other substantive tests directed toward the same specific audit objective, the greater the allowable risk of incorrect acceptance for the substantive test of details being planned and, thus, the smaller the required sample size for the substantive test of details. For example, if the auditor relies neither on internal accounting control nor on other substantive tests directed toward the same specific audit objective, he should allow for a low risk of incorrect acceptance for the substantive test of details.[3] Thus, the auditor would select a larger sample for the test of details than if he allowed for a higher risk of incorrect acceptance.

20. The Appendix illustrates how the auditor may relate the risk of incorrect acceptance for a particular substantive test of details to his evaluations

---

[3] Some auditors prefer to think of risk levels in quantitative terms. For example, in the circumstances described, an auditor might think in terms of a 5 percent risk of incorrect acceptance for the substantive test of details. Risk levels used in sampling applications in other fields are not necessarily relevant in determining appropriate levels for applications in auditing because an audit includes many interrelated tests and sources of evidence.

of both the internal accounting control system and the effectiveness of any other substantive tests related to the same specific audit objective.

21. As discussed in SAS No. 31, the sufficiency of tests of details for a particular account balance or class of transactions is related to the individual importance of the items examined as well as to the potential for material error. When planning a sample for a substantive test of details, the auditor uses his judgment to determine which items, if any, in an account balance or class of transactions should be individually examined and which items, if any, should be subject to sampling. The auditor should examine those items for which, in his judgment, acceptance of some sampling risk is not justified. For example, these may include items for which potential errors could individually equal or exceed the tolerable error. Any items that the auditor has decided to examine 100 percent are not part of the items subject to sampling. Other items that, in the auditor's judgment, need to be tested to fulfill the audit objective but need not be examined 100 percent, would be subject to sampling.

22. The auditor may be able to reduce the required sample size by separating items subject to sampling into relatively homogeneous groups on the basis of some characteristic related to the specific audit objective. For example, common bases for such groupings are the recorded or book value of the items, the nature of internal accounting control related to processing the items, and special considerations associated with certain items. An appropriate number of items is then selected from each group.

23. To determine the number of items to be selected in a sample for a particular substantive test of details, the auditor should consider the tolerable error, the allowable risk of incorrect acceptance, and the characteristics of the population. An auditor applies professional judgment to relate these factors in determining the appropriate sample size. The Appendix illustrates the effect these factors may have on sample size.

SAMPLE SELECTION

24. Sample items should be selected in such a way that the sample can be expected to be representative of the population. Therefore, all items in the population should have an opportunity to be selected. For example, random-based selection of items represents one means of obtaining such samples.[4]

---

[4] Random-based selection includes, for example, random sampling, stratified random sampling, sampling with probability proportional to size, and systematic sampling (for example, every hundredth item) with one or more random starts.

PERFORMANCE AND EVALUATION

25. Auditing procedures that are appropriate to the particular audit objective should be applied to each sample item. In some circumstances the auditor may not be able to apply the planned audit procedures to selected sample items because, for example, supporting documentation may be missing. The auditor's treatment of unexamined items will depend on their effect on his evaluation of the sample. If the auditor's evaluation of the sample results would not be altered by considering those unexamined items to be in error, it is not necessary to examine the items. However, if considering those unexamined items to be misstated would lead to a conclusion that the balance or class is materially in error, the auditor should consider alternative procedures that would provide him with sufficient evidence to form a conclusion. The auditor also should consider whether the reasons for his inability to examine the items have implications in relation to his planned reliance on internal accounting control or his degree of reliance on management representations.

26. The auditor should project the error results of the sample to the items from which the sample was selected.[5] There are several acceptable ways to project errors from a sample. For example, an auditor may have selected a sample of every twentieth item (50 items) from a population containing 1000 items. If he discovered overstatement errors of $3000 in that sample, the auditor could project a $60,000 overstatement by dividing the amount of error in the sample by the fraction of total items from the population included in the sample. The auditor should add that projection to the errors discovered in any items examined 100 percent. This total projected error should be compared with the tolerable error for the account balance or class of transactions, and appropriate consideration should be given to sampling risk. If the total projected error is less than tolerable error for the account balance or class of transactions, the auditor should consider the risk that such a result might be obtained, even though the true monetary error for the population exceeds tolerable error. For example, if the tolerable error in an account balance of $1 million is $50,000 and the total projected error based on an appropriate sample (see paragraph 23) is $10,000, he may be reasonably assured that there is an acceptably low sampling risk that the true monetary error for the population exceeds tolerable error. On the other hand, if the total projected error is close to the tolerable error, the auditor may conclude that there is an unacceptably high risk that the actual errors in the population exceed the tolerable error. An auditor uses professional judgment in making such evaluations.

---

[5] If the auditor has separated the items subject to sampling into relatively homogeneous groups (see paragraph 22), he separately projects the error results of each group and sums them.

27. In addition to the evaluation of the frequency and amounts of monetary misstatements, consideration should be given to the qualitative aspects of the errors. These include (a) the nature and cause of misstatements, such as whether they are differences in principle or in application, are errors or irregularities, or are due to misunderstanding of instructions or to carelessness, and (b) the possible relationship of the misstatements to other phases of the audit. The discovery of an irregularity ordinarily requires a broader consideration of possible implications than does the discovery of an error.

28. If the sample results suggest that the auditor's planning assumptions were in error, he should take appropriate action. For example, if monetary errors are discovered in a substantive test of details in amounts or frequency that is greater than is consistent with the degree of reliance initially placed on internal accounting control, the auditor should alter his preliminary evaluation of the internal accounting control system. The auditor also should consider whether to modify the audit tests of other accounts that were designed with reliance placed on those internal accounting controls. For example, a large number of errors discovered in confirmation of receivables may indicate the need to reconsider the initial evaluation of the reliance to be placed on internal accounting control for purposes of designing substantive tests of sales or cash receipts.

29. The auditor should relate the evaluation of the sample to other relevant audit evidence when forming a conclusion about the related account balance or class of transactions.

30. Projected error results for all audit sampling applications and all known errors from nonsampling applications should be considered in the aggregate along with other relevant audit evidence when the auditor evaluates whether the financial statements taken as a whole may be materially misstated.

SAMPLING IN COMPLIANCE TESTS OF INTERNAL ACCOUNTING CONTROLS

PLANNING SAMPLES

31. When planning a particular audit sample for a compliance test of details, the auditor should consider

  - The relationship of the sample to the objective of the compliance test.
  - The maximum rate of deviations from prescribed control procedures that would support his planned reliance.

- The auditor's allowable risk of overreliance.
- Characteristics of the population, that is, the items comprising the account balance or class of transactions of interest.

32. Sampling generally is not applicable to tests of compliance with internal accounting control procedures that depend primarily on appropriate segregation of duties or that otherwise provide no documentary evidence of performance (see SAS No. 1, section 320.67). When designing samples for the purpose of testing compliance with internal accounting control procedures that leave an audit trail of documentary evidence, the auditor ordinarily should plan to evaluate compliance in terms of deviations from (or compliance with) pertinent control procedures, as to either the rate of such deviations or the monetary amount of the related transactions.[6] In this context, pertinent control procedures are ones that, had they not been included in the design of the internal accounting control system, would have adversely affected the auditor's preliminary evaluation of the system. The auditor's overall evaluation of controls for a particular purpose involves combining judgments about the prescribed controls, the sample results of compliance tests, and the results of observation and inquiry about controls not leaving an audit trail of documentary evidence.

33. The auditor should assess the maximum rate of deviations from a prescribed control procedure that he would be willing to accept without altering his planned reliance on the control. This is the *tolerable rate*. In assessing the tolerable rate, the auditor should consider the relationship of procedural deviations to (a) the accounting records being tested, (b) any related internal accounting control procedures, and (c) the purpose of the auditor's evaluation. For example, if substantial reliance is to be placed on the control procedures, he may decide that a tolerable rate of 5 percent or possibly less would be reasonable; if less reliance is planned, the auditor may decide that a tolerable rate of 10 percent is reasonable.

34. In assessing the tolerable rate of deviations, the auditor should consider that, while deviations from pertinent control procedures increase the risk of material errors in the accounting records, such deviations do not necessarily result in errors. For example, a recorded disbursement that does not show evidence of required approval may nevertheless be a transaction that is properly authorized and recorded. Deviations would result in errors in the accounting records only if the deviations and the errors occurred on the same transactions. Deviations from pertinent control procedures at a given rate ordinarily would be expected to result in errors at a lower rate.

---

[6] For simplicity, the remainder of this Statement will refer to only the rate of deviations.

35. In some situations, an internal accounting control objective may be achieved by a combination of procedures. If a combination of two or more control procedures is necessary to achieve an internal accounting control objective, those control procedures should be regarded as a single procedure, and deviations from any procedure in the combination should be evaluated on that basis. If both control procedures are designed to achieve the objective individually, the significance of compliance deviations from a control procedure on which the auditor intends to rely is affected by the potential effectiveness of the related control procedure.

36. Samples taken for compliance tests are intended to provide a basis for the auditor to conclude whether internal accounting control procedures are being applied as prescribed. Because the compliance test is the primary source of evidence of whether the procedure is being applied as prescribed, the auditor should allow for a low level of risk of over-reliance.[7]

37. To determine the number of items to be selected for a particular sample for a compliance test, the auditor should consider the tolerable rate of deviation from the control(s) being tested, based on the planned degree of reliance; the likely rate of deviations; and the allowable risk of over-reliance on internal accounting controls. An auditor applies professional judgment to relate these factors in determining the appropriate sample size.

SAMPLE SELECTION

38. Sample items should be selected in such a way that the sample can be expected to be representative of the population. Therefore, all items in the population should have an opportunity to be selected. Random-based selection of items represents one means of obtaining such samples. Ideally, the auditor should use a selection method that has the potential for selecting items from the entire period under audit. SAS No. 1, section 320.70, provides guidance applicable to the auditor's use of sampling during interim and remaining periods.

PERFORMANCE AND EVALUATION

39. Auditing procedures that are appropriate to achieve the objective of the compliance test should be applied to each sample item. If the auditor is not able to apply the planned audit procedures or appropriate alternative

---

[7] The auditor who prefers to think of risk levels in quantitative terms might consider, for example, a 5 to 10 percent risk of overreliance on internal accounting control.

procedures to selected items, he should consider the reasons for this limitation, and he should ordinarily consider those selected items to be deviations from the procedures for the purpose of evaluating the sample.

40. The deviation rate in the sample is the auditor's best estimate of the deviation rate in the population from which it was selected. If the estimated deviation rate is less than the tolerable rate for the population, the auditor should consider the risk that such a result might be obtained, even though the true deviation rate for the population exceeds the tolerable rate for the population. For example, if the tolerable rate for a population is 5 percent and no deviations are found in a sample of 60 items, the auditor may include that there is an acceptably low sampling risk that the true deviation rate in the population exceeds the tolerable rate of 5 percent. On the other hand, if the sample includes, for example, two or more deviations, the auditor may conclude that there is an unacceptably high sampling risk that the rate of deviations in the population exceeds the tolerable rate of 5 percent. An auditor applies professional judgment in making such an evaluation.

41. In addition to the evaluation of the frequency of deviations from pertinent procedures, consideration should be given to the qualitative aspects of the deviations. These include (a) the nature and cause of the deviations, such as whether they are errors or irregularities or are due to misunderstanding of instructions or to carelessness, and (b) the possible relationship of the deviations to other phases of the audit. The discovery of an irregularity ordinarily requires a broader consideration of possible implications than does the discovery of an error.

42. If the auditor concludes that the sample results do not support the planned degree of reliance on the control procedure, planned substantive tests should be altered.

DUAL-PURPOSE SAMPLES

43. In some circumstances the auditor may design a sample that will be used for dual purposes: testing compliance with a control procedure that provides documentary evidence of performance and testing whether the recorded monetary amount of transactions is correct. In general, an auditor planning to use a dual-purpose sample would have made a preliminary assessment that there is an acceptably low risk that the rate of compliance deviations in the population exceeds the tolerable rate. For example, an auditor designing a compliance test of a control procedure over entries in the voucher register may plan a related substantive test at a risk level that anticipates reliance on that internal accounting control. The size of a sample designed for dual purposes should be the larger of

the samples that would otherwise have been designed for the two separate purposes. In evaluating such tests, deviations from pertinent procedures and monetary errors should be evaluated separately using the risk levels applicable for the respective purposes.

SELECTING A SAMPLING APPROACH

44. As discussed in paragraph 4, either a nonstatistical or statistical approach to audit sampling, when properly applied, can provide sufficient evidential matter.

45. Statistical sampling helps the auditor (a) to design an efficient sample,[8] (b) to measure the sufficiency of the evidential matter obtained, and (c) to evaluate the sample results. By using statistical theory the auditor can quantify sampling risk to assist himself in limiting it to a level he considers acceptable. However, statistical sampling involves additional costs of training auditors, designing individual samples to meet the statistical requirements, and selecting the items to be examined. Because either nonstatistical or statistical sampling can provide sufficient evidential matter, the auditor chooses between them after considering their relative cost and effectiveness in the circumstances.

APPENDIX

RELATING THE RISK OF INCORRECT ACCEPTANCE FOR A SUBSTANTIVE TEST OF DETAILS TO OTHER SOURCES OF AUDIT RELIANCE

1. Audit risk, with respect to a particular account balance or class of transactions, is the risk that there is a monetary error greater than tolerable error in the balance or class that the auditor fails to detect. The auditor uses professional judgment in determining the allowable audit risk for a particular examination after he considers such factors as the

---

[8] SAS No. 1, sections 320A and 320B, which are superseded by this Statement, used the terms **reliability** and **precision** to discuss the design of statistical audit samples. This Statement uses the word **risk** instead of reliability (risk is the complement of reliability) and the concepts of **tolerable error** and an **allowance for sampling risk** instead of precision. There are two reasons for this change: First, this Statement applies to both statistical and nonstatistical sampling and therefore requires nontechnical terms, and, second, the words **reliability** and **precision** each have been used to mean different things. Auditors may, of course, use whatever terms they prefer as long as they understand the relationship of those terms to the concepts in this Statement.

risk of material misstatement in the financial statements, the cost to reduce the risk, and the effect of the potential misstatement on the use and understanding of the financial statements.

2. An auditor relies on the internal accounting controls, analytical review procedures, and substantive tests of details in whatever combination he believes adequately controls audit risk. However, the second standard of field work does not contemplate that the auditor will place complete reliance on internal accounting control to the exclusion of other auditing procedures with respect to material amounts in the financial statements.

3. The sufficiency of audit sample sizes, whether nonstatistical or statistical, is influenced by several factors. Table 1 illustrates how several of these factors may affect sample sizes for a substantive test of details.

TABLE 1 Factors Influencing Sample Sizes for a Substantive Test of Details in Sample Planning

Factor	Conditions leading to		Related factor for substantive sample planning
	Smaller sample size	Larger sample size	
a. Reliance on internal accounting controls.	Greater reliance on internal accounting controls.	Lesser reliance on internal accounting controls.	Allowable risk of incorrect acceptance.
b. Reliance on other substantive tests related to same account balance or class of transactions (including analytical review procedures and other relevant substantive tests).	Substantial reliance to be placed on other relevant substantive tests.	Little or no reliance to be placed on other relevant substantive tests.	Allowable risk of incorrect acceptance.
c. Measure of tolerable error for a specific account.	Larger measure of tolerable error.	Smaller measure of tolerable error.	Tolerable error.
d. Expected size and frequency of errors.	Smaller errors or lower frequency.	Larger errors or higher frequency.	Assessment of population characteristics.
e. Number of items in population.	Virtually no effect on sample size unless population is very small.		

Factors *a* and *b* in Table 1 should be considered together (see paragraph 8 of the SAS). For example, weak internal accounting controls and the absence of other substantive tests related to the same audit objective ordinarily require larger sample sizes for related substantive tests of details than if there were other sources of reliance. Alternatively, strong internal accounting controls in combination with highly effective analytical review procedures and other relevant substantive tests may lead the auditor to conclude that the sample, if any, needed for an additional test of details can be small.

4. The following model expresses the general relationship of the risks associated with the auditor's evaluation of internal accounting controls, substantive tests of details, and analytical review procedures and other relevant substantive tests. The model is not intended to be a mathematical formula including all factors that may influence the determination of individual risk components; however, some auditors find such a model to be useful when planning appropriate risk levels for audit procedures to achieve the auditor's desired audit risk.

$$UR = IC \times AR \times TD$$

An auditor might use this model to obtain an understanding of an appropriate risk of incorrect acceptance for a substantive test of details as follows:

$TD = UR/(IC \times AR)$

$UR =$ The allowable audit risk that monetary errors equal to tolerable error might remain undetected in the account balance or class of transactions after the auditor has completed all audit procedures deemed necessary.[1] The auditor uses his professional judgment to determine the allowable ultimate risk after considering factors such as those discussed in paragraph 1 of this appendix.

$IC =$ The auditor's assessment of the risk that, given that errors equal to tolerable error occur, the system of internal accounting control fails to detect them, whether because of poorly designed controls or lack of compliance. The auditor would assign this risk for control procedures on which he intends to rely in establishing the scope of the substantive test of details.[2] The quan-

---

[1] For purposes of this appendix, the nonsampling risk aspect of audit risk is assumed to be negligible, based on the level of quality controls in effect.

[2] The risk that monetary errors equal to tolerable error would have occurred in the absence of internal accounting controls related to the account balance or class of transactions under audit is difficult and potentially costly to quantify. For this reason in this model it is implicitly set conservatively at one, although audit experience indicates clearly that it is substantially lower. Accordingly, it is not a factor in the relationship expressed above. Therefore, the actual risk will ordinarily be less than **UR**.

tification for this model relates to the auditor's evaluation of the overall effectiveness of those internal accounting controls that would prevent or detect material errors equal to tolerable error in the related account balance or class of transactions. For example, if the auditor believes that pertinent controls would prevent or detect errors equal to tolerable error about half the time, he would assess this risk as 50 percent. (*IC* is not the same as the risk of overreliance on internal accounting control.)

AR = The auditor's assessment of the risk that analytical review procedures and other relevant substantive tests would fail to detect errors equal to tolerable error, given that such errors occur and are not detected by the system of internal accounting control.

TD = The allowable risk of incorrect acceptance for the substantive test of details, given that errors equal to tolerable error occur and are not detected by the system of internal accounting control or analytical review procedures and other relevant substantive tests.

5. The auditor planning a statistical sample can use the relationship in paragraph 4 of this appendix to assist in planning his allowable risk of incorrect acceptance for a specific substantive test of details. To do so,

TABLE 2 Allowable Risk of Incorrect Acceptance (*TD*) for Various Assessments of *IC* and *AR* for *UR*= .05

Auditor's subjective assessment of risk that internal accounting control might fail to detect aggregate errors equal to tolerable error.	Auditor's subjective assessment of risk that analytical review procedures and other relevant substantive tests might fail to detect aggregate errors equal to tolerable error.			
IC	AR			
	10%	30%	50%	100%
			TD	
10%	*	*	*	50%
30%	*	55%	33%	16%
50%	*	33%	20%	10%
100%	50%	16%	10%	5%

*The allowable level of **UR** of 5 percent exceeds the product of **IC** and **AR**, and, thus, the planned substantive test of details may not be necessary.

Note: Table entries for **TD** are computed from the illustrative model: **TD** equals **UR**/(**IC** × **AR**). For example, for **IC** = .50 and **AR** = .30, **TD** = .05/(.50 × .30) or .33 (equals 33%).

he selects an acceptable audit risk (*UR*) and subjectively quantifies his judgment of risks *IC* and *AR*. Some levels of these risks are implicit in evaluating audit evidence and reaching conclusions. Auditors using the relationship prefer to evaluate these judgment risks explicitly.

6. The relationships between these independent risks are illustrated in Table 2. In Table 2 it is assumed, for illustrative purposes, that the auditor has chosen an audit risk of 5 percent. Table 2 incorporates the premise that no system of internal accounting control can be expected to be completely effective in detecting aggregate errors equal to tolerable error that might occur (see SAS No. 1, section 320.35). The table also illustrates the fact that the risk level for substantive tests of particular account balances or classes of transactions is not an isolated decision. Rather, it is a direct consequence of the auditor's evaluation of reliance on internal accounting control and analytical review procedures and other relevant substantive tests, and it cannot be properly considered out of this context.

INDEX

255